AUSTRALIA
AND
THE MIDDLE EAST

AUSTRALIA
AND THE MIDDLE EAST
A FRONT-LINE RELATIONSHIP

EDITED BY

FETHI MANSOURI

Revised paperback edition published in 2011 by I.B.Tauris & Co Ltd
6 Salem Road, London W2 4BU
175 Fifth Avenue, New York NY 10010
www.ibtauris.com

Distributed in the United States and Canada
Exclusively by Palgrave Macmillan
175 Fifth Avenue, New York NY 10010

ISBN: 978 1 84885 968 5

A full CIP record for this book is available from the British Library
A full CIP record for this book is available from the Library of Congress

Library of Congress catalog card: available

Printed and bound by CPI Group (UK) Ltd, Croydon, CR0 4YY
camera-ready copy edited and supplied by the editor

CONTENTS

PREFACE

The idea for this book emanated from a series of seminars and conferences that dealt with various aspects of the political and social conditions of the contemporary Middle East from a uniquely Australian perspective. One such conference was held in May 2003 and dealt with media representations of Arab-Australians in the wake of the Iraq war and a second organised in December 2004 focussed specifically on civil society and human rights in post-Saddam Iraq. In November 2005 a third international conference on 'Islam, human security and xenophobia' was convened around many inter-related themes including the increasingly visible Australia–Middle East connection. A number of the contributors to this volume took part in discussions on the current political and security conundrum in the region and the role played by foreign powers including Australia. It was during these discussions that many of the book's themes were inspired and, more importantly, where it was felt that such a broad-ranging publication was needed to allow a proper contextualization of events in the Middle East and the subsequent discursive responses from Australia.

Despite the increasing strategic and economic significance of the Middle East region to Australia, very few serious publications have been produced to examine this growing relationship. The current dearth of scholarship on the Middle East reminds me of similar concerns raised in a collection of papers published in 1976 by the Canberra Branch of the Australian Institute of International Affairs titled *Australia and the Middle East: Papers and Documents*. In the introductory chapter, Sir Laurence McIntyre, Australia's permanent representative to the UN between 1970 and 1975, observed that 'of all the numerous arenas of political and martial turbulence around the world today, the longest lasting, most intractable and most productive of violence and terrorism reaching into every part of the globe must, without doubt, be the Middle East.'[1] Sadly, thirty years later, the Middle East seems even more perturbed by intra-state political violence, inter-state conflicts and the post 9/11 global 'war on terror' that is taking place largely in Iraq and Afghanistan.

Historically, Australia's interests in the Middle East related primarily to its role in the imperial defence system led by Britain which resulted in the deployment of Australian forces in the Middle East during both the First and Second World Wars. Similarly, the current involvement of Australian troops in Iraq and Afghanistan is driven by the country's strategic alliance with the US. Yet, as this volume attempts to illustrate, Australia's current relationship with the Middle East is more than a series of historical military encounters. Indeed, the contributors collectively paint a complex multifaceted relationship that spans the cultural, economic, political and strategic spheres. The book's structure and content reflect this multifaceted relationship and brings together a broad array of themes ranging from early settlement of Syrians and Afghans in pre-Federation Australia, to the current plight of Iraqi asylum seekers in 'multicultural' — yet increasingly 'fortress' — Australia.

This volume's main objective is to provide a coherent set of perspectives on the state of Australia's relationship with the countries of the Middle East. It is in no way an exhaustive survey of all the variables that construct and shape this relationship, nor does it encompass all the countries of the greater Middle East region. But it is an attempt to provide a contextualised multi-dimensional understanding of a region that has recently been reduced in the public imaginary to terrorism, corruption and political disarray. Therefore, it is hoped that this volume will engender a greater awareness and a more objective understanding of the Middle East as a region of increasing strategic and economic importance to Australia.

Whilst this book looks at the Middle East from an Australian perspective, it nevertheless engages with common themes and questions that are being formulated as part of the 'what went wrong?' debate that relates to the current lack of progress in the Islamic world in general and the Middle East in particular. The apparent static nature of Islamic and Middle Eastern societies — in terms of philosophical modes of thought and the information technology revolution — stands in sharp contrast to its glorious dynamic past civilizations which were 'in the forefront of knowledge, human thought and civility.'[2] In discussing political violence and economic stagnation in the region, this book identifies an urgent need for foreign players, including Australia, to 'address expression of grievances and demands on the part of those who affirm their Islamic identity, and those who increasingly adopt a critical stance of normative and emotional distance from the imposed Western structures and processes of world order, while themselves affirming the quest for worldwide peace and justice.'[3] Failure to consider this imperative will inevitably paint current interventions in the Middle East as yet further evidence of increasing Western hegemony and opportunism at the expense of local societies and cultures.

As some theorists have argued, the reason Huntington's clash of civilizations thesis has had such extraordinary resonance around the world is because it is closely related to 'the emergent importance at this historical moment of *civilizational* identity as a potent political, moral, and psychological force [which] is an aspect of a more multifaceted challenge to the hegemonic, almost monopolistic, dominance of *statist* identity.'[4] A deep understanding of this *civilizational* identity in the Islamic and Middle Eastern context would lessen the prospects of simplistic, stereotypical, and often implausible, assertions about the cultural 'other' being the only source of discursive reference.

As with any project of this nature, the debts of the editor to so many people are numerous. The editor wishes to thank all the contributors for their professional approach to collaborating on this project and their preparedness to respond in a timely manner to the various requests and questions. A special mention to Sally Percival Wood for her excellent work on many tedious editorial tasks at various stages of the volume's preparation, without which this volume would not have been completed within the expected timeline. Similarly, the editor would like to thank Abdullah Saeed for his support and involvement in the early phases of the project. Finally, I would like to thank a number of colleagues who read and commented on various chapters of this book, in particular, Shahram Akbarzadeh, Samuel Hasan, Julien Barbara and Lucas Walsh. Needless to say, the final production of this book was facilitated and supported by Deakin University's Faculty of Arts, the able assistance of Karen Gillen who worked tirelessly on formatting the final copy and the professional approach displayed by the I.B.Tauris staff.

Fethi Mansouri
Melbourne, March 2006

1

EXPLORING THE AUSTRALIA–MIDDLE EAST CONNECTION

Fethi Mansouri and Sally Percival Wood

For much of its relatively short history Australia has looked to Britain,[1] and more recently the US, for a sense of national identity, economic prosperity and security. Until the mid-1970s the 'White Australia' Policy shaped the cultural image to which Australia aspired in a predominantly non-European region and was a clear reflection of its projected regional and international relationships. Times have certainly changed with Asia looming as a serious economic partner and further afield the Middle East emerging as a critical region for both security and economic objectives. This book focuses on Australia's increasingly multifaceted engagement with the Middle East, highlighting the need to unlock the complex nature of this region and the potential for improved bilateral exchanges.

Australia's involvement in Middle Eastern affairs — manifested in its current military engagement in both Iraq and Afghanistan — is not a new phenomenon, though discussions of this relationship have unfortunately tended to be ahistorical. In fact, Australia's role in the emergence of the Palestinian question could not have been more central. Australia played a leading role in post–Second World War deliberations within the newly established United Nations (UN) and 'in 1947 participated in the creation of a United Nations Special Committee on Palestine (UNSCOP) when Britain announced on 20 September 1947 that it planned to withdraw from Palestine by My 1948.'[2] In addition to the leading role played by Australia's then–Foreign Minister Dr Herbert Vere 'Doc' Evatt in ensuring that UNSCOP's proposed partition plan was adopted by a majority of UN members, 'early in 1948 Australia was the first western nation to accord full recognition to Israel.'[3] Given this early involvement in Middle Eastern affairs, it is a surprise that Australia's subsequent interactions with the region have been constrained by what Foreign Minister William McMahon in 1970 called 'a position of strict neutrality'[4] towards events in the region. One would, of course, need to question this neutrality claim given Australia's strong alignment with the US position on all matters involving Israel. Nevertheless, over the past 50 years, the Middle East in Australian thinking continued to be associated with international conflicts, global economic crises and more recently the flow of forced migrants. The current relationship, therefore, needs to be viewed as a reflection of all of these historical encounters with the recent addition of a strong trade dimension.

On the surface, Australia's engagement with the Middle East appears to be steadily building: bilateral trade agreements with the Gulf States and the United Arab Emirates (UAE) are currently under fresh negotiation; a diplomatic presence has been established in Kuwait with the opening of an Embassy there in late 2004; Algeria appointed an Ambassador to Canberra in February 2005; and a further contingent of Australian troops was dispatched in 2005 to augment its military support of the US intervention in Iraq. While historically Australia has always had a relationship with the Middle East, it is one that has tended to be ideologically filtered through its external relationships: firstly via its commitment to the British Empire and engagement in the Middle East during the First World War; secondly, and more recently, through its strategic alliance with the United States (US) which, this book will argue, shadows the foreign policy interests of the US, rather than an authentically Australian association. Internally, Australia's relationship with the Middle East has been filtered through the ideology of the White Australia Policy which, dating from 1901 through to 1973, reflected an enduring Anglo-Celtic priority that some argue has been difficult to dislodge from the Australian psyche. The foundations of Australia's direct engagement with the Middle East therefore remain either circumscribed by its military engagements in the region (from Gallipoli in 1915 to Iraq in 2006) or somewhat apprehensive in terms of its acceptance of Middle Eastern migrants from Afghan cameleers circa 1860 to asylum seekers and refugees in the present.

Historically, Australia's external relationships have been reflective of a somewhat tenuous sense of identity, which was evident in a 1999 federal referendum when Australians opted to retain constitutional links with Britain's monarchy rather than move to a republic. An Anglo-Celtic conservatism and wariness of difference thus hovers in the margins of Australia's embrace of multiculturalism, and this is most tellingly demonstrated in Australia's at times difficult relationship with its Asian neighbours. Walker, in *Australia and Asia*, reflects on this relationship as one in which, historically, Australia has revealed a certain anxiety that its 'fragile culture … might easily be overwhelmed by the populous nations to its north.'[5] Though comprehensive studies of Australia's relationship with the Middle East have not been undertaken to anywhere near the extent to which Australia's relationship with Asia has been analysed, similar cultural apprehensions, particularly in relation to Arab and Muslim migrants to this country, would not be too extravagant a claim.

This book aims to fill the significant gap that exists in literature on the Australia–Middle East relationship, not only by bringing together these major aspects of the relationship in one volume, but by exploring new areas of potential which have hitherto remained rather fragmented areas of discourse. Still, despite the broad range of inquiry attempted in this volume, some areas remain ripe for further investigation. For example, few scholars have developed a thorough study of Australia's political response, and contribution, to the Middle East Peace Process, which remains an underdeveloped area of academic investigation in Australia. Similarly, any substantial investigation into the nature of the trade relationship, taking it beyond its current import–export parameters with specific existing trading partners, is difficult to locate. This is highlighted in MacQueen's chapter which explores the untapped potential of Australia's trading relationship with North Africa, followed by Mansouri and Sankari's identification of the need for Australia to take a more comprehensive approach to trade by developing the broader links to human rights in advancing economic relations with the Middle East. Through ambassadorial and consular representation, Australia maintains a presence in the wealthier Middle Eastern states of Saudi Arabia, Iran, Kuwait and the UAE, but among the region's less affluent nations, such as some Maghrib states (Tunisia, Algeria, Morocco and Mauritania), Australia has no presence at all.[6] The potential for a deepening mutual relationship is, of course, also dictated by the requirement within much of the Gulf that agents or representatives, who are required to be nationals, must be engaged by offshore companies to facilitate trade negotiations.[7] And in the UAE, for example, business is frequently conducted via the South Asians who occupy many of the senior and middle management positions there,[8] which erects a barrier to direct engagement with Middle Eastern counterparts. An analysis of this aspect of the Australia–Middle East relationship is again an area that is under-scrutinized by Australian academia.

The momentum of Australia's relationship with the Middle East appears to remain set within the paradigm of economic and military activity, somewhat reminiscent of the imperial age. While closer trade ties with the Middle East are an important priority in expanding bilateral collaborations, as with Australia's military engagement in Iraq, these externally projected enterprises appear to operate 'out there'. Any potential misgivings about the trade relationship have been exacerbated in recent years with a dispute that saw the suspension of live sheep exports to Saudi Arabia in 2003 and the latest scandal involving the Australian Wheat Board's secret payments to Saddam Hussein under the UN's oil-for-food program. We have recently seen Australia inject additional military support into Iraq, a move that further circumscribes its Middle East relationship within military parameters. However, closer to the centre of public and political dialogue domestically is pressure around asylum seekers, a discourse that had, until recently, appeared to have stagnated. Since 2000 Iraqi, Iranian and Afghani refugees have been among the main nationalities held in Australian immigration detention centres.[9] Their presence has fuelled a media-driven fear of an 'influx' of a new 'other', replacing an earlier paranoia — with roots stretching back to the nineteenth-century gold rush era — characterized by the 'Asian invasion' or 'yellow peril'. This coincides with a significant hardening of Australians towards onshore asylum seekers. For example, during the 1970s, Australia accepted some 2000 refugees or 'boat people' from Vietnam[10] and when polled in 1979, only 28 per cent of the population believed that refugees arriving by boat should be put back to sea. In 2001, that figure had ballooned to 68 per cent and a substantial 76 per cent agreed that the *Tampa* 'boat people' should not be allowed to return to Australia.[11] This pinpoints Australia's Achilles heel in its relationship with the Middle East and the area where a more erudite and scholarly discourse is needed to move it beyond the confines of economic and military priorities and into a more sensitive, perceptive engagement.

Another point of contact between Australia and the Middle East is aid, which is generally provided via multilateral organizations such as the World Food Programme and UNICEF. Australia's direct involvement is, however, minimal when compared with the financial support that it provides to states in its own region. Australian aid assistance to the Middle East is limited to Palestine and Iraq: support for Palestine in 2003–2004 was around AUD $11 million and this will be increased to AUD $16 million in 2005–2006;[12] aid for the rebuilding of Iraq has been estimated at AUD $126 million for the same period,[13] but even this more generous amount is modest compared to Australia's commitment to regions closer to home. For example, in the wake of the Indian Ocean tsunami disaster Australia has committed AUD $1 billion over the next five years to Indonesia,[14] and Papua New Guinea will receive AUD $492.3 million in ongoing financial aid during the 2005–06 period.[15] This rather uneven approach to aid is reflective of the overall discourse on Australia's relationship with the Middle East.

There have been some publications focusing on specific, particularized aspects of Australia's engagement with the Middle East, such as military, economic or demographic studies, but in both historical and contemporary terms, this complex relationship remains academically underdeveloped.[16] *Australia and the Middle East: A Frontline Relationship* aims to develop the first comprehensive scholarly text to trace through the history of the Australia–Middle East engagement, from the First World War, to areas of potential strengthening of the engagement post-9/11. This objective is all the more important in the current political climate. Insight into the multi-layered nature of the relationship, past encounters, evaluating present policies and developing a framework for future interactions, will provide an essential basis for improved understanding and more articulate discourse. Rather than focusing on one single aspect of the relationship, this book seeks to draw together its various dimensions across three themes, beginning with Australia's military and migration relationship with the Middle East in pre-Federation days. The challenges posed by 9/11 and the West's response, with which Australia has been allied, informs the second half of the book, exploring Australia's relationships with Arabs and Muslims both at home and abroad. The final section examines future trade potentials, Australia's increasing strategic interest, and current military involvement in the region, which will include its approach to humanitarian interventions.

What is 'the Middle East'?

If one is to understand Australia's relationship with a region as diverse and complex as the Middle East, then it is crucial to outline from the outset what precisely is meant by this term. The 'Middle East' entered geopolitical parlance at the turn of the twentieth century when it was identified loosely as the region lying between the 'Near East' (the region of the Ottoman Empire) and the 'Far East' (India, China and Japan), an area of strategic significance to the imperial interests of Britain and France. *The Middle Eastern Question or Some Political Problems of Indian Defence* published in 1903[17] alerted Europe to the changing nature of land and sea defence with the establishment of railway networks across Asia, which provided new possibilities for access and the need for greater geopolitical definition. In 1921, Britain's 'Middle East Department' was established by its Secretary of State for Colonies, Winston Churchill, and subsequently became a more tangible geographical region encompassing Iraq, Palestine, Trans-Jordan and Aden.[18] The 'Middle East' was an area delineated at that time 'to denote a non-Western space, a region to be controlled, ruled or confined by the West but not assimilated.'[19]

Among the first countries to extricate themselves from European imperialism were Egypt in 1922, Iraq in 1932, and Trans-Jordan, Syria and Lebanon in 1946, leading the decolonization momentum as it then swept across Asia and Africa. Once Tunisia and Morocco freed themselves from France in 1956, followed by Algeria in 1962, this group of independent nation-states consolidated a newly defined Middle East albeit within redrawn borders. A definitive demarcation of the Middle East, however, remains somewhat elastic, even more so since the dissolution of the Soviet Union which saw the emergence of Muslim nation-states Azerbaijan, Kazakhstan, Kyrgyzstan, Tajikistan, Turkmenistan and Uzbekistan, states which might potentially be seen as enlarging the current Middle East. For the purposes of this book, however, the Middle East includes those nation-states which share a number of key cultural, linguistic and religious attributes, most notably Islam and the Arabic language, with the obvious exception of Israel. In the adoption of this broad definition of the Middle East, one notes that all but Israel are Muslim countries with nearly 90 per cent of the region's population identified as such, although Lebanon, Egypt and Syria are all multi-confessional societies with varying proportions of Muslim and Christian denominations. Moreover, and with the exception of Turkey, Iran, Afghanistan and Israel, the region's states are all Arab, which explains the dominant status of Arabic language, at least at the cultural level.

In addition to this cultural and linguistic diversity, the region is also characterized by a significant disparity in wealth distribution between major oil-producing countries such as Saudi Arabia and Kuwait and the non-producers of oil such as Jordan, Sudan, Yemen and Syria. In fact, the oil-rich countries rank among the world's wealthiest in terms of GNP, while the non-producers of oil are among the world's poorest states. This economic gap is manifested in the level of investment different countries in the region are able to make in key areas such as the development of infrastructure, health, education and other social benefits.

Both the cultural diversity and the economic gap among many countries within the region means that the potential for disharmony exists both internally, because of this cultural and religious diversity, as well as externally, because of the region's natural resources and its increased importance to the global economy. Internally, the Iraq conflicts of 1991 and 2003, in particular, created a polarity in the Arab world leaving it 'deeply divided and incapable of any collective action'[20] despite Shimon Peres' optimistic vision post-1991 for a 'New Middle East' modelled on the European Union.[21] In terms of its external relationships, the Middle East, as the site of over half the world's oil resources, exerts considerable economic influence over oil dependent economies, particularly China, India and the US where demand for oil has boomed in 2005. But the recipients of oil's largesse is restricted to the Middle East's oil producing nations which are, in turn, the nations with which Australia covets an increasing economic interest, such as Iraq, Saudi Arabia, Qatar and the UAE.

Key Themes

This exploration of Australia's relationship with the Middle East begins by looking at a history framed by immigration and multicultural diversity extending back to Australia's period of settlement in the nineteenth century. Walker begins in Chapter 2 with his study of an inherent anxiety about the 'other' in Australian history. Australian representations of the Middle East, while differently inflected, can hardly be separated from the cultural anxieties evident in its response to Asia. 'Perilous Encounters: Australia, Asia and the Middle East' provides an historical overview of the ways in which Asia has been represented in Australia along with a discussion of the process by which 'Australia' was understood to be different from 'Asia'. Walker then goes on to consider the representation of the Middle East in Australia: whether it was historically conceived as being a part of Asia or whether it was differently represented in Australia. The chapter addresses the cultural dynamics of representation and the imagery associated with the societies, religions, and landscapes of the Middle East. It comments both on the changes in this imagery over time and the persistence of cultural stereotypes.

These enduring stereotypes, as Lowe explains in Chapter 3, have their origins in Australia's military involvement in the Middle East around a century ago when a revealing taxonomy of identifiers was established. In his chapter 'From Sudan to Suez: Strategic Encounters', as the title suggests, Lowe further elucidates themes of Australia's military involvement in the Middle East established by Walker. While Australia's current relationship with the Middle East is largely characterized by its support of the US in its 'war on terror' in Afghanistan and Iraq, direct Australian strategic involvement in the Middle East can be dated from 1885, before Australia was a federal nation-state. It was in the late nineteenth century that the self-governing Colony of New South Wales sent a military contingent in support of imperial forces countering the Mahdi-led revolt, a milestone also highlighted by Lowe in this volume. Not only was this a defining moment in terms of an intertwining between Australian nation-making and service in imperial causes, but it also stands at the beginning of a line of significant Australian episodes of military encounters with, and strategic planning for, the Middle East. When Australian expeditionary forces sailed to the cause of empire in the First and Second World Wars, they went first to Egypt, for training and preparation. Then, at the height of Cold War fears about a third world war in the early 1950s, Australian military planners again agreed to send an expeditionary force to the Middle East in order to safeguard British air bases that would be used to launch atomic strikes on the Soviet Union. Similarly in 1956, Australia became directly involved in efforts to resolve the Suez Crisis. Cumulatively, the story up to 1956 is one of close involvement in imperial defence plans involving the Middle East, and of the Middle East becoming an important source of Australians' assumptions about their role in world affairs.

After the Second World War the make up of Australia's migrant intake shifted considerably. Middle Eastern émigrés, however, remained something of a classification conundrum for the Australian authorities. Neither European nor Asian, this group was compelled to work around an immigration policy that was constrained by notions of race. In Chapter 4 Batrouney explores patterns in migration and settlement over the last 120 or so years by identifying government policies across four historical periods: the White Australia Policy (1880s–1920s); the period of assimilation (1950s–1970s); the period of multiculturalism (1970s–1990s); and the last decade of the twentieth century referred to as 'beyond multiculturalism'. Batrouney aims to situate the story of Middle Eastern migration and settlement within the broader picture of the Australian story and, in doing so, discovers the mutual efforts made towards building an enduring relationship. While Arab-Australians have made efforts to become accepted and respected as citizens, and at the same time strived to maintain valued elements of their cultural identity, the post-9/11 climate has presented significant challenges.

The post-9/11 invasions of Afghanistan and Iraq, with which Australia was (and remains) militarily involved, have significantly destabilised infrastructure, security remains fragile, and have done nothing to temper the flow of refugees from those two states. Though the repatriation of Afghan or Iraqi refugees therefore remains tenuous at best, the temporary nature of Australia's policy toward onshore asylum seekers provides no guarantee of any lasting refuge in Australia, to their severe psychological detriment. In mid-2002, after the Taliban regime had been toppled in Afghanistan, Australia's then–Immigration Minister Phillip Ruddock set about planning the return of Afghan refugees, which included a monetary incentive of AUD $2000 for individuals and AUD $10,000 for families. This coincided with the Australian Government's assessment of the situation in Afghanistan which, according to Maley (Australia's leading expert on Afghanistan and a contributor to this volume), 'should be regarded not simply as misleading, but as highly irresponsible.'[22] Maley's appraisal proved correct, if the fact that only 33 of Australia's 3400 Afghan refugees' (less than one per cent) acceptance of the offer is any indication.[23] Similarly, immediately after the fall of Saddam Hussein in May 2003, and despite the UNHCR's recommendation that repatriation of Iraqis would be premature before 2005, the Australian Government began urging their return. Twenty-three agreed, more because life in Iraq would hold less fears than the 'present horrors in Australian detention'[24] than their willingness to do so. Australia's flagrant disregard of the UNHCR's advice was followed in December 2003 by Iraq's exhortations to allow refugees to stay in Australia until security had improved and 'until we have the capability for receiving these people and providing them with housing.'[25]

In Chapter 5, Saeed explores the history of migration from the Middle East rather more specifically as he surveys the presence of Islam and Muslims in Australia, and how these groups have made conscious moves towards firmly establishing themselves socially. Beginning in the mid-nineteenth century, Saeed traverses the various phases of Australian immigration from 'White Australia' through to recent patterns of Islamic migration, assimilation and integration. The impact of a series of external events, such as the Gulf War in 1991 and 9/11 a decade later, which was closely followed by the Bali bombing on 12 October 2002 and an attack on the Australian Embassy in Jakarta, is examined. This series of events, apparently establishing a 'clash of civilizations' or a 'West and the rest' mentality, has culminated in the so-called 'war on terror'. The creation of deep philosophical and ideological opposition framed by 'terror' has shifted an already at times tentative equilibrium within Muslim communities living in the West. Since those external events, the presence of onshore asylum seekers in Australia has taken an unsettling turn towards regressive, 'Islamicized' fears of the 'other'. The Lowy Institute's poll found that the Middle East, Iran and Iraq are the least favourably viewed countries or regions by Australians: 69 per cent of those polled had negative feelings about the Middle East; 68 per cent about Iran; and 72 per cent about Iraq.[26]

Such negative responses confirm the harmful cultural stereotypes perpetuated in the Australian media, a phenomenon that Saeed addresses in Chapter 5. Such media representations do not go unnoticed by Middle Eastern states with which Australia simultaneously covets closer trade ties. In particular, Arabic media sources such as *Al-Jazeera* and the *Khaleej Times* have kept pace with Australia's treatment of refugees and mandatory detention policies, and often respond to these issues. For example, the infamous 'children overboard' episode prompted scathing editorial in the *Khaleej Times* which questioned Australians' projected self-image[27] and a gruesome image of an Afghan refugee with lips sewn together appeared in the Middle East's highest profile media outlet, *Al-Jazeera*.[28] The mounting desperation of Arabs and Muslims held in remote detention centres reached a climax in mid-2005 and families with children were finally released from detention at the end of July. The labyrinth of Australia's increasingly complex visa regime for refugees and asylum seekers, a topic that Mansouri investigates in Chapter 6, however, remains. In March 2005 Australia's Immigration Minister Amanda Vanstone introduced measures intended to release long term detainees awaiting removal from detention and release them into the community. This move was welcomed as an important, albeit small, step in the right direction but it was roundly criticised for the significant obstacles which would make the new visa accessible to only very few detainees. Enthusiasm was also tempered by the fact that this new sub-class visa removes none of the inhumanity of uncertainty under the temporary visa regime. The minimalism of the Minister's attempt to breathe some compassion into the burning issue of refugee detention has recently been characterised as Australia's 'new politics of indifference'.[29]

Mansouri ventures more deeply into the re-emergence of a culture of 'otherness' in Australia and examines Australia's policy responses during its recent encounters with asylum seekers from the Middle East. He focuses on the social and political contexts within which exclusionary policies have been formulated and justified in the public domain in the wake of 9/11 and the terrorist attacks in Indonesia, first in Bali in 2002 and then the Australian Embassy bombing in 2004, which brought the spectre of terrorism much closer to home. Specifically, he focuses on the Federal Government's introduction of 'deterrence' measures which include temporary protection visas, offshore mandatory detention of asylum seekers in Pacific island nations, and the deliberate linking of treatment of refugees to border protection and security threats. Mansouri argues that this episode in Australia's long history of accepting humanitarian entrants has undermined its reputation in the region and internationally, raised serious questions about its commitment to multiculturalism, and exacerbated an existing undercurrent of exclusion and denigration among members of Arabic and Muslim communities. This sense of anxiety about the direction of Australia's refugee policies targeted at Middle Eastern asylum seekers has been intensified by media coverage which, Mansouri explains, focuses on Muslim asylum seekers as deviant, undeserving and troublesome. They have been deliberately represented not only as the undeserving other but also as potentially hostile strangers.

Batrouney, Saeed and Mansouri's chapters clearly expose the need for Australia, in developing its relationship with the Middle East, to come to a more sophisticated understanding of Islam and Muslim culture. Currently, Australia's most immediate external engagement with Islam is experienced through its relationship with Indonesia, where the world's largest population of Muslims live. Australia's historical relationship with Indonesia is therefore reflective of the nature of its perceptions of Islam, which had to become rapidly more acute after 9/11 and, more particularly, after October 12. As Barton explains in Chapter 7, if 9/11 changed Australia's view of the Middle East then October 12 changed its view of Islam and its need to engage with Islamic issues. 9/11 was a brutal reminder that neo-Wahhabi extremism in Saudi Arabia is not something the world can simply close its eyes to and hope that it will go away, while the Bali attack awoke Australia to the fact that *Jihadi* extremism is no longer neatly contained at 'the other end' of the Islamic world. Barton points out that Australia has long been accustomed to believing that 'our region' on the eastern periphery of the Islamic world was different from, and unconnected to, the Middle East. Unfortunately, Australia also took this to mean that it did not need to seriously concern itself with understanding, much less engage with, Islam in Southeast Asia. Australia is now becoming increasingly aware that globalization is not just about American fast food franchises and MTV. Barton goes on to analyse Southeast Asian Islam and its own exposure to globalization, which absorbs influences from the Middle East and its environs. This means that Australia, he concludes, needs to pay greater heed to a raft of much more complex issues than it had previously imagined. This is particularly pertinent as Australia ramps up both its military presence in Iraq and its trade negotiations in the Middle East region.

In Chapter 8, Burchill moves the discussion of Australia's military presence in the Middle East to the current situation when he analyses the events of 9/11 and the ongoing Israel–Palestine conflict. He points out the significance of 9/11 and its impact upon Canberra's policy towards the Middle East and, in particular, towards the Israel–Palestine conflict and Iraq. Australian foreign policy, he suggests, has shifted from a pre-9/11 approach that favoured Israel and was framed within the pretence of even-handedness. Post-9/11, policy towards the dispute has dropped any such pretence to become almost indistinguishable from Washington's neo-conservative 'Likudnik' approach. In reality, he concludes, Australian policy is now vicariously formed. In its response to each terrorist attack in Israel, Australia's reflexive support for the so called 'roadmap', its attitude to the Palestinian leadership, and more recently in an altered voting pattern in the United Nations, Australia has accepted Tel Aviv's claim that Palestinian militancy should be conflated with the global threat of militant Islam, and that Israel's response should be seen as part of President Bush's 'war on terror'. This is a departure from previous Labor Party and earlier Coalition (Liberal and National party) policy which was overtly sympathetic to Israel, conscious of the power and influence of the Jewish lobby, but recognised the legitimate aspirations of the Palestinians and the need for a settlement that was fair to both sides. Ignoring the impact of 35 years of brutal occupation, refusing to accept the legitimacy of anti-colonial resistance and insisting on an end to Palestinian attacks as a pre-requisite to any peace negotiations is the approach of Washington, Tel Aviv and now Canberra, towards the Middle East.

Australia's contribution to the war against Iraq in 2003 was a significant escalation from its minor role in 1990–91. Burchill explains that this should not be seen as a new found interest in the region, which has been and remains primarily commercial. Iraq was not a security threat to Australia, nor was it a regional priority. British and US pretexts for the war, copied by the Australian Government, proved to be either fatuous, imaginary or based on poor intelligence. In particular, Saddam's weapons of mass destruction (WMD) were not found and belated humanitarian concerns expressed in 2003 were not raised in the 1980s at the peak of Saddam's crimes. Australia's joint invasion and occupation of Iraq in March–April 2003 should therefore be understood as a reflection of the growing alignment in the global outlook shared by Canberra and Washington. Australia is not a main player in the Middle East, however, via the close public relationship established between the Howard Government and the Bush Administration, Burchill asserts that Australia is building itself a profile in the region which might well run counter to its long term interests.

Australia's involvement in major military operations in the Middle East continues to raise important questions about the foundations of Australian foreign policy. In Chapter 9, Maley points out that the geographical propinquity of Afghanistan and Iraq should not disguise the fundamental differences between these two cases. In the case of Afghanistan, the 9/11 attacks provided a strong basis for international action (Operation Enduring Freedom), which had firm grounding in international law. In the case of Iraq, international action (Operation Iraqi Freedom) was based on shaky legal grounds, and even shakier factual premises. On 31 March 2005, the Commission on the Intelligence Capabilities of the United States Regarding Weapons of Mass Destruction, established in February 2004 to examine the veracity of military intelligence used to support the coalition invasion of Iraq, released its report to the President. The report found the invasion to be 'one of the most public — and most damaging — intelligence failures in recent American history' and the US intelligence community to be seriously deficient.[30] Australia's Prime Minister commissioned a similar report on 4 March 2004 a few days after a Parliamentary inquiry into its intelligence agencies ASIO (Australian Security Intelligence Organisation), ASIS (Australian Security Intelligence Service) and DSD (Defence Signals Directories) was released.[31] While the *Report of the Inquiry into Australian Intelligence Agencies*, released in July 2004, found the Australian Government had not applied pressure to intelligence agencies to support the coalition case against Iraq, it did conclude that Australian 'Intelligence was thin, ambiguous and incomplete.'[32] This report followed a furore a year earlier when former senior intelligence analyst Andrew Wilkie resigned in protest over the Australian Government's actions in relation to the Iraq war, claiming that 'Australia's spies knew the United States was lying about Iraq's WMD programme.'[33] Australian involvement in Iraq derives neither from specific interest in the Middle East, nor a wider interest in being a good international citizen. Rather, it reflects the lengths to which Australia is prepared to go to persuade the Bush Administration that Australia is a reliable ally. Echoing Burchill, Maley concludes that the risks of such open-ended commitments, both for Australia and for Australians, are considerable.

Despite growing unease in several quarters over Australia's support of the US in Iraq, Prime Minister John Howard confirmed in April 2005 that Australia would deploy more troops to Iraq, doubling its military presence there. This came despite wide criticism domestically of Australia's further entrenchment in Iraq after an explicit 2004 election campaign pledge that this was not envisaged. Howard's public acknowledgment that the decision would be an unpopular one[34] did nothing to assuage the deepening sense that Australia's foreign policy alignment is increasingly a shadow of US policy. When the Lowy Institute asked Australians in February 2005 whether Australia takes too much or too little notice of US foreign policy, 68 per cent said 'too much'. Heading off such criticism, the Prime Minister explained in an address to the Lowy Institute the following month that Australian troops would be offering security protection to Japanese personnel in *Al-Muthanna* province in response to a formal request from its regional partner, Japan, and providing further training of Iraqi security forces.[35] This decision to 'lend a hand for freedom'[36] made no mention of the Australia–US alliance, though the rhetoric was rather familiar. What *is* transparent, however, is that Australia's deepening support of the US in Iraq helps to fill a military, and increasingly an ideological, void left by the withdrawal of 14 member states from the original 'coalition of the willing', including Spain and the Philippines in 2004, followed by the Netherlands in 2005, and Italy's intended departure by June 2006. In February 2006, while British Parliament debated its possible commencement of a military withdrawal by the end of the year, it was reported that Japan would leave Iraq 'within months'. But in Australia it was reported that, after discussions in Washington between Australia, Britain, the US and Japan, Australia was considering keeping its troops in Iraq after imminent the Japanese withdrawal.

As the Federal Government pondered its continued military presence in Iraq, the country's most damning corruption scandal ever continued to unfold. In order to secure contracts during the post–Gulf War UN sanctions against Iraq, the Australian Wheat Board (AWB), which has a monopoly over Australian wheat exports, allegedly siphoned off AUD $300 million to Saddam Hussein through inflated wheat prices and bogus transport costs. Prickly military involvement and shady transactions notwithstanding, in 2005 Australia stimulated a burst of trade activity with the Middle East. At the time of the 1991 Gulf War, Australian exports to the Middle East amounted to just over AUD $2 billion but this figure had climbed to around AUD $5.2 billion by 2004.[37] The Australian Government is in the midst of concerted efforts to establish a more coherent working relationship with nation-states in the Middle East and a Joint Standing Committee reported in February 2005 on strategies for the expansion of Australia's trade and investment relations with the Gulf States. This was followed in March by the Australian Trade Minister's announcement of the initiation of negotiations on a bilateral Free Trade Agreement (FTA) with the UAE, Australia's first for the Middle East region. It would also be the first FTA entered into by the UAE.[38] The 'Expanding Australia's trade and investment relations with the Gulf States' report makes key recommendations for increasing Australia's trade representation in the Gulf and developing areas of technical co-operation, such as in mining and agriculture, but also to develop strategies for the export of defence-related hardware and services. The latter seeks to expand the trade parameters of the Australia–UAE relationship, which substantially turns on crude petroleum imports[39] and motor vehicle exports.[40] The volume of these two main areas of import–export in the UAE dwarf trade on other resources and products, ranging from liquefied propane to jewellery and glassware, and Australian zinc and meat.[41]

In terms of Australia's current trade relationships with the Gulf States, the most lucrative activity takes place with Saudi Arabia. Motor vehicle exports to Saudi Arabia are four times higher than to the UAE,[42] while petroleum imports, both crude and refined, are on a par with the UAE,[43] accounting for the greater part of Australian imports from Saudi Arabia. Motor vehicle exports to the Middle East are strong — one in five cars sold in the Middle East is Australian-made[44] — but otherwise trade data with the Gulf States generally is uninspiring. Australian imports and exports between Jordan, Iran and Iraq, for example, are negligible. Trade activity between Australia and the North African Arab States slides even further into insignificance. Only Mauritania and Morocco show some signs of life in terms of projected growth while Tunisia and Algeria seem destined for stagnation by current estimations.[45] MacQueen sets out to explore the 'missing link' of Australian trade activity with North Africa in Chapter 10.

As MacQueen points out, while trade and investment continue to take precedence in the nurturing of the Australia–Middle East relationship, political, social and cultural exchanges remain insubstantial. The relationship between Australia and the North African Arab States (those of the Arab Maghrib Union or AMU) have been negligible. Outside the areas of trade in primary products (principally oil and gas from the region and agricultural products to the region) each of the respective partners has a minimal impact on and presence in each other's region. However, as Australia seeks to boost its presence in the Arab world in the realms of trade and political and cultural relations, the Maghrib provides a fertile ground in which both parties could benefit greatly. MacQueen focuses on the history of the relationship between Australia and the states of the AMU and seeks to single out areas in which this association can be fostered in order to promote a relationship that can take a valuable and prominent place in the broader relationship between Australia and the Arab world.

The volume concludes with a discussion of Australia's strategic interests in the Middle East and the human rights challenge. Mansouri and Sankari discuss current trends and future prospects in the economic and trade relationships between Australia and the Middle East and propose a new approach that links in a principled manner economic interests to local discourses on democratization and human rights. The chapter places the economic relationship in its wider social and political contexts arguing that a narrow focus on short term trade opportunities will not serve Australia's long term strategic interests in the region. Chapter 11 concludes by suggesting that, should Australia widen the strategic sphere of its engagement with the region by incorporating a consistent and systematic approach to human rights and other humanitarian issues, it would do greater justice to its stated commitment to global human rights and democracy. As the situation currently stands, Australian foreign policy has neither been equivocal nor consistent on the issue of linking trade to human rights, but the time is ripe for such a move to take place.

Events continue to move with such speed that it has been impossible to incorporate all the current shifts, not only in Australian immigration and foreign policy, but in the broader world context. Coordinated bomb attacks in London on 7 and 21 July 2005 took terrorism debates into a new direction when it was found that young Pakistanis born in Britain were responsible, adding further to the intricate nature of identity politics and social discontent. In Australia, the much publicised terror plots aborted in late 2005 in Melbourne coupled with Sydney's 'race riots' reinforced the notion of Arab and Muslim migrants as potentially 'hostile strangers' unable or unwilling to integrate into the nation state. The Sydney riots in particular, where attack and counter-attack between Middle Eastern and Anglo-Australians climaxed when 'an angry crowd of 5,000 Anglo-Australians staged vicious mob attacks on dark-skinned beachgoers and on people they believed to be Muslims', revealed a deep antagonism and hostility toward Arab and Muslim migrants.[46] The situation was exploited by a 'neo-Nazi group known as the Patriotic Youth League, which has links to the German-based skinhead group Volksfront and the British National party, also used the rally to promote white supremacism'.[47] While the Federal Government insisted that racism is not an underlying factor in the Sydney riots, opinion polls showed that 75 per cent of those surveyed think that there is underlying racism in Australia[48].

It is ironic that the very neo-liberal policies pursued by Western countries such as Britain and Australia and their globalization agenda are presenting new challenges to the concept of citizenship as conceived in the modern nation-state. Indeed, British youth of Muslim background, like Australian youth of Muslim background, may challenge the exclusionary juridical and social nature of citizenship and often articulate dual forms of attachment that reflect their hyphenated identities. Yet, the hybridity of Arab and Muslim youth in increasingly multicultural Western societies such as Australia should also be seen as a proof that rapprochement between the Middle East and the West is not only possible but ultimately unavoidable. It is for this reason that a deeper understanding of the Australia–Middle East connection is a timely endeavour. The Middle East, a complex region that has remained peripheral in much of Australia's history, is destined to always come to prominence in times of wars, conflicts or terrorist activities. The chapters in this book make a collective attempt to unlock the complexity of the Australia–Middle East connection not only at the level of military engagements but also the level of cultural encounters and economic interests.

2

PERILOUS ENCOUNTERS:
AUSTRALIA, ASIA AND THE MIDDLE EAST

David Walker

The processes by which the West sought to control the Orient by imposing generic characteristics on diverse cultures and peoples is a central theme of Edward Said's *Orientalism*. Said contends that the West not only claimed the right to define the Orient, a considerable power in itself, but did so in persistently negative terms. It followed that the degraded Orient of Western discourse had to be brought to order by the West. Said's focus was the Middle East and the representational and territorial conflicts between Christianity and Islam.[1] In the Australian case, the battle between the European and Arab worlds was less of an issue than the conflict between the West and Asia or, in the language of the late nineteenth century, the conflict between 'white' and 'yellow'. Prior to the current war on terrorism the 'yellow peril' gripped the popular imagination in Australia more forcibly than the real and perceived threats from Islam and the Middle East. In this chapter I examine why an Asian threat always appeared more potent and more capable of generating the desired nation-building response among Australians than a Middle Eastern one.

From at least the 1880s, Australia has a history of concern about threats from the north.[2] These concerns are more complex than they might at first appear. Warnings of dangers ahead might suggest no more than a determination to counter a threat to national security, but the process of identifying enemies at the gate is commonly accompanied by an assessment of national strengths and vulnerabilities. The presence of an enemy beyond the borders demands a domestic response and an assessment of who can be trusted to defend the nation in its hour of need. In this dialogue, confidence in the effectiveness of the nation to resist an enemy matters at least as much as awareness of the threat itself. Indeed, the threat may simply present a dramatically satisfying opportunity to speculate upon the cohesion of the nation, its military capacities and the quality of its leaders.

To be truly serviceable an imagined enemy must appear capable of mounting and delivering a threat, but the threat must also have cultural resonance. The creation of the 'yellow peril' is a case in point. In the mid-1890s the diverse threats and challenges represented by 'awakening Asia' were accorded a new power and immediacy when encapsulated as the 'yellow peril'. Kaiser Wilhelm first coined the term in 1895.[3] The phrase struck an immediate chord and quickly entered the language. The precise nature of the peril would change over the years, although it was always clear that the threat in question was 'Asian' and 'yellow' rather than generically oriental. It was definitely not Middle Eastern.

In January 1898 the influential American journal, *Harpers Weekly*, published an essay disputing the Kaiser's warning of an impending threat. The author, French painter J.F. Raffaelli, believed that the 'yellow peril' was little more than a product of the Kaiser's fevered imagination. Raffaelli spoke from a classically orientalist position of a kind thoroughly documented by Said. Raffaelli argued that the civilizations of China, India and Egypt had died out long ago, leaving only degenerate remnants of what had gone before. 'History' ordained that these dead civilizations would never rise again, but were doomed to 'mere animalism and vegetation.'[4] Dead civilizations demanded European intervention and governance, but posed no threats as enemies. In sharp contrast, the Kaiser's impending 'yellow peril' reconstituted Asia as an active force in world affairs and an enemy to be taken seriously.

No sooner had the 'yellow peril' entered the language as one of the defining phrases of the late nineteenth century, than sinister figures embodying the threatening East found their way into *fin-de-siecle* popular culture. Guy Boothby, the Australian expatriate writer, created the mysteriously Eastern Dr. Nikola who made his first appearance in 1895 and his last, seven novels later, in *The Curse of the Snake*.[5] Nikola, with his imposing brow and mesmeric gaze, was devoted to sinister medical experimentation. Albert Dorrington, another expatriate Australian, created Dr. Tsarka, a Japanese 'nerve specialist' working in the heart of London. There was the same capacious brow and destructive medical genius, motivated by resentment of the white races.[6] The most enduring expression of this stereotype, Sax Rohmer's Dr. Fu Manchu, appeared in 1913. In the twelve Fu Manchu novels and many short stories featuring the Doctor that were published regularly until 1959, Rohmer invariably introduced Fu Manchu as the 'embodiment of the yellow peril.'[7] Like

Dr. Tsarka, Fu Manchu worked in London, devoting his mighty intellectual energies (again denoted by an astonishing cranium) to the destruction of the white races. Rohmer's novels proved to be immensely popular statements on the theme of race war, where the only races that mattered were the 'white' and the 'yellow'.

The Fu Manchu figure was a reminder that, even though China was not then a modern nation, the Chinese were thought to be very well equipped intellectually to master the modern world. Fu Manchu drew upon the ancient wisdom of the Chinese, but Rohmer is at pains to point out that the Doctor was also the greatest medical scientist of modern times and a formidable linguist. While Japan at that time provided the most convincing real-world demonstration of modernizing Asia, Rohmer warned that it was a mistake to assume that China was incapable of transforming itself into a modern power, albeit one with few scruples about how that power might be exercised.

In the 1890s when Australia was a small white community at the edge of the British Empire, the idea of the yellow peril had particular resonance. In its various manifestations it served as a cultural template for the survivalist anxieties of a new and insecurely established young nation, a white settler society far removed from its racial homeland. The yellow peril evoked the dynamic energies and avenging spirit of long suppressed races freeing themselves from European domination. Rudyard Kipling warned Australians in the 1890s that the Chinese had a long memory for the insults they had suffered at the hands of Europeans and that a day of reckoning was drawing closer.[8] The *Morning Post* made a similar point when it reported on a lecture delivered by Australia's most famous figure in Asia at the time, George Ernest Morrison, Peking correspondent for the London *Times*. Morrison had told his London audience that the Chinese were a gifted people who would not tolerate their lowly position in the world for much longer. The *Morning Post* then reminded its readers of a famous prediction by Britain's leading Sinologist, Sir Robert Hart, that the Chinese 'would repay with interest all the injuries and insults they had suffered at the hands of European powers.'[9] Race war seemed inevitable, as did the prospect of Australia becoming a rich prize for the victor.

In the speculative literature on race war of that time the invasive forces are invariably Asian and for the most part Chinese or Japanese. In *National Life and Character: A Forecast* (1893), Charles Pearson's wide-ranging and influential study of future trends, the Chinese loom large as an emerging force, while the Muslim world is barely mentioned.[10]

Similarly, the best-known American exponent of the race war theme, Homer Lea, author of *The Valor of Ignorance* (1909) and *The Day of the Saxon* (1912) was pre-occupied with Japan.[11] In the contrasts between dynamic Asia and the degenerate Orient, the Muslim world was generally assigned a place among the defeated races. Islam and the Arab world are certainly conspicuous by their absence from the Australian literature of invasion.

The invasion narrative is typically concerned to identify national strengths and weaknesses. By the late nineteenth century Australia had already been identified as a highly urbanized society at a time when city living was considered softening. Males who had become too habituated to the creature comforts of the city were thought to be in danger of losing their military prowess, whereas urban women ran the risk of failing to produce families big enough to guarantee steady population growth. A timely reminder that crowded and desperate Asian nations to Australia's north might value Australia more highly than its comfortable white inhabitants helped focus popular sentiment on defence, security and population growth. In doing so, the real men from the interior of the continent were accorded a higher value in defending the nation than their urban brothers. A potential threat of Asian invasion helped promote masculinist causes on the home front at a time when the 'new woman' was regarded as an increasing threat to the old order.[12]

At certain points in a nation's history some enemies are likely to be more convincing than others and therefore more likely to elicit the desired patriotic responses. As Australia approached formal nationhood in the last decades of the nineteenth century, questions of development, legitimacy and national cohesion were critically important. In these circumstances the ideal enemy was one that made colonial Australians aware of the urgent need to populate, develop and value their continent. Empty spaces were central to this drama. It was no longer acceptable to allow large parts of the continent to remain empty when overcrowded nations to Australia's north required, so it seemed, new lands for their surplus populations. The Asian nations to Australia's north were routinely represented as adaptable peoples hungry for space. If Australians chose not to settle their continent others, notably the Chinese and Japanese, could be expected to do it for them. If this challenge to Australian territories could also be represented as part of a larger struggle between East and West for racial supremacy, so much the better. Such an enemy demanded disciplined resistance, calling for racial cohesion, effective settlement and national development. In a struggle that made race and space central issues, a nearby Asian enemy served the specific requirements of the nation well. An enemy so tenacious had to be excluded altogether on the grounds that the new nation needed time to settle the continent and create its own distinctive civilization.

'Asia' became Australia's indispensable enemy in the late nineteenth century and largely remained so until the post 9/11 'war on terror'. Whenever the racial grounds for exclusion were deemed unacceptably provocative, the case for keeping Asia at bay was couched in economic terms. Asian labour was represented as a threat to high standards of living and the Australian way of life. But the Asian threat had the further advantage of being located at the centre of a battle between East and West. Australia was assigned an important role in this encounter as a continent well-suited to the propagation and renewal of the European race. The encounter with Asia was at once local and specific and, at the same time, global and civilizational. Given the global nature of this conflict it was considered unlikely that Australia would have to confront this enemy alone and unaided. Predicting a future Asian enemy, therefore, had the further advantage of making Australia a central player and one that European nations and America would notice, in the coming world struggle between the 'white' and the 'yellow' races.

While Islamic peoples were not the main focus of Australian insecurities in the early twentieth century it cannot be said that they were welcomed in Australia or were exempt from orientalizing stereotypes. If they were not high on the list of perceived threats it was largely because whatever threat they were thought to pose was not considered geo-politically sustainable. Where Asia was 'awakening,' the Arab world and the crumbling Ottoman Empire were declining. In contrast to an Asian country like Japan, the Muslim world did not appear to have the capacity or the will to marshal its forces for a challenge to Australian sovereignty.

The people who introduced Islam to Australia and were its most public face up to the Second World War were the Afghans, a widely dispersed and all male community reaching a peak of 3000 in the 1890s, mainly confined to the remote outback. The first Afghans had entered Australia in 1860 as camel drivers for the Burke and Wills expedition. Thereafter they were closely associated with outback transport until the spread of motor vehicles from the 1930s displaced these cameleers, though not the camels. Over 100,000 wild camels now roam outback Australia.[13]

In her detailed and illuminating history of Australia's Afghan camel drivers, Christine Stevens documents a number of cases of anti-Afghan prejudice.[14] In arid conditions camel teams were much better suited to the harsh climate than horse or bullock teams. The cameleers were deeply resented as foreign competitors. Bitter feuds often developed between the Afghans and their European rivals. The tensions were exacerbated by hostilities within the animal kingdom itself as horses react skittishly to camels. F.C.B. Vosper, editor of the *Coolgardie Miner*, campaigned against the Afghans with a malevolent passion and helped form an Anti-Afghan League in 1894.[15] Later in this decade a West Australian journalist warned that Australians might well be endangered if a *Jihad* (Holy War) were ever to be proclaimed.[16] The observation was lodged in the mass of evidence gathered in the course of a Western Australian Royal Commission into Mining. It is a fascinating comment on how ideas of a Muslim peril might have developed, but it is also clear that this *Jihadi* threat and its accompanying theological intricacies were not widely understood and did not resonate in Australian popular culture. What mattered more to Europeans were claims that the Afghans were dirty, that they took jobs from European workers and that their supercilious camels were alien and malodorous. (For further reflections upon the experience of Afghan cameleers in nineteenth- and early twentieth-century Australia, see Chapter 5.)

Stevens also notes the views of R.S. Ross, editor of the Barrier *Truth* and later of the Melbourne *Socialist*. In 1903 Ross raised the spectre of 'The Afghan Menace' in the Barrier *Truth*, focusing on the superstition, sexual depravity and predatory characteristics that were said to typify the Afghan community.[17] While these were advanced as solid reasons for excluding Afghans under the terms of the recently enacted White Australia legislation there is nothing to suggest that this 'menace' was equivalent to that attributed to the Japanese. At the time Ross's story appeared, the New South Wales Bookstall Company, famous for its cheap paperbacks with arresting covers, had rushed out an edition of T.R. Roydhouse's novel of the Japanese invasion of Australia, *The Coloured Conquest*.[18] Australians may well have believed that the Afghans were everything Ross alleged against them, but when it came to menaces they were a long way behind the progressive and militarily strong Japanese. Afghans might be considered wholly undesirable as settlers, but Afghanistan itself was too remote, poor and powerless to be regarded as a geo-political threat even among popular writers with an outrageous talent for speculative fiction.

It must also be conceded that the Afghans occupied an important but very specialized niche in the colonial economy. The vast majority were cameleers, confined to outback transport. The same is true of the people who were often loosely and inaccurately designated as Lebanese. Many preferred to be known as Syrians, but however described the great majority worked as hawkers and for the most part in remote districts.[19] By contrast the Chinese had a much greater reputation as versatile settlers and for that reason appeared to pose a greater threat to the European community. They were thought capable of working in almost any conditions from the hottest and most tropical regions to the coldest. They were to be found in rural Australia and in the towns and cities. They were skilled miners, agriculturalists, storekeepers and traders and even their harshest critics acknowledged that the Chinese were a capable and enduring race.[20] While it was commonly the case that Arab and Islamic peoples were categorized as oriental, along with the Chinese and Japanese, there remained an important distinction between the awakening 'yellow' races and the decaying Orient identified with the Middle East and Islam. Moreover, while China and Japan had a certain racial and geographical coherence in the eyes of the colonial Australians, the Middle East was at once more inchoate and more remote. Turkey might be proffered as an exception and it is certainly true that the Gallipoli campaign drew attention to the fighting prowess of Turkish troops, but their numbers in Australia were small, peaking at just over 300 in 1911 and not rising appreciably above that number until the 1960s.[21]

Another critical point of contrast between 'yellow peril' and Middle Eastern threats resides in the Australian self-image in 1901. As citizens of the first new nation of the twentieth century, Australians took considerable pride in being modern and sensibly progressive. Although there was a good deal of resistance to the parallels drawn between Australia and Japan, some commentators noted that both nations could be considered forward looking and for all their many differences, both were deemed to have an impressive future. By its very presence Japan challenged Australia to become a stronger and more internationally aware nation. No country in the Middle East provided a similar challenge. The Australian priest, Father J.J. Malone, author of *The Purple East* (1911), summed up the case against Islam in terms that found broad agreement at the time and since. 'Islamism,' Malone wrote, is 'one of the narrowest and most unprogressive' creeds: 'It is the creed of a nomadic and semi-barbarous race, and can never become the cult of progressive peoples.' Malone's claim that Islam 'had assimilated nothing new' in twelve centuries provided ample reason to dismiss it outright. There was a suggestion in Malone's characterization that the backward tribes of the Arab world were not far removed from the Aborigines who had been so comprehensively displaced by white Australia. Malone believed that Islam was not only a 'creed' that had nothing to say to progressive Australians, it seemed to be opposed to everything they stood for.[22] Even more to the point, tribal societies posed no geo-political threat.

It was not until the First World War that Australians were exposed in any numbers to the Middle East and Islam, but the encounter only intensified existing stereotypes of degeneracy, depravity and backwardness. Egypt was the focus of Australian interest as troops began arriving in Cairo from December 1914. This encounter largely confirmed Australian perceptions of Arab inferiority, which in turn reinforced the view that it was very desirable to keep both Islamic people and Islam itself out of Australia. One soldier was so shocked by Egyptian dirt that it improved his opinion of Australian Aborigines: 'I must say my regard for the Australian Aboriginal has greatly improved since coming into contact with the lower grade of the Egyptian race.'[23] Belief in Middle Eastern degeneracy was reinforced by the grandeur of the Pyramids and the contrasting squalor of modern Cairo, leading many to conclude that a finer and cleverer race must have been responsible for the Pyramids. Even so, as Richard White notes, many soldiers were deeply impressed by Islamic architecture, if not by the religion itself.[24] Indeed, Islam may well have been an architectural experience rather than a religious encounter. Islam was undeniably imposing and exotic, but it remained resolutely alien, particularly in its religious teachings.

Through the inter-war years a variety of government instrumentalities and private organizations sought to build Australia's population. Typical of the period was the extravagant developmentalist hyperbole of the 'Millions Club,' which set as its goal the settlement of a million farmers on a million farms across Australia. It was one of many schemes designed to fill 'empty' Australia as quickly as possible before the long-anticipated threat from the north materialized. The imagined threat was invariably either generically Asian or specifically Chinese or Japanese. The much nearer Muslim population in the Netherlands East Indies (now Indonesia) was not considered a cause for concern. It was taken for granted that they were completely subjugated by the Dutch. Climate also played a part in these speculations. The indigenous population of the Netherlands East Indies was thought to have been reduced to passivity by their tropical climate. Not so the enterprising Japanese. There were worried reports about a growing Japanese presence in the

Netherlands East Indies accompanied by a lively apprehension that they had also set their sights on empty Australia.[25]

One of the purposes of identifying threats was to quicken the process of settling the continent and transforming it into an advanced, white, European nation. A rapid Europeanization of Australia was considered vital. In this context, nationalists roundly rejected any suggestion that Australia had oriental characteristics or affinities whether in landscapes or climate. The *Bulletin* writer, entrepreneur and politician, Randolph Bedford, was prominent among those who repudiated all suggestions that Australia was in any sense oriental. He claimed that Australian heat was not enervatingly Asian, as some commentators suggested, but invigoratingly Australian. The process of differentiating Australia from Asia was also apparent in Bedford's insistence that Australia's arid zones were not deserts of the kind found in the Arab world. He believed that country identified as desert would be transformed into productive farmland as settlement spread further into the interior.[26] The geographer, Edgeworth David, believed that there was considerable hostility to representations of Australia as a dry continent characterized by extensive deserts. David speculated that the hostility derived from the association between deserts and nomadic Arab populations, the antithesis of progressive settlement.[27] In his classic and now largely forgotten text on the landscape of Australian poetry, Brian Elliott noted that Australian antiquity was commonly framed as Egyptian.[28] But Egypt typically invoked the classically orientalist tropes of exhaustion and timelessness; a world without history or progress, condemned to endless repetition or, recalling Raffaelli's formulation of the backward Orient, a world of 'mere animalism and vegetation.' Clearly, these were associations that a modernizing young nation would have to escape.

An Australia drawn to Egyptian associations could hardly be expected to fulfil its promise as a new and progressive society. Egypt was dismissed as a poor model and a contemptible adversary and as such could play no useful role in shaping Australia's future. The Japanese were another matter. Though commonly disparaged, they were also seen as a clever, adaptable and disciplined people. The more Japan succeeded, the more likely it was that Australia would have to improve its own performance as a nation. These contrasting perceptions are clear in two Australian travel books published in the inter-war years, M.H. Ellis's *Express to Hindustan* (1929) and Florence Taylor's *A Pot-Pourri of Eastern Asia* (1935). The cover of Ellis's book shows a sleek, late model car (the 'express' of the title), with camels and palms in the background:

Australian speed and modernity is here framed against the lethargic and 'timeless' Orient. Ellis had robust ideas on the need to rule the Arab world with a rod of iron, but his experiences in the Middle East had little direct relevance for Australians, except to highlight Australian modernity. For Taylor, on the other hand, modern Japan was full of portents and at almost every turn she found new grounds for Australians to become as disciplined and efficient as the Japanese. Moreover, whereas Ellis was one of only a very few Australian travel writers to discuss the Middle East outside of the war experience, Florence Taylor joined a growing fraternity of writers who had marvelled at the ominous speed of Japan's industrial development.[29]

While there were occasional warnings about Islamic developments to Australia's north, there is little evidence that they were taken seriously or reached a wide audience. Harriet Ponder, an imperious traveller with strong family connections in Australia, wrote two impressive travel books on the Indies in the 1930s, *Java Pageant* and *Javanese Panorama*. In the former she noted the presence in Java of a 'New Islamic Movement' that seemed to be spreading with 'tremendously potent force' and working with a 'resistless power of religious appeal.' Ponder linked these developments to a 'gigantic reawakening of Islamic fervour' in the Near East, India and Africa, but made no direct reference to any dangers this might pose for Australia.[30] Paul McGuire's *Westward the Course: The New World of Oceania*, first published in 1942 and written for an Australian audience, similarly noted that pan-Islamic sentiments were widespread in the Netherlands East Indies, but added: 'if Islam is the garment of Indonesian society: the way of life is still richly Animistic.'[31] McGuire was more inclined to admire the spiritual intensity of Javanese Islam than to identify a danger in the spread of Islamic teachings. Moreover, Islam in the Indies was softened and made more pliable in McGuire's view by its close association with Javanese spiritual traditions. (A full discussion of Islam in Indonesia can be found in Chapter 8.)

The Second World War again returned Australian soldiers to the Middle East where many of the tropes of the First World War were again affirmed and repeated. Eric Lambert's *The Twenty Thousand Thieves*, by far the most popular Australian novel to emerge from the Second World War with sales of over 700,000 copies, opens in Egypt in January 1941. The first descriptions of the population are of a 'few ragged Arabs' and an alluring Egyptian woman whose 'dark, liquid eyes' surveyed the troops from 'above her *yashmak*'.[32] The Australian soldiers were contemptuous of the ragged males, whereas the sight of the woman put many of them into a state of palpitating sexual excitement. The dark, liquid eyes provided an instantly recognizable reference to the submissive sensuality attributed to Eastern women. While many of Lambert's soldiers were not much more than sexual predators, there is nonetheless a familiar contrast between progressive Australian attitudes towards women and the backwardness attributed to the East. One soldier defined Egypt as a country where a man valued his donkey more highly than his wife. Lambert's more reflective soldiers are fascinated by what they regard as 'Eastern scenes,' but it is the dirt of the Arab world that strikes them most forcefully. Arab villages are 'filthy, diseased things' and, as if the message needed reinforcing: 'The Arab village was filth made out of filth.'[33] Close up the dirt is repellent, but 'Eastern scenes' still had their impact. One of Lambert's soldiers is 'thrilled by the actuality of … the date palms, the hot, dusty villages, the blind ox on the water wheel, the minaret of some distant mosque.'[34] This was the picturesque Middle East celebrated in paintings and post cards alike. But in *The Twenty Thousand Thieves* the Arab world is no more than an exotic backdrop. This is first and foremost a novel about the Australian soldier.

An impression of the place of the Arab world in the Australian imaginary from the 1930s to the 1960s can be gained from the writings of Frank Clune, one of Australia's most successful travel writers. From the late 1930s Clune cast himself in the role of man of the people and popular educator. One of his pet themes was the need for Australians to understand their place as a Pacific nation. For twenty years from the late 1930s he travelled the countries to Australia's north, writing travel books as he went beginning with *Sky High to Shanghai* (1939) and ending with *Flight to Formosa* (1958). In the intervening years there were books on the Netherlands East Indies, Singapore, Japan and India, all of them presented in Clune's idiosyncratic and populist style. Clune was convinced that Australia's trading future lay in Asia, but he also worried that turmoil and unrest in Asia might lead to Australia being engulfed by war and invasion. Clune insisted that Australians had to know Asia better than they did because their survival as a nation depended on a stable Asia, preferably under European tutelage. The 'Asia' that Clune identified as crucial to Australian interests, the Asia that Australia had to know better, was a geo-political entity rather than a religious one. The force of numbers and political instability made Asia dangerous. Accordingly, anything that might help stabilize Asia found favour with Clune.

One of the striking features of Clune's considerable output on Asia and regional identity is the marginal role of Islam. Although it could be expected to loom large, the Islamic presence is barely acknowledged in *To the Isles of Spice*, Clune's account of the Netherlands East Indies. He visits a mosque in Surabaya, an occasion for some general observations about Islam: 'Muslims must not drink wine or eat pork, but they can have as many wives as they can afford to keep. And they believe that if they die fighting the infidel they go straight to Paradise.'[35] Islam is quickly disposed of as an awkward and intractable subject. When he comes to summarize what his visit means for Australians, Clune focuses on the benefits of Australia being a 'White Man's Country': 'Thanks to the foresight of our political fathers, Australia has no colour-bar and no colour-phobias. It is different in the Indies where all sorts have intermingled.'[36] It was clearly better in Clune's view to be a racially cohesive white nation than a racially mixed one like the Netherlands East Indies, but there is no suggestion that in proclaiming their whiteness, Australians ran a greater risk of being cast as 'infidels'. Moreover, while Clune insisted that Australians needed to know more about Asia, including Asian languages, he showed very little interest in Islam as a religion and at no stage recommended the teaching of Arabic. It is quite possible that many of Clune's readers may have finished *To the Isles of Spice* without knowing that the isles in question were predominantly Islamic.

Islam proved harder to overlook in Clune's *Tobruk to Turkey*, a book written to support the Australian war effort. Flying over Oman, Clune looked down upon some of the worst country he had ever seen. Dry, harsh and inhospitable, it seemed no place to find human beings, but he had no doubt there would be people down there: 'Arabs ... living on a date or two, with a stray goat on Sundays; and if lucky, a gargle of arrack as they kneel and strike the earth with their forehead towards Mecca and thank Allah for his benevolence and beneficence.'[37] It was a typically dismissive commentary designed to reinforce the view that Arab peoples were backward, credulous and enslaved by a laughably crackpot religion, a suitable subject for dismissive larrikin humour.

For Frank Clune, the Cairo of World War Two was not much different from the Cairo he had known in the First World War: 'Every one is out to rob the soldier: barber, café, souvenir shops, hotels, stores...Cairo is still the home of touts, taxis and trollops.'[38] Clune also met the Australian war artist William Dargie and observed that from an artist's point of view the Middle East had its attractions. Like Lambert's soldier attracted by 'Eastern scenes,' Clune could see how 'a shrubless desert of red sand' could be transformed into something more temptingly exotic 'when that desert is peopled by Arabs and airmen, camels and donkeys, date palms, mud-built villages and age-old wells, it is a romantic sort of desert to a city born painter.'[39] Dargie's painting was of a crashed plane with an Arab looking on. From Dargie's account of the painting this was just another moment in the chronicle of the timeless Orient: 'To the simple Muslim it is only another incident — a passing phase — in the wars that have been fought over these deserts in the past millenniums.' On his departure Clune summed up this Arab world as the 'Muddle East'.[40]

The only point at which Islam displayed any redeeming features in Clune's view was in India and largely because he found there a people he liked even less than the followers of Islam. Clune finally made his long-awaited trip to India after the Second World War, but he soon developed a powerful antipathy to 'slimy Hindus' who kept asking him about the White Australia Policy.[41] Surrounded by some of the world's greatest talkers, Clune discovered a preference for the sterner Muslim leadership. Never one to avoid prophesy, especially in countries he knew little about, Clune declared that the Muslim leader, Muhammad Ali Jinnah, would lead his people to victory in the subcontinent and that India would become a Muslim country.[42] Clune was not at all unhappy about the prospect and there is nothing to suggest that he considered a Muslim India a threat to Australia.

As the Cold War deepened, Islam (along with Buddhism) emerged as a useful antidote to the primary enemy, communism. Any set of beliefs that directed peoples' thoughts to the spiritual plane and tied them to the authority of religious leaders in the search for a better world appeared to offer a barrier to the temptations of communist doctrine. This may not have been a prominent theme in the Australian Department of External Affairs, but it is nonetheless clear that religious adherence in countries vulnerable to communism was considered something worth encouraging.[43] This stance was no doubt strengthened by the fact that Pakistan was a member of the South East Asian Treaty Organization (SEATO) and was seen as an ally of the West. By contrast, the largely secular and this-worldly orientation of the overseas Chinese made them an object of concern to Cold War strategists. Even so, Islam was not widely examined. In the many discussions surrounding the implications for Australia of the Afro–Asian Conference in Bandung in 1955, the presence of Islamic nations, not least Indonesia itself, was barely mentioned. Australian reports of the conference focused on the presence of India's Jawaharlal Nehru and China's Chou En-lai, while race and colonialism were identified as the key conference themes. While Australian journalist reported a range of threats associated with the spirit of Bandung, resurgent Islam was not among them.[44]

Australia's leading post-war diplomat and an observer at the Bandung conference, Walter Crocker, was also disinclined to see Islam as a key issue for Australia. In 1956 Crocker published a reflection on the international order and the trend of world events, perhaps the most important statement of its kind to come out of Australia in the 1950s. Titled 'The Racial Factor in International Relations' and written in the shadow of the Bandung conference, Crocker addressed 'the darkening peril under which we are living, a peril that is scarcely less than the death of civilization, perhaps the death of the human race.'[45] Crocker feared that a world increasingly governed by moral absolutes ran the risk of nuclear destruction. Crocker's major preoccupation was the danger that might flow from a widening gulf between the 'white world' and 'awakening' Asia, a gulf that he believed communist powers were eager to exploit. Where Crocker refers at length to racial sensitivities and the legacy of colonialism in India and Africa, Islam attracts only a single passing comment, though it is an illuminating one. Comparing communism with Islam, Crocker notes that both subordinated 'race to faith'.[46] Crocker was convinced that this gave communism an enormous propaganda advantage throughout the third world because it enabled racial antagonism against the West to be converted into passionate support for communist causes. Islam had the opposite effect by supplanting potentially dangerous racial passions with an altogether deeper commitment to Islam. The Islamic faith that Father Malone had dismissed as a narrow and backward creed had emerged half a century later as an effective antidote to that most dangerous of 'moral absolutes': communism. Islam may have been a 'moral absolute,' but it was a moral absolute that Crocker viewed with favour.

Paradoxically perhaps, one effect of Crocker's analysis of the international order was to affirm Islam's status as a religion that posed no major threat to the West in general and Australian interests in particular. And because Islam was said to subordinate race to faith the need to assuage Islamic opinion was reduced. With R.G. Casey as his Minister for External Affairs, Crocker was convinced that Australia had to do all it could to persuade Asian opinion, particularly in India and Indonesia, that Australia saw itself as part of Asia and wanted to be regarded as a friendly neighbour. In doing so, Crocker adhered to the official view that Australia was a country without colour prejudice. The task was to persuade Asian leaders that this was the case, no simple undertaking given that Australia's restrictive immigration laws were not about to change. What Crocker did want to change was the way Australians spoke about race. He maintained that it was 'common sense and a matter of self-interest to be scrupulously courteous, always avoiding the provocative and always cultivating the conciliatory approach on both sides.'[47] Critical Asian nations and their more outspoken citizens, the people who were most likely to criticize the White Australia Policy, were to be the focal point of the new era of racial courtesy and conciliation.

Because the Arab world was not regarded as a direct threat to Australian interests, the 'other' that Australians were encouraged to know and conciliate was predominantly Asian. The nations to Australia's north had long been regarded as a danger to Australia's security and a continuing pattern of indifference to cultures and languages that were geographically close could be deemed arrogant and provocative. Knowing the neighbours encouraged a new Asia-related emphasis with the introduction of modest but significant Asian Studies programs in universities, ongoing (if sometimes begrudging) support for the Colombo Plan and, at Casey's urging, the formation of Asian Australian Associations in the late 1950s designed to show a conciliatory face to Asian visitors. While it was clear that the Middle East as a region was considered important to peace and stability, there was no corresponding drive to promote Arabic as a language, to introduce Arabic Studies or to foster a deeper knowledge of Islam.

In the period since the Second World War, and particularly the fifty years since the Bandung conference, the need to know Asia has been invoked on a regular basis by governments on all sides of politics. It could hardly be argued that anxieties about Asia are now a thing of the past, but there has been over fifty years of familiarization with the nations to Australia's north. These processes, not least travel to the region, have lessened much of the menacing exoticism that was once associated with unknown Asia. The demonic energies and moral depravity freely attributed to communist China in the 1950s, for example, has largely disappeared. While many still regard China as a seriously flawed, authoritarian regime it nonetheless belongs within the global community. It is precisely because the Arab world and Islam have not been subjected to the same familiarizing processes or the same level of sympathetic scrutiny that Islam can so powerfully represent the new, dark unknown, a world to be dismissed and repudiated rather than studied or understood. Moreover, in a world of non-State actors the 'crazed' Arab bent on dragging the civilized world back into darkness has both a new power and renewed cultural resonance.

3

FROM SUDAN TO SUEZ:
STRATEGIC ENCOUNTERS
David Lowe

For around 70 years, the Middle East occupied a special place in Australian strategic planning, and in thinking that connected Australian military and diplomatic activity with ideas about identity and nationhood. From the mid-1880s to the mid-1950s a succession of military episodes and international crises prompted such government and popular responses to suggest that the Middle East became a special 'site' for Australian projections overseas. This chapter explores this notion, concentrating especially on the consequences of military episodes and strategic crises for political-strategic planners, and on the significance of these accumulating military experiences in the Middle East for Australians' stories about themselves in war and in the world. I suggest that there grew, and, to some extent, there remains today, a loose but welcome relationship between these two themes: Australians' familiarity with the Middle East as a strategically defined concept and the stories about Australians at war there that help define 'Australianness'.

The basis for exploring connections between foreign and defence policy and constructions of national identity has been well-established by historians. By defining dangers and degrees of foreignness, governments inevitably create mental boundaries for people thinking about their country in relation to others. In his wide-ranging study of American foreign policy, David Campbell's succinct statement that foreign policy/defence policy is an identity-constituting act is now shared by many historians, and provides the basis for analyses ranging from the highly discursive and post-structural to the more causation-focused works that try to incorporate a layer of cultural texture.[1] This chapter is closer to this latter end of the spectrum of possible interpretive approaches. In order to appreciate the intersections between military/diplomatic activity and identity-shaping, I examine the course of the main Australian–Middle Eastern encounters between the 1880s and the 1950s under two main headings: strategic judgments that led to Australians playing a military role in the Middle East; and Australian narratives about their military endeavours in the region, which tended to revolve around the two themes of the Middle East as testing ground for troops destined for more far-reaching conflict and the Middle East as the place where imperialism, tourism and Australian nationalism intermingled. Extending this second theme further, we can also note a developing blend of assumed (usually more than soundly-based) familiarity with the circumstances in the Middle East and contempt for either the societies there or, in the case of critics of government policy, for Australian involvement there. The two episodes serving as bookends here, the dispatch of an Australian contingent to Sudan in 1885, and the diplomacy surrounding the Suez Crisis of 1956 highlight this familiarity/contempt theme in particular.

And although the scope of this chapter does not permit elaboration, it should at least be noted that New Zealand's military, strategic and diplomatic experiences in the Middle East over this period suggest the same type of connections with cultural themes. New Zealanders born around the turn of the century grew up with similar assumptions about Britain's imperial and civilizing mandate in the region, New Zealand soldiers trained and fought there in two world wars, along the way adding to popular, 'orientalist' ways of viewing Egypt and neighbouring countries, and New Zealand politicians and defence planners assumed further possible action in the region until the mid-1950s.[2] As historian Malcolm Templeton has argued, all of these themes need to be taken into account in order to appreciate the blend of emotional and strategic factors behind New Zealand's role in the Suez Crisis of 1956.[3] I argue below that the same applies for Australia, but rather than having the Suez Crisis as a climactic focus, it stands in this account more as a conclusion to a long narrative about Australian strategic thinking and the Middle East, with several consistent threads.

Strategic Viewing

One of the most important things to note at the outset is that throughout the period under examination here, the leaders of other nations did more to define Australia's strategic role in international affairs than Australians did. Both before and after Australian Federation British leaders logically provided the most important analyses of the British Empire's strategic interests. This is a fundamental point that needs to be remembered when considering lively expressions of

Australian nationalism, and particular Australian interests overseas in the late nineteenth- and early twentieth-centuries. Leading Australian politicians, at State-Colony and then federal level, were far from acquiescent when British diplomacy seemed to neglect Australian interests in the Pacific. From the 1880s through to the First World War there were several examples of spirited Australian agitations for the extension of British control in the South Pacific, in order to head off, or reverse, imperial gains of other European powers such as France and Germany in the region. Among these were propositions entailing the spread of a modest Australian empire, preferably one financed and defended by the British. In general, however, British responses were attuned to the strategic priorities in Europe, and therefore not encouraging for adventurous sub-imperialism.[4]

The great naval scares and fleet expansions of the early twentieth century only intensified this position. Nervous Australian opinion-shapers were quick to appreciate the connections between their own defence, whether against other European imperialists or against restless, acquisitive Asia, and the fastest sea route to Australia via the Mediterranean and Middle East. On the eve of the First World War, the Sydney *Daily Telegraph*, contemplating the real prospect of Asian aggression towards Australia and New Zealand, concluded:

> In that event, if Britain is to preserve her Empire, she must be able to dispatch a great navy into the Pacific. And in order to be able to do that with the promptitude essential to success she must command her inner line of communication — the Mediterranean and the Suez Canal.[5]

This was the basic equation for the next thirty years. Australia's security depended heavily on the prestige and real military power, especially naval power, of the British Empire. In the absence of an imperial Pacific fleet, which the Australians agitated for unsuccessfully before the First World War, they remained heavily dependent on the Royal Navy to be able to come to their aid quickly. The Middle East was never the source of direct threat to Australia. As David Walker argues in this volume, the threat would come from Asia, the 'yellow peril' rather than another part of the 'Orient' such as the Middle East, whose military capabilities appeared to be in decline, in contrast to those of the ascendant Japanese.[6] But the Middle East, or more specifically, the naval route through the Suez Canal, formed part of a crucial line of communication which would help speed the Royal Navy towards Australia if and when necessary. Anything which disturbed British imperial prestige in the Middle East was a potential threat to Australia's own security.

Furthermore, there was a comforting clarity about sending Australians to the Middle East. They travelled there to become part of a British imperial force, and thereby drew on the formidable stores, command and organizational expertise and other forms of support that the British armed forces offered. They might sometimes be swallowed up within the great imperial forces in ways that detracted from their distinctiveness, but they were not in danger of appearing too puny and isolated to offer real combat against a foe. And, as part of an imperial force, they were positioned to establish the two sets of credentials dear to Australians, worthiness as transplanted Britons and as successful pioneers. The first instance was in 1885 when a contingent of New South Wales volunteers sailed to the Sudan to help avenge the death of the legendary British General Gordon, and quash the indigenous revolt against the British-backed Egyptian regime. It was a milestone in Australian history, for hitherto no soldier in the pay of a self-governing colony (i.e. New South Wales)[7] had ever served in an imperial war. In contrast to the considerable fanfare accompanying the 758 volunteers, their service in the Sudan consisted mostly of skirmishing and guarding a new railroad project which, in the end, was abandoned. The highlight was their inclusion in a 30 kilometre march of 10,000 men, in square formation. The New South Wales artillery component drilled and camped, but did not come close to an enemy. The few Australian casualties were the result of disease.[8]

The scale of conflict and the appalling casualties made the First World War very different from the Sudan experience, but the initial phase saw the basic pattern of Australian volunteers sailing to the Middle East repeated. It might have been otherwise. The original plan was for the First Australian Imperial Force (as they were officially titled) to proceed to England for training, but the main camps there on the Salisbury Plain were already too crowded by late 1914, and the Australian and New Zealand troops undertook their training in Egypt instead. As is discussed below, it was during this period, December 1914 to April 1915, that the larrikin dimension to the image of the ANZAC soldier was fleshed out, and Australian orientalist tales about the Egyptian condition built on stereotypes about this part of the Middle East. (Walker details Australia's literary impressions of the Middle East in the First World War in Chapter 2.)

The Australians' landing at Gallipoli on 25 April 1915 and their subsequent eight month struggle against well-entrenched Turkish defenders was quickly elevated to nation-making significance, and continues to attract greater attention than other aspects of Australian involvement in the First World War. According to popular thinking, this was where the recently-born nation was given its fierce baptism. Part of a bigger and over-ambitious British campaign to enable the Royal Navy through the Dardanelles into the Sea of Marmara and hopefully knock Turkey out of the war, the Gallipoli landings were riddled with errors and too easily-anticipated. The details of how Australian and New Zealand troops clung on to a small beach-head and, in coming months launched desperate, near suicidal attacks in vain, have been well-told elsewhere.[9] For the purposes of our inquiry, it is worth noting that the Australians, although later adept at appropriating the Gallipoli campaign, were outnumbered throughout by British, Indian and French forces. The Dardanelles campaign had little significance in the bigger context of the war, fought largely on two fronts in Europe; and in terms of those Australians killed, the figure of 8141 at Gallipoli was soon dwarfed by the monstrous bloodshed in France. When Prime Minister 'Billy' Hughes demanded reparations and the recognition of Australian interests in the peace-making at the end of the war, he claimed to speak for the 60,000 Australian dead. Gallipoli accounted for less than one-seventh of these.[10]

Having withdrawn from Gallipoli back to Egypt, some Australian troops stayed in defence of the Middle East. The Australian Light Horse, having fought dismounted at Gallipoli, regained their horses and initially, as part of a bigger imperial force under British command, helped guard the Suez Canal. During 1916 this force went on the offensive against Turkish positions in the region. They recaptured Sinai and then pushed into Palestine, taking Jerusalem at the end of 1917; and in the following year they moved into Lebanon and Syria, before the Turkish surrender in October 1918. The Light Horse enjoyed some spectacular successes along the way, most notably their successful charge across open ground in the face of machine guns and artillery at Beersheba in October 1917, and in the same year an Australian, General Henry Chauvel, became commander of the Desert Mounted Corps, comprising British, New Zealand and Indian troops as well as the Australians. The number of Australians killed in the Middle East campaign was very small in the context of the bigger struggle — 1394 — but unlike Gallipoli, casualties in these battles could at least be justified as having helped hasten the Turkish surrender.[11]

In the Second World War, the Second Australian Imperial Force followed the same route as their predecessors, sailing for the Middle East, but the surrounding circumstances were very different. First, although there was broad consensus in Australia about the need to assist in the struggle against Hitler, there was less certainty about how to do so and on what scale at a time when Japan, having already invaded China, was increasing its pressure on Southeast Asia. After some agonizing, Prime Minister Robert Menzies sent the first raised division of volunteers to Egypt at the beginning of 1940, and another followed later in the year.

The Middle East, and especially the Suez Canal, retained its lynch-pin strategic significance for Britain and its allies. More than just the route to India and Australasia, it was adjacent to major oil fields in an era of increasingly mechanized warfare; and after Japan's successful entry into the war in December 1941, the canal and the lands to its east assumed the importance of a region that must not be used as a means of enabling Japanese and German-led forces to join up. Before then, however, in June 1940 (five months after the arrival of the first Australians in Egypt) Italy entered the war in alliance with the Germans, and with colonies in Libya and Ethiopia immediately jeopardized the British hold in Egypt.

In response, Australian troops graduated quickly from larrikins to warriors in the Middle East in a manner similar to their forebears, and built on the image of Australians proving their mettle against the desert backdrop. In September 1940, when the Italians attacked Egypt from neighbouring Libya, the Australian 6th Division countered with immediate success and with a British armoured division notched up a series of rapid victories as they drove the Italians westwards across the North African coastline. These achievements were the more remarkable for the numerical superiority of the Italians. Ten Italian divisions were destroyed and close to 130,000 prisoners taken, at the cost of 500 Australian and British killed.[12] When the Germans joined the battle in North Africa, however, all of these gains were lost. One pocket to hold out against General Rommel's Afrika Corps was in the Libyan city of Tobruk, where four Australian brigades and other allied troops withstood a siege for close to eight months, before being relieved through a successful counter-attack. The Australians were withdrawn before the siege was lifted, at the insistence of the Australian Government, but by then they had, through their tenacious defence, turned Rommel's intended insulting epithet, 'desert rats' into a source of pride.

After the Japanese attack on Pearl Harbour in December 1941 two Australian divisions were withdrawn from the Middle East to help defend Australia and its approaches. The one remaining division in the region was part of the British force that eventually defeated the Germans decisively in October 1942 at El Alamein. The Royal Australian Air Force remained active in the region and ships from the Royal Australian Navy continued to help make up the Royal Navy force operating in the Mediterranean during the war.

Capturing the Australian contribution to the Middle Eastern campaigns of the Second World War is easier than assessing the value of these campaigns in relation to the other theatres. It would be hard to argue that the campaigns were decisive for the course of the war in Europe. The battle between German and Soviet forces dwarfed them for significance, and then the D-Day landings by allied forces in June 1944 opened up the long-awaited second front in Europe. In contrast to their small contributions towards the D-Day landings, Australians had earlier been central to a disastrous attempt to open a new European front from the British position in the Middle East, namely the ill-fated Greek campaign of 1941, which saw over 5000 Australians captured.[13] From December 1941 Australian contributions to the war effort were split between Europe/Middle Eastern and Pacific theatres, and were less significant in both in the latter stages of the war. The war confirmed some fears for Australian strategic planners in relation to the Middle East. The spectacular initial successes of the Japanese from December 1941 to February 1942 confirmed the dangers of depending on the speedy dispatch of the Royal Navy towards Australia in a war fought on several fronts.

Should Australian troops have been kept in Australia, in anticipation of looming conflict with Japan? In tackling this question historians have often divided along the lines of more nationalist-minded arguments versus those interpretations stressing the bigger picture of the global struggle, in which Australia was inevitably caught up. Those focusing on the nationalism, or lack thereof, in Australian wartime policy have tended to be more critical of the decision to send a total of three divisions to the Middle East, while those determined to situate Australia in the context of a global struggle have generally been more sympathetic to the decision.[14]

In the absence of a solid alternative (at least until the conclusion of the ANZUS Treaty with the United States and New Zealand in 1951),

Australians' involvement in Middle Eastern defence during the Second World War threw into sharp relief the need to preserve crucial lines of communication, including that through the Suez Canal, rather than consign Australia's role in British/Commonwealth strategy to the dustbin. The uncomfortable situation of working within a system that has been tested and found wanting persisted into the early 1950s. Its logic rested squarely on the assumption that the next conflict would bear the same global characteristics as the Second World War, and that the Anglo–American alliance would therefore again be able to cover shortcomings in British/Commonwealth defence plans.

Of course, there was no third world war, but there was, until the early-mid 1950s, a real expectation that the new Cold War might suddenly become hot in ways that would reinforce traditional ways of planning for Europe's and the Middle East's defence. There is no doubt that Australia's defence planners envisaged Australia's role in the early stage of another global conflict very much in terms of a replay of 1939–40. From 1948, Australians were treated to a stream of foreboding British analyses of the Soviet threat. The Chifley Labor Government tried to maintain a distinction between the Cold War polarity in Europe and more multi-faceted problems in Southeast Asia, but the global logic of Cold War was formidable, and was positively embraced by the Menzies Government sworn in at the end of 1949. By the middle months of 1950, both before and after the outbreak of the Korean War, leading British and American policy-makers began employing even more climactic metaphors, arguing that the time was fast approaching when a stand had to be taken and communism fought squarely. Menzies agreed.[15] In June 1950 Australia's top defence planning body, the Council of Defence met with Britain's Chief of Imperial General Staff, Field Marshal Sir William Slim, to consider the gravity of the Cold War crisis and its implications for Australians. Slim told the Australians that Europe and the Middle East were the most crucial theatres to hold in the event of a war with the Soviet Union. More specifically, he wanted the Australians to agree to send an expeditionary force to help defend British airbases in the Middle East. Interestingly, he prompted something of a collective excursion into the history of Australia at war. Prime Minister Robert Menzies said, 'The Middle East has been an Australian theatre now in two wars. We raised and sent the 2nd AIF to it and it was our primary preoccupation until Japan entered the war.' His Chief of General Staff, Sidney Rowell, added, 'We did right to help out in M[iddle] East in [the] last war, and [the] situation now resembles this'; while another

Cabinet member suggested that the situation was in fact 'more comparable to [the] first world war than to [the] second.'[16]

Pleased by this historical turn in the conversation, Slim encouraged the Australians to assume that war with the Soviet Union would be global, and he pointedly reminded them of how the British Empire might unravel should the Middle East not be held. If this happened, he said, 'it may open the route to Africa, finish co-operation by Pakistan and India, cut the sea route through the Mediterranean and deny to us oil resources which may be essential to the prosecution of this war.' Menzies agreed, adding that the Russians were also students of history: 'If they take note of the lessons of past history their aim must be to knock us out in the early period of the war.'[17]

And Menzies acted. He doubled the defence budget as a percentage of domestic product, he introduced a big, expensive national service program for 18-year-old men, he led Cabinet into agreeing to send troops and aircraft again to the Middle East when war broke out, and he commenced stockpiling and gearing the economy for war.[18] His Chief of General Staff made ambitious promises about how many troops would be available to travel to the Middle East on the basis that national service trainees had joined up in droves when the First World War had broken out. The trainees of the early 1950s would surely do the same.[19] From 1952, this logic began to unravel in the face of communist-led revolutions and the demise of colonial power in Southeast Asia, and then the death of Stalin. Preparing for another global war never disappeared totally from Australian calculations, but it competed with regional dangers and was complicated by new alliance structures (NATO, ANZUS and other regional security architecture) in ways that made the Middle East recede for Australians.[20]

Thus, after the preliminary localized encounter in Sudan in 1885, it was preparing for, and twice became involved in, global wars that kept the Middle East to the fore in Australian minds. We should not be surprised at this. From the vantage point of the 1950s, the twentieth century appeared to be one of ever widening and cataclysmic wars.

The First World War was extraordinary for its parameters — all of the major powers involved, and many of the smaller ones — its duration, its extravagant use of vast transport and weapons industries, its destruction of property, and the appalling loss of life, mostly European men, numbering nearly 10 million. It left deep scars with the generation who endured it.[21] The Second World War went even further in scope and destructiveness. Air power enabled constant and easy transgression of national boundaries, and aerial bombardment and the concept of total war made a mockery of the distinction between soldiers and citizens. Of the more than 50 million killed, at least half were civilians. Almost as many were uprooted as refugees in Europe, and not all were able to return to their pre-war homelands. Nazi ideology almost brought about the destruction of European Jews, with six million killed. The war ended with the dropping of two atomic bombs, signalling a new high-point in space-time compression, an absurd level of disproportion between the use of weapons and human suffering, and the prospect of human self-destruction.

For the generation of Australian politicians and defence planners who had grown up during this murderous half-century the prospect of another calamitous war was very real. Their main allies in Washington and London agreed, and therefore the Middle East retained its special place in Australian strategic thinking for some time beyond the end of the Second World War.

Testing Ground and Tourists

With an eye towards Australian involvement in future wars, historian Ken Inglis titled his study of Australians in the war in the Sudan, *The Rehearsal.*[22] This was the prelude to bigger forays to come, and there were also strong threads of continuity for the historian to trace from this to subsequent conflicts. The Sudan expedition was, to many Australians, a welcome testing of Australian mettle and imperial worthiness. There was, in the 1880s, a need to build on incipient acts of nationalist pride. The Australian Test Cricket Team had recently triumphed over England in England, and, consistent with the popular assumption of close connection between sporting prowess and warrior, the Sudan presented an opportunity to show that Australia boasted fully fledged men of Empire.

It also inspired one of the most enduring symbolic representations of dissent, the Little Boy of Manly, who rapidly became the symbol of young Australia.[23] As a cartoon character that also found its way into advertising, the little boy arose from the story of nearly-nine-year old Ernest Laurence who bemoaned his youth, which kept him from sailing with the New South Wales contingent that he watched depart from the Heads at Sydney. Not to have his patriotic instinct denied, Laurence sent money to New South Wales Premier William Dalley, as a contribution to a patriotic fund for anticipated widows and orphans resulting from the war. The Little Boy of Manly making his donation was soon penned by the *Bulletin*'s satirical cartoonist, Livingston Hopkins, in April 1885, The *Bulletin*, at the time a champion of radical nationalism, was critical of the dispatch of the New South Wales contingent, and the Little Boy was drawn as an outdated caricature in Sunday School dress.[24] Thereafter the Little Boy was often deployed by Hopkins and increasingly by other cartoonists through the early decades of the new Commonwealth. The mocking tone of an absurd figure prevailed in the earlier cartoons, but, as a representation of young Australia, he became more ambiguous from the late 1880s: regarded with affection but never shaking off a tendency towards the absurd; capable of joining with larger than life figures of the British Empire, but starting to appear a little too young for an Australia moving towards nationhood. The *Bulletin*, in a change of tone and stance generated by new management, applauded the Australian contribution to empire in the First World War and had the Little Boy handing over his role to the image of the rugged Digger.[25] In short, some of the more recognizable imagery associated with Australian nationhood and development can be traced to the Sudan campaign in 1885; and, at the same time, critics' responses to the sending of the New South Wales contingent can logically feature in the annals of dissent in Australian public life.

By the turn of the century, Australians, as travellers and readers of travel tales, were familiar with at least the highlights of the lands surrounding the Suez Canal. They were more accustomed to the Middle East as being a slow transit zone offering tourist excursions than the idea of it being a final destination. From the time ships began using the new canal in 1869, wealthy Australians on their way to London paused briefly in Colombo, Ceylon, and then made a habit of side-trips to Cairo and Luxor in Egypt while their ship made its way up the canal.[26]

In the First World War Australians deposited in Egypt were on their way elsewhere. Expecting to train in England, most were disappointed to be stuck in Egypt for four and a half months, a situation hardly surprising when we recall that more than 20 per cent of those who sailed were born in Britain or elsewhere overseas, and a goodly proportion of the total — the nature of the records prevents a very accurate estimate — were motivated at least partly by the prospect of a paid trip 'home' and other exciting destinations. Several recruiting posters played on this idea of a rare opportunity for young enlistees to see the world.[27]

It was in Egypt that the First AIF established an essential dimension to their stereotypical behaviour which, with added elements of ingenuity, heroism and blinding loyalty to mates on the battlefield, became the

'Anzac legend'. The dimension that grew from Egypt was larrikinism, a feature of their behaviour that went hand in hand with racial stereotyping of the Egyptians they encountered. Journalist, and later official war historian, C.E.W. Bean set the tone at the outset, presenting to soldiers a guidebook in which he warned of prevalent diseases owing to the filth, poor sanitation and foul water used to wash food, of conniving thieves and tricksters anxious to rid Australians of their money, and of 'foreign women riddled with disease,' making Cairo an international capital of gonorrhoea and syphilis.[28] Soldiers writing about their experiences in Egypt, in diaries or letters home and in some published instances after the war, often dwelt on similar themes, and the 'Gyppo' quickly became a well-known and reviled figure. (And older generations today still know that to be 'gypped' is to be cheated or deceived.) Those soldiers who engaged more fully with their surrounds did so mostly either in appreciation of ancient and religious landmarks or in the exotica of the bazaar.[29]

Rather than training and preparing for battle, the most-celebrated behaviour of Australians in Egypt was their instinctive suspicion of authority and officialdom, especially British, and their larrikinism — or, in less benign terms, their boorish racism and vandalism. In April and July 1915 Australians led rampages through the Wazza brothel district of Cairo, terrifying inhabitants, burning property and clashing with military police who tried to intervene. While boredom and the high incidence of venereal disease were identified as likely causes, underlying the rampaging was also a reaction against a land that defied easy understanding by impatient travellers. In the words of historian Richard White, the Australians' actions resulted from 'the generalized frustrations of the gypped tourist, whose Orient had not lived up to the poetry of the tourist brochures.'[30]

In the wake of their first major battle, however, Australians could engage with a much stronger literature. From Gallipoli, news of the Anzacs' bravery and endurance in appalling circumstances was eagerly consumed at home. Arguably, Australian deeds there in 1915 were soon overburdened by public anxiety to see them as having passed a supreme test, signifying virility in an era of Darwinian preoccupations with national survival and decline. Some contemporary commentators and several later ones dwelt on Gallipoli's location as the source of Western civilization, blessing Australian heroism with allusions to the Crusades and to ancient Greece.[31] The Dardanelles' proximity to Greece lent this action a stronger sense of European destination; and it was where the

Middle East met Europe, the special belt of lands from old Mesopotamia to Greece well-known from junior history lessons as producing the cradle of civilization, the origins of democratic rule and Christianity. To allude to such powerful themes in discussion of Australians' feats at Gallipoli was, again, surely overburdening them, but it was also a popular way of linking the campaign to national hopes and anxieties. The Australian Light Horse's successes in the desert fighting of 1917–18 were perfect embellishments as they were rare instances of gallant rapid movements in a war better known for attrition over inches of land.

Australian deeds in the desert in the Second World War were captured fastest by war novelists who went out of their way to draw lines between this batch of Diggers and the First AIF. In his 1944 account of the siege of Tobruk, correspondent and novelist, Chester Wilmot, wrote:

> There was much in common between these men and the original Anzacs. Although the one was a successful defence and the other an offensive which failed, the same spirit was engendered in Tobruk and on Gallipoli. In both, the constant threat of an enemy who hemmed them in with their backs to the sea bound men together in unbreakable comradeship. Because of this, Tobruk and the spirit it typified became woven into the pattern of the Australian heritage, just as surely as Gallipoli was twenty-six years before.[32]

In Lawson Glassop's novel, *We Were the Rats*, published in the same year, the leading characters pause to ponder what makes Australians such good fighters, and settle on virtues such as pioneering spirit, sporting inclinations, and disregard for danger, and 'the virility of young nation' — all qualities that helped tie them to the achievements of the First AIF before them.[33] The Second World War saw Australian soldiers win fame for defence of their own territory, most notably on the Kokoda Trail in Papua New Guinea, but the Pacific theatre did not overshadow stories about deeds elsewhere. As a place where Australian fighting prowess and national pride could both jostle with and sustain British efforts, the Middle East retained its special place in popular ways of understanding Australians at war.

Familiarity and Contempt

The Suez Crisis of 1956 is presented here less as the climax to 70 years of Australian military thinking about and involvement in the Middle

East, than as a reminder of the potency of Australian narratives about the region even at a time of clear change in strategic imperatives for Australians. By 1952, the Anglo–American consensus on Australia playing its familiar role as part of an Imperial/Commonwealth force defending the Middle East was starting to break down in the face of communist successes in Asia, and the emerging new line of thinking that the 'cold war' might not necessarily become 'hot' in the sense of global war in the near future, but that smaller conflicts and acts of 'subversion' might be increasingly damaging to the West. By 1953, the Australians had agreed that they should anticipate sending their first contingent of an expeditionary force to Malaya rather than the Middle East, and in 1955 this had been confirmed through the formation of a Commonwealth Strategic Reserve. The Middle East, although still regarded as a crucial theatre in any general war, and more important than ever for its oil reserves, was no longer logically of immediate security concern for Australians. A new security guarantee struck with the Americans and New Zealanders in 1951, in the form of the ANZUS Treaty, took the weight off the Royal Navy which, in any case, was less important than air power in the 1950s. So, what was this episode over the Suez Canal in 1956, and why, given the changed strategic circumstances, were Australians so caught up in it?

The Suez Crisis is widely regarded as a desperate and unsuccessful throw by Britain and France to halt their decline linked to disintegrating empires; and Australia's unwavering support for Britain, by extension, is often depicted as a final moment of unquestioning filial loyalty, before the realities of Britain's slide in international affairs became too obvious to ignore. The Australian role in the crisis was diplomatic only but, through a mixture of timing and activism, it was also prominent. The details of the crisis are well known. In brief, the Egyptian leader Gamal Abdel-Nasser announced the nationalization of the Canal which to that date had been operated by an international company of French origin and in which the major shareholder was Britain. The British Government led by Anthony Eden quickly came to the conclusion that this assault on their interests in the Middle East had to be resisted, and joined with the French and Israelis to plot an excuse for invasion. According to the plan, Israeli troops invaded Egypt on 29 October and an Anglo–French force followed them a week later, ostensibly to halt the combat and secure the Canal, but the main aim was to secure it permanently for Western interests.

The conspirators' plan went disastrously. The UN General Assembly quickly condemned the Israeli and Anglo–French invasions, and the Americans demonstrated how effectively they could undermine the British pound in the event of continued military action. Eden and his government, and the French, withdrew in humiliation. Throughout the crisis, the Australian Government supported Britain. The only other member of the Commonwealth to do so was New Zealand. Australian support was all the more notable for Australia's membership on the UN Security Council at the time and for Menzies' own service as a spokesman for the Canal users sent to Egypt to put the users' case to Nasser, prior to the invasions. The Australians did not know of the intrigue behind the Anglo–French–Israeli action, but the government held fast to the British position, even when rumours of possible plot grew stronger.

Historians have offered several reasons beyond the simple argument of strong loyalty to explain Menzies' unswerving support for the British. Among those identified by Bill Hudson are economic ones, such as possibly higher Canal charges and qualms on defence (naval) grounds, and, in Hudson's words, 'an incredible contempt for Egyptians and disbelief in their ability to run anything, let alone a great international waterway.'[34] In Menzies' case, this observation is certainly warranted. His references to Nasser around the time of the crisis tended to suggest a connection between racial character and untrustworthiness. Menzies' exuded the manner of a good 'Orientalist,' as later outlined by Edward Said. Clearly, it was significant that of all the countries in the Middle East, Egypt was one that Australians knew, largely through tales arising from military episodes. Earlier encounters with Egyptians, both first-hand and digested written accounts, had established this well before the crisis of 1956. The example used by Said of British politician Arthur Balfour explaining in the House of Commons in 1910 how the British presence in Egypt was raising it from a low point of social and economic degradation might easily have been interchanged with a Menzien mid-century observation.[35] Passing through Egypt in 1950, and speaking with British officials there, Menzies noted, less benevolently, in his dairy; 'These Gyppos are a dangerous lot of backward adolescents mouthing the slogans of democracy, full of self-importance and basic ignorance';[36] and in the wake of his unsuccessful representations in Cairo in 1956, he described Nasser as 'cunning but simple in mind.'[37]

Such remarks, and the air of living in the past about European, Australian and New Zealand actions in relation to the Suez invite dismissive criticism, but it is worth noting also the enduring power of familiarity in Canberra and Wellington. It not only bred contempt but it also provided certainty in a world made uncertain by the spread of communism, the prospect of a third world war in the early 1950s, and the rapidity of change in Asia. Like Balfour in the House of Commons, Australians and New Zealanders knew the Middle East through the lesson of civilizing imperialism; and, furthermore, they had banked their important military deeds relating to national identity and purpose.[38] As Australian historian J.D.B. Miller wrote, for Australians and New Zealanders in 1956, 'there was almost a sense of relief about again being involved in the Middle East.'[39]

Both Australian and New Zealand Governments looked gullible and behind the times in their support for Eden's disastrous adventure in Egypt in 1956. For the Australians especially, it marked something of a turning point in the decline of the Middle East in relative strategic significance. But we need to recall that it was not until the mid-1950s that the idea of a long Cold War replaced expectations of a likely 'hot' one. This slow transition paved the way for harder thinking in Australia about the consequences of past and likely future decolonization in Southeast Asia and the Pacific.[40] It did not mean the end of interdependence between security in a regional context and involvement in British and American global strategy. Such interdependence has never disappeared. The transition was also far from smooth, as was well-illustrated by the Menzies Government's strident support for Britain during the Suez Crisis of 1956. A crisis in the Middle East in which British and French interests were at stake triggered a default setting in government for Australian rallying to preserve the imperial life-line, the sea-lines between Britain and Australia. Significantly, from the late 1950s the numbers of Australians sailing to the Middle East as soldiers and/or tourists also began to decline, largely in response to advances in air travel. The strategic encounters and the self-celebrating narratives about Australians in the Middle East which had sustained each other over 70 years began to assume the less potent force of completed stories about days past.

As we have seen since 2003, however, in the form of clichéd media references to rugged Anzacs again striding out into Middle Eastern deserts, this time in Iraq, they are still capable of being invoked.

4

ARAB MIGRATION FROM THE MIDDLE EAST

Trevor Batrouney

In this chapter the term 'Arab-Australians' is used broadly to refer to a cultural group defined by a common language and common cultural heritage.[1] It encompasses people who have settled in Australia from the Arabic-speaking countries of the Middle East, including Lebanon, Egypt, Iraq, Jordan, Palestine and the Arabian Peninsula. The use of this term is not to deny the distinctive identities of these Middle Eastern nations, which have diverse populations, including different ethnicities, religions and dialects. For example, an Egyptian or Lebanese, while emphasizing their 'Egyptianess' or 'Lebaneseness', can still describe themselves as 'Arabi' or 'Ibn Arab'.

Immigration from Middle East is currently little more than five per cent of all migration to Australia. Until about the 1960s the story of Arab migration to Australia was essentially that of Lebanese migration. Despite variations in countries of migration origin over time, Lebanon has been by far the largest source country, followed by Egypt, with immigrants from Iraq becoming more numerous in recent years. This is illustrated by the following settler arrivals figures from 1996/97 to 2001/02: Iraq (8314), Lebanon (5396) and Egypt (1796), with much smaller numbers for Syria (845) and Jordan (679). At the 2001 Census the number of Lebanese-born in Australia stood at 71,329, over twice the size of the Egyptian-born, which was 33,432. The recent arrival of Iraqi refugees has led to 24,832 Iraqi-born in Australia with smaller numbers of Syrians (6710) and Jordanians (3322). Other Middle Eastern groups, including non-Arab ethnicities such as Turkish and Iranian, number around 9890. A second measure of the size of the Arabic community in Australia is derived from ancestry (identified as having one or both parents born in that country). For example, in 2001 the ancestries of the larger Middle Eastern groupings were as follows: Lebanese (162,239); Egyptian (27,001); and Iraqi (11,190).

A further indication of the size of the Arabic community is given by those who speak Arabic at home. Arabic is used at home by 209,371 Australian residents,[2] making it the fourth most widely spoken community language in Australia, the first community language in Sydney (142,647) and the fifth community language in Melbourne (45,736). The birthplaces of Arabic speakers resident in Australia are: 41.7 per cent born in Australia; 30.9 per cent in Lebanon; 7.5 per cent in Egypt; and 5.2 per cent in Iraq.

In terms of religion, the overseas-born in Australia from Arab countries continue to be predominantly Christian, despite the recent arrival of large numbers of Muslims. At the 2001 Census, 89 per cent of the Egyptian-born and 66 per cent of the Iraqi-born living in Australia were Christian. Among the Lebanese-born around 58 per cent are Christian and 41 per cent are Muslims. Wars and other civil strife in the Middle East has significantly affected the flow of immigrants, especially of refugees and displaced persons, to Australia. These migration waves have made for a more diverse Arab presence in Australia by the end of the century than was the case at the start of the century.

The history of Arab migration is examined according to four defining periods in in terms of government policies related to immigration and citizenship, and the responses by Arab-Australians. The periods defined are: the early years of the White Australia Policy (1880s–1920s); assimilation (1950s–1970s); multiculturalism (1970s–1990s); and the last decade of the twentieth century, which I term 'beyond multiculturalism'. This review reveals changes over time in Australian Government policy and public attitudes as well as changes in the responses and attitudes of Arab-Australians. As such, it provides some insights into the multi-faceted relationship between Australia and the Middle East.

White Australia Policy Period: 1880s–1920s

In many respects the Lebanese (then known as Syrians) who came to Australia in the late 1880s and early 1900s could not have chosen a less propitious time to start a new life in Australia. A combination of economic depression, popular feelings of nationalism and racism, and a pervasive imperialist ideology marked their earliest years in Australia.

By the mid-1890s Australia was in the midst of its worst economic depression ever. In addition to economic decline the country was suffering from a cruel drought that slashed the wheat yield by a third and culled the sheep population by a half. At the depth of the depression unemployment claimed 30 per cent of the skilled workers and even more of the unskilled. The depression had driven many city dwellers into the country areas in search of work. By 1901 the situation had improved somewhat but many Australians remained out of work and desperate.

During the previous thirty years Australia's population had doubled due in largely to the gold rushes in New South Wales and Victoria. This influx of a relatively heterogeneous group of immigrants led to popular feelings of racism within the Anglo-Celtic majority, particularly against the Chinese and other Asians. Thus the push for Australian nationalism, which gained strength in the latter part of the nineteenth century, included, as a powerful element, the notion of 'Australia for the Australians' meaning, of course, Australia for the Anglo-Celtic majority.

The agitation for White Australia was fully developed by the mid-1880s and had moved from labour protection to openly racist arguments. The trend was sustained by growing popular journalism, particularly in the *Bulletin* and the *Boomerang*. Their development of a racist ideology through articles and cartoons exerted a powerful effect on the population. White Australia moved from being originally concerned with the Chinese to being a crusade against all non-European immigrants. Writers such as Henry Lawson and Banjo Patterson contributed to this dominant ideology by idealizing shearers, farmhands and other itinerants in the Australian bush as model Australians. Lebanese hawkers were not only excluded from this idealized group but were also the subject of popular agitation and parliamentary criticism.

The Boer War and the First World War gave rise to a powerful expression of nationalist and imperialist ideology among Australians. Not only was Australia white and British but it would fight alongside the mother country in protection of the Empire of which it was a proud member. At the time of Federation the greater part of Australia's sense of identity came from its connection with the British Empire.

Immigration and Citizenship Policy

The birth of the Australian nation in 1901 was accompanied by two Acts of Parliament, both of which were intended to ensure that Australia remained predominantly British. The *Immigration Restriction Act* of 1901 was designed to preserve racial purity and the protection of labour conditions by limiting the immigration of non-Europeans through the introduction of a dictation test in any European language. This was followed by the Commonwealth *Naturalisation Act 1903*, which denied

Asians and other non-Europeans the right to apply for naturalization. Similarly, they were prohibited from receiving the pension and enrolling as electors. In this way the new Federal Government assumed control of immigration and vigorously pursued policies of *exclusionism*, that is, debarring entry of immigrants to Australia on criteria based explicitly or implicitly on racial characteristics and *exclusivism,* which involved preferential treatment for particular nationalities.[3]

When the new Federal Government passed the *Immigration Restriction Act* in 1901, Australia aspired to a racial and cultural homogeneity through the establishment of the White Australia Policy. Thus the first attempt to ensure social cohesion was by exclusion of those who were not British. The notion of 'Australia as British' provided the basis for Australia's social cohesion until the onset of mass migration after the Second World War. The *Immigration Restriction Act*, the first major piece of Commonwealth legislation, was only part of the legislative armoury of White Australia. Colonial and state laws relating to immigration, occupation, citizenship and Aborigines were all part of a consistent campaign to prevent anyone from contributing to Australian nation-building who was not of European descent and appearance.[4]

The attitudes of Australian Government officials towards Lebanese citizenship were equivocal. Officially the Lebanese were grouped together with Asians; unofficially they were recognized as being different. The Secretary for the Department of External Affairs, Attlee Hunt, indicated that Lebanese were suitable as immigrants and settlers on several grounds. The comparatively high number of Lebanese female immigrants, (38 per cent of the total Lebanese-born in 1901), meant that they could not be considered a threat to the safety of Australian women or racial purity. They also appeared more similar to Europeans than Asians and because of these attributes it was felt that they could quite easily blend with the racial mix in the young Australia. In addition, they were considered to have a relatively high educational standard compared with other immigrant groups. Hunt gave examples of this in the bi-lingual ability of some of the early Lebanese settlers. This contributed to the view that the Lebanese were a unique group. They were familiar with French, English, Italian and other European languages and customs, owing to the presence of European educational and religious institutions in Lebanon. In this limbo where they were defined as not quite Asian and not quite European, no one was quite sure how the Lebanese, or Syrians, should be treated administratively. They were arbitrarily classified with Asians, not by race but by region. Therefore, any restrictive legislation worked against them and, as a result, they presented something of a dilemma to the immigration authorities.

The outbreak of the First World War was detrimental to relations between the Australian Government and Lebanese immigrants. Although the majority of Lebanese settlers came from the district of Mt Lebanon and were described as Syrians, the Australian Government classified them as Turkish subjects. Consequently, they had to register each week at their local police stations as enemy aliens while, ironically, at the same time, some second generation Lebanese-Australians were fighting as members of the Australian Imperial Army against the Turks.

Responses of Arab-Australians

As indicated above, the Lebanese revealed a number of characteristics that distinguished them from Asian immigrants with whom they were classified. As a result, the Lebanese strongly rejected their classification as Asians. A Lebanese community leader in Melbourne wrote to Alfred Deakin in 1911, urging the entry of his countrymen to Australia on the grounds that, as he claimed, 'Syrians are Caucasians, and they are as white a race as the English. Their looks, habits, customs, religion, blood etc., are those of Europeans but they are more intelligent.'[5] Many Lebanese applied unsuccessfully for citizenship until the passing of the *Nationality Act 1920* which allowed people who had been resident in Australia for five years or more to become naturalized. However, even after gaining naturalization, Lebanese, being classified as Asians, were not permitted to enrol and vote in elections. During this period the Lebanese only challenged the prevailing public norms around race, and discriminatory immigration and citizenship legislation, on moral grounds, when it applied to them. In other words, their desire was simply to be accepted and respected as members of British Australia.

A sample of letters to government departments from Lebanese seeking Australian citizenship reveals the depth of feeling with which the Lebanese responded to their alien status.[6] It also exhibits a growing sense of confidence and assertion with which Lebanese community leaders approached authorities directly or requested others to intercede on their behalf in their attempts to gain full citizenship status. They based their claims on a number of factors: their racial similarity to Europeans and their distinctiveness from Asian races; their commercial endeavours; and their integration into Australian society.

The small Lebanese communities of Sydney and Melbourne were keen to demonstrate their public spiritedness and loyalty, which they did through community collections for hospitals and charities, activities that were carried on by descendants of first wave settlers until the 1980s. As early as 1914 the small Lebanese community in Sydney subscribed over 400 pounds to the Lord Mayor's Patriotic Fund and 600 pounds to the building of the South Sydney Hospital. At the end of the First World War the Syrian community of New South Wales sent the following message of congratulations to the Australian Governor-General:

> Please accept for your Excellency and convey to His Gracious Majesty the King our humble congratulations of the Syrian community of New South Wales at the great victory achieved by the British Empire and its Allies, and our unswerving loyalty to His Majesty's person and throne.

If the ultimate test of loyalty is to fight for one's country, then membership of Australian-born Lebanese in the armed forces during both war and peace also met that requirement. In 1914, out of a Lebanese-born population of 1527 and their descendants, an estimated 60 young Lebanese Australians joined the Australian Imperial Army and fought in the various battlefields of the First World War.

The Lebanese underwent two identity changes during this period: one related to their home country and the other related to their adopted country. Lebanon was a semi-autonomous district in the Ottoman province of Syria until the French Mandate of 1920. After semi-autonomous statehood was achieved in 1926 individuals began migrating with Lebanese passports. But it was not until 1954 that Australian Census officials classified Lebanese and Syrian immigrants in separate categories. The second change of identity was achieved in 1920 when immigrants from Syria began to be accepted as British subjects.

The difficult times and the negative social attitudes endured by many of the first wave settlers produced a number of defensive responses among Lebanese descendants. These sometimes involved obscuring and, at other times, outright denial of their ethnic and religious backgrounds. This led, for example, some second generation Lebanese to claim a presumably higher status 'French' or 'Mediterranean' background in preference to their Lebanese one. Another partly defensive response was the Anglicizing of both surnames and first-names, to more or less approximate with their Lebanese names. Another common occurrence was changing religious affiliation from one of the Lebanese Christian churches such as Antiochian Orthodox, Maronite and Melkite Catholic Rites to affiliation with Anglican and Latin Catholic churches.

Yet another strategy did not involve denial of Lebanese background but enhancing of it. This applied to the practice of 'claiming', whereby prominent individuals, who may have some Lebanese background, were 'claimed' as members of their group. This is intended to have the effect of adding worth to their group and, by extension, to them as individuals.

Assimilation: 1950s–1970s
Immigration and Citizenship Policy

Although Australia's population has been marked by diversity since 1788, by 1947 the country could still be termed ethnically homogenous and monocultural. However, in the immediate post–Second World War years, Australia embarked on a campaign to achieve a population growth of two per cent per annum, of which one half was anticipated to come through natural increase and one half through immigration. The objective of immigration in the 1950s and '60s was to create a labour force, which could help to expand Australia's manufacturing industries.

Between 1947 and 1971 the Australian population grew from 7.6 million to 12.7 million with net immigration contributing 2.2 million, or 43 per cent, of the total population growth. With the addition of the children of these immigrants, some 60 per cent of the population increase during this period can be attributed to immigration.[7] This post-war migration included not only British settlers but also increasing numbers of immigrants from a diverse range of European countries.

The initial government policy response was that of assimilation. Immigrants, especially those from non-British backgrounds, were expected to abandon their languages and cultures and conform to the dominant Australian values and become citizens as quickly as possible. The major emphasis was on shedding national loyalties and affiliations and adopting the language, culture and institutions of the host society. The motivation was not primarily economic or political but essentially cultural and the culture to which immigrants were expected to assimilate was essentially British–Australian. There was no place for cultural diversity within this definition of Australia.

A single important value underpinned Australian citizenship law and practice during this period: the definition of Australia as British. Australia's *Nationality and Citizenship Act 1948* came into effect on 26 January 1949. It created a distinct status of Australian citizen which, in addition, ensured that Australian citizens also retained the status of

British subject. This British link was so durable that it was not until 1984 that Australian citizens could no longer be considered as British subjects. Despite the passing of this Act, aliens were confronted with a number of restrictions such as the right to claim certain pensions, access to public housing, and the full range of political rights. During this period the White Australia Policy was securely intact, with resident non-Europeans ineligible to apply for naturalization until 1956. Even then, while the qualifying period for others was five years, the residential qualifying period for non-Europeans was fifteen years.

It is important to note that Australian citizenship at this time was still expressed in terms of British culture and ethnicity, not in terms of the rights and responsibilities of citizens of the state. Thus the Act defines an 'alien' as a person who does not have the status of British subject and is not a protected person. The definition of an Australian in the Act was therefore a person descended from an Anglo-Celtic people.[8]

Responses of Arab-Australians

The self-perception of Lebanese settlers as Syrians in Australia persisted until the arrival of a second wave of immigrants after the Second World War. The early settlers defined themselves as Syrians due to their classification under the Turkish Empire as being part of the administrative division of Syria. On many applications for naturalization dating back to the 1920s, the place of birth is shown as Mt. Lebanon, Syria. This was in marked contrast to those immigrating after 1920, when Lebanon became a French Mandate. These immigrants saw themselves as Lebanese and quite distinct from Syria. On the other hand, Lebanese settlers in Australia seemed quite unaware of the change of status of Lebanon as a nation. Thus the seeds were sown for conflict between the pioneer groups and later groups of Lebanese settlers.

The period of assimilation brought with it a diversity of Arab immigrants to Australia. Not only was there considerable growth in the numbers of Lebanese immigrants but also the arrival of Egyptians and small numbers of other Arab immigrants. While their settlement during this period was marked by a preoccupation with the practical matters of settling and establishing their families in Australia, they were instrumental in establishing some, and rejuvenating other, religious and community organizations.

They continued, under the influence of descendants of first wave settlers, to participate in displays of public spiritedness and collections for charity. Sometimes this involved donning traditional dress to attend the Red Cross International Ball or similar events, which stressed the exotic nature of Arabic culture. Like many other culturally and linguistically diverse groups at the time, through establishing their own ethnic organizations, they sought to preserve their own languages, religions and cultural practices and, in doing so, rejected the policy of assimilation, but quietly.

Multiculturalism: 1970s–1990s
Immigration and Citizenship Policy

By the 1970s, after several decades of non-British immigration, Australia was moving from an essentially monocultural society to becoming a multicultural one. Not only had its population become much more multicultural since the 1940s but public policy developed in response to this shift.[9] The election of the Whitlam Labor Government in 1972 was accompanied by a change in official ideology towards immigration. For example, in 1973 it was proclaimed that future immigration policy would not distinguish between immigrants on the basis of race, ethnicity, religion, colour or nationality, beginning the abandonment of the last vestiges of the White Australia Policy.[10] During this period Australia continued its policy of admitting some refugees, with those from Indochina now replacing the earlier post-war intake from Eastern Europe. Although Lebanese were not officially designated as refugees, special arrangements were made in 1976 to resettle persons displaced by the Civil War in Lebanon.

Modification of the White Australia Policy began in 1966 with a reduction of the citizenship requirement to only five years of residence, but the open abolition of the policy had to wait until the Whitlam Government declared in 1973 that future admissions would be universal. The decisive year, confirming that the White Australia Policy had broken down, was 1976 when the first 'boat people' arrived in Darwin, the same year that special concessions were extended to Lebanese.[11]

The policy of assimilation was clearly giving way to the emerging policy of multiculturalism. By the mid-1970s Australian Governments had adopted a policy of multiculturalism, which is based on the idea that ethnic communities are legitimate and consistent with Australian citizenship, so long as certain principles (such as respect for basic institutions and democratic values) are adhered to. This formal recognition of Australia as a multicultural society is the most recent of Australia's cultural transformations, each of which has been brought about by immigration.

As a result of immigration and the growing diversity among the Australian population, Australian citizenship law and practice were altered progressively from the late 1960s, when the impact of immigration was first felt. In the 45 years after its original enactment, the *Nationality and Citizenship Act* was altered some 27 times. The changes over recent decades reflect a general movement from an Anglo-Celtic, monocultural conception of citizenship to one that recognizes the multicultural character of the Australian community, encourages a broader basis for inclusion, and seeks to extend access to the rights that accompany Australian citizenship to all.[12]

Amendments in 1993 to the *Australian Citizenship Act* 1948 incorporated a preamble and introduced a new pledge of commitment to persons acquiring Australian citizenship. These amendments aimed 'to give proper recognition to the significance of Australian citizenship as a common bond which unites all Australians.' Thus the qualifications for the grant of Australian citizenship reflect an inclusive approach to prospective citizens including: residency of two years (of the previous five); a basic knowledge of the English language; an understanding of the responsibilities and privileges of Australian citizenship in relation to the political and legal systems; understanding of entitlements such as the right to vote and stand for election, serve on juries, to apply for certain government jobs, and to obtain an Australian passport.

A number of important developments in citizenship policy took place during the 1970s to '90s, which I frame as the period of multiculturalism. These included the gradual movement from exclusion to inclusion; government invitations to citizenship; abolition of renunciation of former allegiance; and the introduction of dual citizenship. With the gradual elimination of the barriers to citizenship confronting aliens, today the general approach towards Australian citizenship is inclusive and non-discriminatory with minimal eligibility requirements.

Responses of Arab-Australians

During the period of multiculturalism, a substantial number of Arab-Australians entered Australia under the humanitarian program. They included humanitarian entrants from Lebanon during the Civil War, Palestinian refugees, as well as refugees from the Iran–Iraq and Gulf Wars. Despite coming from the strife torn Middle East and despite evidence of some current and historical discrimination against them, Arab immigrants have revealed great commitment to settle in Australia.

Evidence for this is to be found in their establishment of two types of community organization. The first may be termed 'cultural maintenance organizations' where the primary focus is to preserve and maintain aspects of the former culture such as language, religion, music, and dance. Churches, mosques, social groups and village organizations fall into this group. The second type includes those community organizations which seek to engage directly on behalf of their members with the wider society. These include community welfare organizations, which typically seek to meet the welfare needs of Arab-Australians, and socio-political organizations, which ensure that the political interests of Arab-Australians are brought to the attention of both the public and the authorities. The establishment of these organizations reveals a growing degree of self-confidence and assertion on the part of Arab-Australians to ensure their rights in a multicultural society.

Further evidence can be found in the high take-up rates of Australian citizenship by the major Arab immigrant groups which, by 1995–96, were: Lebanese (96.2 per cent), Egyptian (95.1 per cent); Iraqi (82.5 per cent) and other Middle East and North Africans (90.3 per cent).[13] These rank among the highest of all immigrant groups. One explanation for these high rates of citizenship take-up may be found in the fact that a number of Arab countries allow dual citizenship, such as Lebanon, Egypt, Syria and Jordan. Citizens of these countries do not, therefore, have to choose between their country of birth and their adopted country.

Beyond Multiculturalism: 1990s–

This section examines a range of attacks on multiculturalism and the impact of various government policies, which together have made for a policy regime that goes 'beyond multiculturalism'. In a recent work, Jupp[14] outlined the conservative critiques of multiculturalism which have been mounted by various groups: academics, such as Blainey and Betts; politicians, such as John Howard and Stone; journalists and popularizers, such as Barnett, Sheehan and Piers Ackerman; and assorted talk back radio hosts. Critics of multiculturalism put forward four main arguments. First, it is claimed that the immigration and multiculturalism debate has been suppressed in the interests of political correctness as critics of multicultural policy were denounced as racists. A second critique asserts that multiculturalism is a divisive force that risks dividing Australia into warring tribes. A third accusation is that multiculturalism is advocated mainly by elites, or the 'new class', and is less supported by working class Australians. A final criticism identifies a dominant culture within the

Anglo-Celtic majority and questions whether recently arrived immigrants are likely to share this culture. Although these criticisms were expressed most strongly and consistently by conservative critics, they were also to be found in certain elements of the Labor Party during the 1990s.

Some sections of the Coalition Government were either open or closet supporters of these views. For example, during the first few years of his tenure as Prime Minister, John Howard appeared to be a reluctant supporter of multiculturalism. With the abolition of the Bureau of Immigration, Multicultural and Population Research, and the Office of Multicultural Affairs, support for multicultural policy was to be found at grassroots level among community workers, ethnic communities and, in more muted form, by government departments and inquiries.

A major threat to multiculturalism was Pauline Hanson's election to Federal Parliament in the 1996 election. She campaigned on a policy of limiting immigration and abolishing multiculturalism, Aboriginal reconciliation, and a humane refugee policy. These views attracted widespread international and national criticism and seriously damaged Australia's reputation abroad, leading to a bipartisan statement to the Parliament on 30 October 1996 reaffirming Australia's commitment to a non-discriminatory immigration policy and to maintaining Australia as a culturally diverse, tolerant and open society.[15]

Pauline Hanson's One Nation party was established in April 1997 after she was forced out of the Liberal Party. This political party did not arise in a vacuum, but reflected the negative views on Asian migration and multiculturalism which had become more acceptable in conservative ranks after the demise of the Fraser Government and during the 13 years of Labor rule from 1984 to 1996. Although support for One Nation began to diminish after a popularity peak in 1998, it exerted an indirect but significant impact on government policy. Its policy proposals, which were later implemented, included a move from permanent residence to temporary protection for some refugees, a change in the status of New Zealanders and the excision of Christmas Island from the Australian 'immigration zone'. It also encouraged the public expression of views on immigration, Asians, multiculturalism and refugees, which had heretofore been unfashionable. The Liberals adopted much of One Nation's refugee policy and pursued their own similar agenda against multiculturalism and Aboriginal reconciliation. By the election of 2001, One Nation had contributed to the policy agenda of the Howard Government which could be described as 'conservative, assimilationist, reactionary and nationalistic.'[16]

The forces of economic rationalism had been exerting a growing influence on immigration and settlement policies from the 1980s and particularly since the election of the Howard Government in 1996. Economic rationalism made an impact on migrant selection criteria through the introduction of user pays and cost-free migration, the sale of facilities, the outsourcing of services and the abolition of the Department's research and multicultural policy bodies. These administrative changes after 1996 revealed the government's weaker commitment to the policy of multiculturalism.

The impact of changes to the points system led to the increased significance of economic measures in the selection of migrants so that by 1999, non-economic factors had largely been eliminated from this system of selection. Family reunion numbers were capped at the level of 500 and now require higher payments and guarantees of support than ever before. The points system effective from 1 July 1999 requires applicants to be under 45 years, to understand vocational English and to have a skilled occupation with qualifications recognized in Australia.[17]

The economic rationalist ideology made inroads into immigrant settlement services, with changes including: the denial of welfare (other than Medicare) to all non-humanitarian arrivals for two years; the pre-payment of bonds against future welfare dependency by migrants or their sponsors; and a requirement for some to pay for their English language tuition. Asylum seekers on temporary protection visas (TPVs) have been particularly hard hit, facing restrictions on welfare, work and education, and denied any administrative assistance from the Department of Immigration and Multicultural and Indigenous Affairs (DIMIA). The 'user pays' principle was even extended to the charging of detention costs to failed refugee applicants which, if not recovered, prevented them from returning to Australia.[18]

Jupp summarized the elements of Australia's 'economically rational' immigration policies thus:

> selection on employability criteria; abolition of assisted passages; restriction of family reunion; limitation of welfare rights and services; selling of on-arrival hostels; competitive tendering and charges for English tuition; agency user pays for translating and interpreting; and, finally in 1997, the privatization of detention centres and deportation.[19]

Refugees and Asylum Seekers

A new era in the treatment of refugees and asylum seekers commenced with the opening of the Port Hedland detention centre in 1991 for the internment of those arriving without documentation or authorization. This alone did not discourage small numbers of asylum seekers continuing to arrive in Australia. However, three decisions taken by the Howard Government in the late 1990s ushered in a more rigorous, if not punitive, approach. These included: the outsourcing of detention centres to a private American prison corporation; the opening of the Woomera detention centre in the South Australian desert; and the change from permanent to temporary visas for unauthorized arrivals deemed to be refugees. This means that asylum seekers are to be detained until all assessment processes are concluded, including appeals. Although the detention of asylum seekers and their children has attracted widespread national and international criticism, it has enjoyed considerable public support within Australia.

Temporary protection visas (TPV), which had been introduced and later abolished by the Hawke Labor Government, were reintroduced by the Liberal–National Government in 1996. The current version of the TPV scheme means that those arriving without a visa and being interned were to be issued only with three-year visas which can be renewed but never be replaced by permanent residence. This group is denied family reunion and many settlement services. Instead, official encouragement and financial assistance is offered to them to return home when the Australian Government considers conditions in their home countries to be safe. The impact of the scheme and the Government's proposal to send Iraqis and Afghanis home is detailed by Mansouri in Chapter 6.

A key event in Australia's action against asylum seekers was the *Tampa* incident in August 2001. This involved the Australian Government refusing permission to the *Tampa*, a Norwegian ship which had rescued a number of asylum seekers bound for Australia, to enter Australian territorial waters. This stringent action was intended to deny asylum seekers the opportunity to apply for refugee status. It is important to place the *Tampa* incident in context. First, at the time of the *Tampa* confrontation the government was already disposed to establish detention centres for asylum seekers in remote areas within Australia, such as Port Hedland and Woomera. Second, the numbers of refugees from Iraq and Afghanistan were on the increase, numbering 3800 by the year 2000. These numbers, although small by international standards, alarmed DIMIA, sections of the Australian public, the media and some politicians. Third, government spokespersons had been propagating negative views for some years about 'queue-jumpers' and 'wealthy illegals', which had fuelled popular prejudice and prepared the public for this action. Furthermore, as many of the recent asylum seekers were Arabs and most were Muslims, fears of links with terrorism after 9/11 were inferred and, in some cases, openly stated by sections of the Australian community.

Australia's action against the *Tampa* led immediately to the *Border Protection (Validation and Enforcement Powers) Act* passed in September 2001 declaring Christmas Island, Ashmore Reef and Cocos Island to be outside Australia's 'migration zone'. This was followed by agreements reached with Papua New Guinea and Nauru to house asylum seekers at Australia's expense. The full deterrent system against asylum seekers was now in place. In addition to legitimizing the *Tampa* incident through legislation, excising offshore territories from the migration zone, permanently denying full residence status to those coming without documentation, it also denied them any of the social or educational benefits extended to other refugees.[20] (See Chapter 7 for further detail on the *Tampa* incident and the resulting 'Pacific Solution'.)

Twin forces have been at work on Australia's immigration, settlement and multicultural policies during the 1990s. On the one hand, policy has been rationalized in purely economic terms with some immediate benefits to DIMIA's 'bottom line' and to the immediate employability of selected immigrants. A second force is that of bureaucratic rationality and control, which has led to a range of increasingly stringent deterrent procedures directed against asylum seekers. These 'rational' approaches have, at times, been carried to extremes and have led to a weakening of Australia's non-discriminatory immigration policy, its range of settlement services, its adherence to international refugee protocols, its commitment to human rights and its support for the policy of multiculturalism. These government policies reflect, and to some extent foster, negative public attitudes to immigration and multiculturalism.

Responses of Arab-Australians

Arab-Australians are marked by great diversity such as: countries of origin; length of time in Australia; religious affiliation; size of communities; mode of arrival; settlement needs; ethnic community organizations and so on. Their responses to government policies can be considered at three levels. At one level, their responses to policies in the 1990s were as varied and as complex as any other large segment of the

Australian population. At a second level, particular Arab communities (such as Lebanese, Egyptian and Iraqi) reflect the concerns and preoccupations of their communities. For example, Palestinians in Australia are particularly concerned with Australian Government policies and responses to events in the Palestinian territories. Likewise, Iraqi Australians tend to focus on the Australian Government's role in the enforcement of sanctions and participation in conflicts in Iraq. Lebanese-Australians are particularly concerned with vilification of their community as a result of some violent crimes in Sydney. A third level of analysis, the one taken in this chapter, involves examining Arab-Australian responses to government policies through the activities of those organizations that serve the Arab-Australian community as a whole. Gaining insights into this third level involved the item analyses of annual reports, journals, media releases and other publications.

Three Arab-Australian community organizations established in Melbourne are the Victorian Arabic Social Services (VASS), Australian Lebanese Welfare Inc. (ALW) and Australian Arabic Council (AAC). Each of these bodies is non-religious, non-party political and committed to serve the Arabic community as a whole. The first of these bodies to be established was VASS (formerly the Victorian Arabic Network) in 1981 with the aim of bringing Arabic community workers together for support, exchange of information, and joint action on specific issues. Its activities include monitoring welfare service provision and advocating on behalf of the Arabic community; providing information and cross cultural training sessions on issues related to the Arabic community; and working in partnership with mainstream organizations, such as schools, to meet the needs of the Arabic community.

ALW Inc. was established in 1983 to meet the extensive welfare needs of the humanitarian settlers who fled Lebanon before and during the Civil War. In 1995 it extended its work into the employment field. Through both its welfare and employment activities it complements the work of mainstream organizations and acts as an intermediary with them for Lebanese and other Arabic-speaking migrants.

The AAC was established in 1992 as a direct response to the racism experienced by members of the Arabic Community in Australia during the Gulf War. The Council has engaged in a range of activities to promote Arabic culture and language, eradicate racial vilification, raise public awareness on international human rights issues, oppose negative depictions of Arabs in the media, encourage accurate reporting on Arabs and Arabic issues, engage in educational activities, and respond to government inquiries.

The responses of Arab-Australians to government policies fall into a number of categories. Perhaps welfare is the longest-standing area in which Arabic community organizations have sought to complement government services and, where necessary, compensate for the withdrawal or denial of services to Arabic migrants and refugees. The ALW, in particular, has worked closely with DIMIA, complementing its services to vulnerable groups in the Australian Arab community. An example of compensatory services is the establishment of the Asylum Seeker Resource Centre in Preston by a consortium of volunteer individuals and organizations led by an activist from the Australian Lebanese community. The Centre provides free legal aid, material aid, English classes, social and recreational programs and counselling services for asylum seekers and people on TPVs. Interestingly, the Centre is housed in the centre of a Lebanese Christian village organization. In addition to the provision of complementary or compensatory services, Arabic community organizations also monitor mainstream service provision and advocate for the needs of Arab-Australians. Welfare activities conducted by ALW and VASS are provided on a non-political and non-sectarian basis and have a large volunteer component.

A second activity, largely undertaken by the AAC, is opposition to racist and religious stereotyping and vilification in person or through the media. Vilification can take the form of comments revealing 'Arabphobia' or 'Islamophobia' or a wrongheaded conflation of both terms. Particularly since the ending of the Cold War, Arabs and Muslims have become used to being cast as the 'enemy,' the 'villains' or the 'other' of the West. The Gulf War, 9/11 and the Bali bombing have accentuated this trend. Opposition to racial and religious vilification involves close monitoring of all media, the publication of letters and articles in mainstream and Arabic media, the conduct of forums and giving talks on these topics at conferences. The AAC media awards have become well known as a means of encouraging accurate and fair writing and depictions of Arabs. The AAC has also led opposition to police ethnic descriptors with some success in Victoria. Another initiative has been the compilation of a register of acts of racial vilification and violence against Arab-Australians. The AAC has also been active in making submissions to government inquiries and legislation proposals, with a particular emphasis on the need for educational programs to combat discrimination and vilification.

A third activity, undertaken by each of the organizations, is in the field of education and research. This has involved Arabic language campaigns, cross-cultural communication classes, production of videos on Arabic history and culture, talks in schools and universities, the conduct of Arabic quiz competitions and public seminars, as well as liaising and counselling of Arabic students in schools. Educational activities go beyond formal education to embrace cultural activities, which have included two exhibitions and an Open Day at Melbourne's Immigration Museum as well as theatre and video productions. These activities are intended to counter negative depictions and provide accurate accounts of Arabs and Muslims to the wider community and, in so doing, raise Arab community and individual esteem. Research sponsored by one or other of these Arabic organizations, such as a study for VASS entitled *Politics of Social Exclusion: Refugees on Temporary Protection Visa in Victoria* is also an important part of their community activities.

The AAC has been vocal in providing commentary and advocacy on a range of government policies on international affairs. For example, the Council strongly opposed the sanctions imposed on Iraq following the Gulf War and Australian involvement in any future war against Iraq. It has also sought to influence government policy towards an even-handed stance in the Israel–Palestine conflict. This has involved highlighting atrocities committed against Palestinians and countering public statements made by the Jewish lobby in Australia. In the aftermath of 9/11, the AAC was concerned to warn against and highlight any vilification or physical attacks that might be directed against Arab Australians. While these have been the major preoccupations of the AAC, it has also opposed vilification of French Australians during France's nuclear testing and supported the plight of Kosovo refugees.

A major thrust of the AAC has been the need to foster Australia's relations with the Middle East and the Gulf Region. In response to a government inquiry, the AAC produced a report which resulted in the establishment of an Australia Arabic Foundation. The Foundation is a government-funded organization to further develop and guide multilateral strategic relations between the Arab world and Australia. This is an example of constructive co-operation between government and community organizations.

The sharpest criticisms of government policy in internal matters came with the government's treatment of asylum seekers, its policy of mandatory detention, the *Tampa* incident and the introduction of the so-called 'Pacific Solution'. Criticism of these policies was given the added force of the Arabic community's experience and detailed knowledge of the needs and sufferings of many Arabs among detainees and TPV holders. As shown above, the Arab community not only opposes these policies, but also actively seeks to mitigate their negative impact on asylum seekers. The AAC sees these as a continuation of the views of Pauline Hanson and One Nation, which it strongly opposed from their first appearance on Australia's political landscape.

Conclusion

Arab-Australian responses to government policies in the 'beyond multiculturalism' era range from close co-operation to intense opposition. One area of co-operation is support for and contribution to government inquiries and legislation in the fields of racial vilification and discrimination. A second example is to be found in international relations where members of the Arab Australian community are able to facilitate trade, educational and other contacts with the Middle East. Education represents the third area where there is co-operation between government departments and Arab-Australian community organizations to the benefit of Arab-Australian and other students in schools and universities in both Australia and the Middle East. In the area of welfare services government and community relations are generally complementary and co-operative, despite the vigorous advocacy that community members engage in. Two other matters reveal a co-operative relationship: the government's provision of funding to Arab community organizations and its recognition of them as points of inquiry and referral in matters affecting the Arab-Australian community.

The 'beyond multiculturalism' period has also witnessed intense opposition to government policies. This opposition is evident where the interests of Arab-Australians, or one of the constituent communities in Australia or overseas, is at stake. Examples include opposition to the government's stringent rules for family reunion; costs associated with some settlement services; problems facing asylum seekers in detention and those seeking to assist them; the adoption by government of some of One Nation's policies; the vilification of Arab and Muslim asylum seekers; the introduction of TPVs; the *Tampa* affair and the Pacific Solution. In international affairs there is opposition to the government's policy stance on the Palestine question as well as to the imposition of sanctions and Australia's participation in the second invasion of Iraq.

In a sign of growing maturity, Arab-Australian community organizations reflect an increased degree of altruism and principle. Their responses to the above issues are no longer solely pragmatic and focused on their own community. Examples include the AAC involvement in the movement for Aboriginal reconciliation, in advocating human rights for many different groups, such as the Kosovars under temporary protection and French Australians during nuclear testing. The AAC has become an Australian, as much as an Arab, organization.

Over the one hundred and more years of Arab-Australian settlement in Australia, several continuities and changes can be discerned in relation to issues of identity and citizenship. First, over each of the periods examined, Arab-Australians have not only chosen to settle in Australia but have evinced a strong desire to be accepted and respected members of the community. During the White Australia Policy period they continued to bring their families and establish themselves economically in Australia, while strenuously rejecting their status as aliens and seeking to gain citizenship of British Australia. This pattern of early commitment to settle and seek an attachment to Australia was repeated in both the assimilation and multicultural periods, revealed through displays of public spiritedness, loyalty and high take-up rates of Australian citizenship. The same desire to settle is to be found in the 'beyond multiculturalism' period, however for the reasons outlined, it is less able to be realized by sections of the community because of the current emphases of certain government policies. A second example of continuity is to be found in Arab-Australians' readiness over each of the periods to accept the prevailing public mores and government policies, only to opposing them when their interests were manifestly at stake. For example, during the White Australia period, they accepted the notion of British Australia based on the policies of exclusionism and exclusivism, but understandably wished to be included among the favoured group.

Likewise, during the period of assimilation, they engaged in assimilatory behaviour which, for some, involved shedding their religion, changing their Arab names to Anglo ones and engaging in host society cultural practices, both in wider society groupings and even in their own community organizations. During the assimilation period when cultural practices were maintained, this was done within the private sphere of life. During the multicultural period they were adaptable to public and policy changes, asserting their Arabic culture and establishing more ethnic community organizations to provide services to their members. For example, during this period there was increasing usage of the terms 'Arab' and 'Arabic' as an all embracing term for the various national groupings and cultures from the Middle East. Thus we have the birth of community organizations such as the AAC and VASS. During this period they also showed themselves to be capable of using host society structures to defend their interests. Thus Arab community organizations made submissions directly to Commonwealth and State Governments and to agencies such as the Human Rights and Equal Opportunity Commission (HREOC), as well as on occasions using the law to defend their interests. The 'beyond multiculturalism' period saw the Arab-Australian community continue to offer support to the government on certain issues but, to vigorously oppose it not only when the community's interests were at stake but also as a matter of principle on a range of issues of concern to the Australian community as a whole.

A third continuity over time has been the strong commitment to take up Australian citizenship. At the 2001 Census the take-up rate by people born in the Middle East was generally above the average citizenship take-up rate (74 per cent) of all overseas-born Australians. The citizenship take-up rate is highest for longer established groups such as those born in Lebanon (91.3 per cent); Egypt (91.6 per cent); Syria (86.2 per cent); Iraq (68.1 per cent). Likely reasons for high take-up rates include the perceived higher status of Australian citizenship and passport (compared to those of their countries of origin). For refugees and those fleeing turbulent political environments, gaining Australian citizenship provides much needed security. Pragmatic factors, including dual citizenship and ease of return visits to their countries of origin, are also reasons why people choose to take up Australian citizenship. Family reasons, that is, the desire to become Australians like their children or other family members born here, can also be influential in taking up citizenship.

This chapter has explored changes to government immigration and citizenship policies over four key periods in Australian history. In doing so it has charted the pathway to both a non-discriminatory immigration policy and an inclusive citizenship policy. At the same time it recognizes the weakening of government commitment to non-discriminatory immigration and multicultural policies during the 'beyond multiculturalism' period. It identifies across each of the periods the consistent desire of Arab-Australians to make an early commitment to settle in Australia and accept the prevailing public mores and government policies. However, it notes also that, when their interests have been at stake, Arab-Australians, with a growth in community self-confidence evident by the end of the century, are willing to defend and assert their interests. Finally, it demonstrates that, in recent times, their activities have gone beyond self interest in their embrace of issues of concern to the wider Australian community.

5

MUSLIMS IN AUSTRALIA

Abdullah Saeed

Muslim contact with Australia is said to date back to the 1750s, well before Europeans arrived, when Muslims from the Indonesian archipelago, particularly Macassan fishermen, regularly visited the north in search of *trepang* (sea slugs). These fishermen settled in beach camps for months at a time and lived peacefully with local Aboriginal communities. This interaction was hindered with the European colonization of northern Australia and eventually ceased in 1907 with the full implementation of the White Australia Policy.[1]

A second wave of Muslim contact came with the Afghan camel drivers who were brought to Australia between 1860 and 1910.[2] Realising the advantages of camel transport for Australia, Thomas Elder and Samuel Stuckey imported 122 camels and their 31 Afghan attendants in 1866.[3] The Afghans and their camels were based at Beltana sheep station in South Australia's Flinders Ranges, and here the first Muslim settlement in the inland developed.[4] Reports indicate that during the second half of nineteenth century and early twentieth century, between two and four thousand men were brought to Australia to work in the camel-based transportation industry which linked the outback to the major settlements of Australia. The Afghans worked in the desert heartland of the separate colonies of South Australia (which then included parts of what is now in the Northern Territory), Western Australia, Queensland and New South Wales, providing a vital lifeline for the developing continent. They formed tight communities on the outskirts of outback towns.[5] Since the Afghan camel drivers were not seen as permanent settlers, they came without their families. Some married Aboriginal women or other disadvantaged or marginalised women.[6] In the 1860s, they built Australia's first mosque in Broken Hill, New South Wales. The mosque is now a museum maintained by the Broken Hill Historical Society.[7]

The introduction of motorised transport at the turn of the century led to the collapse of camel transportation. Coupled with this, the commitment of the newly formed Commonwealth Government to a White Australia Policy meant that the Afghans could not apply for naturalization. The White Australia Policy was an implicitly racist strategy (the aim was to keep Australia 'racially pure')[8] and aimed at excluding Asiatics/Coloureds from living and working in Australia. Bigotry emanated from the highest levels of Australian society. In the 1901 Parliamentary debates Australia's second Prime Minister Deakin, who was instrumental in Australia's Federation, warned against 'the probability of racial contamination'[9] and Prime Minister Hughes, well known for his pugnacious views, stated in 1919 that this policy was 'the greatest thing we [the Commonwealth] have achieved'.[10] The policy was implemented by the newly created Commonwealth Government and placed migration restrictions on non-Anglo-Saxons.[11] As a consequence of this policy and the environment it engendered for non-Whites, many Afghans decided to leave; those who remained were denied citizenship and experienced enormous difficulties.

Many Afghans were subjected to racial persecution. They were prevented from working in certain sectors of the economy and efforts to remove them from the goldfields in the last decade of the nineteenth century incited specifically anti-Afghan sentiment. Afghans were considered alien, dangerous, and 'traitorous by nature'. Some, like the editor of Broken Hill's *Barrier Truth* (1903), held the view that Afghans were a 'menace', a 'threat to the morals of the community, filthy, savages and that non-white races could not blend with the whites.[12] According to Christine Stevens the term 'Afghan' began to embody a notion of contempt, of racial inferiority, of uncleanliness, brutality, strangeness and fear; Afghans became untouchables in a white Australia.[13]

The departure of many Afghans did not help those left behind to retain their Islamic identity and it seems that many with links to Islam drifted away from their faith. Commenting on the importance of these Afghan camel drivers, Christine Stevens says:

For nearly fifty years these Muslim men and their animals criss-crossed three-quarters of the Australian continent to service and sustain life and industry in the harsh interior. Without the exceptional skills and perseverance of these hardy Muslims — among the first Muslims to become part of the cultural mix of contemporary Australian society — much of Australia's traditional wealth would have remained undeveloped for many decades.[14]

There were other Afghans, however, whose contribution so impressed Europeans that streets were named in their honour. Elsewhere, traces of Afghan history linger, such as in the Sadadeen Primary School in Alice Springs which bears the name of the legendary Afghani cameleer Charlie Sadadeen, and 'The Ghan' train, running from Adelaide to Alice Springs was named after the Afghan cameleers who helped establish the first transport system across arid central Australia in 1879.[15]

Under the White Australia Policy, preference was given to white migrants of largely Christian backgrounds from Britain and Europe, in the name of keeping the community uniform, both ethnically and culturally. Of the few Muslims who arrived in Australia from Europe, most were of Albanian origin. Between 1930 and 1939 some 400 Albanians arrived[16] and, after the Afghans, were considered the second major Muslim group to migrate to Australia. Albanian émigrés were predominantly young, single and male and worked as casual labourers in Western Australia, Queensland and Victoria throughout the 1920s and 1930s. This group was visually 'acceptable' because of their 'lighter European complexion.'[17]

Due to economic necessity in the aftermath of the Second World War, substantial changes were made to Australia's immigration policy, bringing about the slow demise of the White Australia Policy.[18] In the late 1940s, the Australian Government began to promote immigration to rebuild and develop the economy, but the White Australia Policy still dominated thinking on migration. Unable to attract sufficient numbers of British migrants, however, the government expanded the intake to include large numbers of other European migrants. More liberalization followed due to the need for imported 'cheap' labour as a result of strong growth of the economy in the 1950s and 1960s.[19]

With the signing of an agreement between Australia and Turkey in the 1960s, a significant number of Turkish Muslims formed the first large-scale Muslim migration to Australia in the twentieth century. Approximately 10,000 Turkish migrants arrived in Australia between 1967 and 1971.[20] In the early 1970s, Muslims began to arrive in large numbers from the Middle East, particularly Lebanon in response to the civil war, and Egypt. More recent Muslim migrants include refugees from Bosnia, Somalia and Afghanistan.[21]

The debate about the efficacy and appropriateness of the White Australia Policy was further spurred on by the emergence of vocal migrant communities who were against assimilation and in favour of a more tolerant multiculturalism (unity through cultural diversity).[22] These pressures were raised by increased migration subsequent to the Second World War and the migrant communities' desires to express their own identity which gradually led to the complete abolition of the White Australia Policy by the Whitlam Government in 1973.[23]

Australia from then on experimented with the idea of multiculturalism, giving a voice to various ethnic, linguistic, cultural and religious minorities and assisting them by providing an opportunity to retain their distinct identities within an Australian context. The 1970s saw the emergence of a number of publicly funded multicultural institutions which gave an important say to minorities and helped build institutions to support the maintenance of their ethnic, linguistic and cultural identities.[24] Important institutions were either consolidated or established, such as: the Adult Migrant English Program, which was instigated as an experiment in 1948, and came to be considered a right rather than a privilege under the new multicultural policies being developed in the '70s;[25] multicultural television and radio broadcaster the SBS (Special Broadcasting Service);[26] and the Department of Immigration and Multicultural and Indigenous Affairs (whose name has changed several times overtime).[27] Government-funded research projects on settlement in Australia as well as additional facilities for migrants were also set up. This development of 'multicultural' institutions was undertaken in order to provide sturdy foundations for a 'united' society prefaced on cultural diversity.[28]

Subsequent to the Second World War, and with an acceleration since the late 1960s, there has been a rapid growth of the Muslim population in Australia to over 280,000 (based on 2001 Australian Census figures). These migrants came from all corners of the world with the largest contingents coming from Lebanon, Turkey, Afghanistan, Bosnia, Pakistan, Indonesia, Iraq and Bangladesh.[29] The eclectic origins of Muslims in Australia has had a real impact upon the nature, languages spoken, sectarian groupings, institutional structures, development of mosques and understandings of Islam that exist in Australia.[30]

Aspects of Community Building Post-1970

The 1960s, '70s and '80s saw the most important practical shifts in the provision of opportunities for Muslim migrants in beginning to strengthen their identity as Muslim-Australians. This was due to a series of programs aimed at migrants in general, from which Muslims significantly benefited. This period consolidated Muslim-Australian identity in a number of ways and through several developments.

Islamic Societies and Centres

An important aspect of Muslim community building was the establishment of the community organizations.[31] First, various Islamic societies which mushroomed from the mid-1960s began to consolidate their position.[32] Each state had a number of Islamic societies. Each community was centred around a mosque or prayer facility or around a particular issue of interest to the Muslim community where it was established.[33] These societies, although initially poorly structured or organized, began to develop well in the 1980s.[34]

The Muslim community is organised at the local, state and federal levels. Consolidation of the Islamic societies into state-wide Islamic councils began in the 1960s when the Islamic societies of each state joined the Islamic council of that state. Each council has its own agenda and activities such as welfare, educational and religious facilities. Today, well-established councils such as the Islamic Council of Victoria offer a broad range of activities related to weekend school, inter-faith dialogue, welfare services, media monitoring, educational programs and chaplaincy projects (such as sending *imam*s to prisons).[35] They also have a board of *imam*s and mechanisms for representing Muslims at state level.[36]

At the federal level, all Islamic councils are represented in the Australian Federation of Islamic Councils (AFIC), an umbrella organization for Australian Muslims.[37] While divisions along sectarian and ethno-linguistic lines persist, the AFIC provides symbolic unity and acts as an Islamic representative body at national level. Initially, AFIC's activities were largely funded by the issuing of *halal* certificates (these certificates verify that foods sold are in accordance with Islamic dietary laws), by donations from oil-rich Muslim countries, such as Saudi Arabia, and by its own investments. AFIC increasingly assists with purchasing educational facilities for Muslim children, building mosques and prayer facilities, providing *imam*s, and making lobbying services available to promote Muslim community interests in state and federal politics.[38] This latter point is important as the community develops and its political needs change — these issues have been heightened since 9/11 and the subsequent rekindling of negative stereotypes.

Educational Facilities

Many Muslims saw early on that education was the key to the maintenance of Islamic identity in Australia. They commenced weekend schooling with very few resources as early as the 1950s. Similar efforts continued throughout the 1960s and 1970s, then in the early 1980s the first regular Islamic schools were established in Australia with increased government funding/support from both the Commonwealth and States for community-based schooling.[39] Muslim primary and secondary schools were able to provide Islamic education, language studies such as Arabic and Turkish,[40] as well as teaching the core curriculum of each state; in other words, a secular education within an Islamic environment. The standards of these schools have gradually improved and a number of them, particularly well-established ones like King Khaled Islamic College and Minaret College in Melbourne, Malik Fahd Islamic School of Sydney, and the Islamic College of Perth, compete with other schools to provide a high quality education, especially in the core curricula.

With the initial infrastructure for the schools funded mainly from outside sources and with something of an Islamic school system running in Victoria, New South Wales and Western Australia, the subsequent funding from the Commonwealth and State Governments was used to further expand the Islamic education system in the 1990s. By 2005, there are over 26 Islamic schools with a student population of over 12,000. In addition, there are many weekend Islamic schools and *Qur'an* classes at most mosques and Islamic centres. Students who do not have the opportunity to attend regular Islamic schools can attend these weekend schools to learn more about Islam and the Arabic language.[41]

Unlike many other Western countries, such as the United States, where there is no taxpayer-funded Islamic school system, Australia provides substantial support to private schools, including Islamic schools. The number of children in private ethnic, religious and Christian schools in Australia grew by more than 50 percent between 1986 and 1994. It has been growing steadily since then partly as a result of the Commonwealth Government's decision to end the minimum and maximum enrolment limits on private schools, and to provide increased funding for those schools.[42] This has, however, led to significant public debate within the broader Australian community as to the role of public (state) education and private education. In this context, the growth of Islamic education in Australia has its critics. Much of this is connected to the broader debate on school funding and the recent increases in the government funding of private schools at the expense of public schools.

At the peak of debates in the late 1990s about private education funding Pamela Bone wrote in *The Age* that a:

> just released study of migrant students carried out for the federal government cautiously questions whether some ethnic schools are creating a less tolerant society. The author of the report, Professor Desmond Cahill of RMIT, said concerns had been expressed about the "pervading ethnocentricity" of the schools, "historically dubious curricular material", and whether some ethnic schools might be teaching "negative attitudes" about other Australians.[43]

In response Irene Donohoue Clyne, a researcher on Islamic education in Australia, felt that:

> Headlines such as "A new school of social division" and "Report questions curriculum of ethnic schools" in *The Age*, clearly link these to an Islamic school in Victoria. Moreover, language such as "educational ghetto", "ethno-nationalist or ethnic bias" and "historically dubious curriculum material" imply that these schools somehow are separating Muslim Australians from mainstream society and indoctrinating them with un-Australian values. [44]

As has been seen through the quotations above, an argument about the appropriate balance between educational systems (public and private) has the possibility of entering directly into the public debate about what it means to be an 'Australian' and the type of community that is hopefully developing. Unfortunately, however, this has the possibility of leading to a blaming of those who are culturally different from the mainstream, and therefore creating a less tolerant society.[45] Importantly this means that Islamic education can not be disconnected from broader public debates about education and its role within Australian society.

Despite financial support and growing academic success, Islamic schools still face some significant problems, particularly in the area of Islamic education and the Arabic language curriculum: for example, suitable teaching materials are needed, as are qualified teachers who are familiar with modern methods of teaching appropriate to Australian culture. These problems are also common elsewhere in Western countries, such as the United Kingdom. Nevertheless, Islamic schools provide for many Muslims a way of retaining and strengthening their religious and cultural traditions within an Australian context. Often the objective of an Islamic school is to train and nurture the generation of Muslims who are at home with both mainstream Australian society and Islamic tradition; in other words, to nurture a generation who are proud to be Muslims and Australians at the same time.

Mosques and Religious Leadership

Mosques play a pivotal role within the religious and cultural lives of Muslims and many early mosques in Australia were funded by countries such as Saudi Arabia, the United Arab Emirates, Kuwait and Libya. Since the late 1960s, the number of mosques in Australia has grown with the increase in size of the Muslim community. There are currently over 68 significant mosques in Australia, with the largest numbers located in Victoria and New South Wales,[46] and an increasing number of prayer rooms in workplaces, educational institutions and community centres.

The 1980s saw an influx of graduates of Islamic religious studies, mainly from Islamic universities located in Saudi Arabia, Egypt, Pakistan and India, into Australian mosques. The presence of *imams* from overseas also stems from the large-scale Turkish migration in the late 1960s, which prompted official interest from the Turkish Government which has sent *imams* to Australian mosques. A significant number of *imams* within the Australian Muslim community are therefore imported. As a consequence, Muslim religious leadership in Australia often lacks the necessary cultural understanding of the Australian context, and may not speak English. This creates a significant, persistent problem for Muslim Australians.

Some well-established *imams* have spent a considerable time in Australia and have familiarised themselves with the needs of the Australian Muslim community and culture as well as that of the wider society. Religious leaders who are fluent in English do play a significant role mediating and facilitating the Muslim communities' position within the wider society and greatly assist the relationship between the State and Federal Governments and the Muslim communities. There are also signs of the emergence of a small number of younger religious leaders born and educated in Australia, but it may take some time before a home-grown professional religious leadership emerges here.[47]

Islamic Financial Institutions

A significant achievement in the area of infrastructure was the establishment of an Islamic financial institution in the 1980s — the Muslim Community Cooperative (Australia) (MCCA). This has since developed into a fully-fledged Islamic financial institution of great importance for the Muslim community. The MCCA was established in 1989 in Melbourne with ten members and capital of AUD $22,300. By 2005, membership had grown to 7000 with over AUD $24 million invested.[48] It aims to present a practical model of Islamic banking to the Muslim community and to the Australian society at large, and to provide Muslims in Australia with an alternative to existing interest-based financial products and services.

In its financial dealings, the MCCA does not pay or charge interest (regarded as *riba* which is prohibited by Islam), and its transactions and dealings are deemed to be *halal* (this means 'lawful' in Arabic — these are types of transactions and commercial activities permitted to be undertaken by Muslims). The MCCA's primary areas of activity are housing finance, purchase of consumer products, and finance for business ventures. The MCCA made a profit for the 2004 financial year of AUD $509,927 and it is projecting profits of over AUD $680,000 in the next financial year.[49] Within ten years of its establishment, the MCCA succeeded in establishing a second branch in Sydney and diversifying its products. Although its services are mostly provided to Muslims, an increasing number of non-Muslims are also customers. The MCCA has thus become an important link between Muslims and the wider community.

Muslims and the Media in Difficult Times

As in many other Western countries, Islam has an image problem in the Australian print and electronic media. Headlines such as 'Muslim leader jailed in Egypt',[50] 'Mujahedeen from Hallam',[51] 'Muslims brace for the next backlash',[52] 'Anger at Islamophobia',[53] and 'Arab extremists could threaten order — expert'[54] exemplify the significant lack of understanding of Islam and Muslims. The stereotyping results in mistrust and misapprehension on the part of a significant section of the Australian population about Islam and Muslims. (For a further discussion of media representation of Arabs and Muslims in Australia, see Mansouri in Chapter 6.) This is accentuated by a bombardment through the international electronic media of images of Muslims as prime suspects in global terrorism, drug smuggling and the oppression of women. In taking the worst aspects of Muslim behaviour and presenting them as the normative standard rather than the exception, an understanding of the cultural, linguistic and ethnic richness and diversity of Muslim communities is discouraged.

Awareness of this problem is increasing within the Muslim community. At the Islamic State Council and Federal Council levels, attempts are being made to respond to perceived attacks on Islam and/or Muslims in the media, as was the case during the Gulf War, the American Embassy bombings in Africa, and the Indonesian military's involvement in the destruction of East Timor. As *The Age* wrote in the aftermath of the Gulf War:

> One of the by-products of the Gulf crisis has been an upsurge of racist attacks against Arabic and Islamic communities in Australia. The attacks led the [then] Prime Minister, Mr Hawke, to issue a statement recently, describing them as 'utterly repugnant'. His concern is shared by the [then] president of the Human Rights and Equal Opportunity Commission, Sir Ronald Wilson.[55]

Despite this, in the second Gulf crisis, the issue came to haunt Muslims again. Prime Minister Howard urged Australians not to take retribution on Arab- and Muslim-Australians for the actions of Iraq's then President Saddam Hussein.[56] The Australian Federation of Islamic Councils called on the media to exercise restraint in the reporting of the American Embassy bombings in Kenya and Tanzania, because they were deeply concerned that Australian Muslims would be stereotyped inappropriately as 'violent' and 'terrorist', therefore becoming the subject of abuse.[57] In 2003, public and political dialogue around the war in Iraq and the media representation of Arab-Muslim Australians became particularly heated during the Sydney peace protests, a phenomenon Mansouri explores in Chapter 6.

While media focus groups within state Islamic councils and the Australian Federation of Islamic Councils are beginning to more proactively respond to media characterizations of Islam, it must be said that the efforts on the part of the Muslim community to manage the response to the stereotyping of Muslims is still in its early stages and it may take some time for the community to develop a sophisticated infrastructure to respond to such issues in a more co-ordinated and organised fashion. With the development of such an infrastructure, progress is being made on a number of other fronts, such as the establishment of small-scale community radio stations in the major metropolitan areas of Melbourne and Sydney. Local Muslim newspapers and magazines are also gaining a foothold. The *Australian Muslim News* has been in circulation for some time, while other publications, mostly distributed in Sydney and Melbourne, include *Salam* magazine and a series of student newsletters.

Conclusion

The experiment of multiculturalism has successfully taken root in Australian society over the last 30 years, and so one should not exaggerate incidences of intolerance at the expense of the overall tolerance demonstrated by the wider community. There will always be isolated incidents and these increase proportionately to the raising of political tension between Australia and a particular Muslim country, for example, Iraq or Indonesia. This does not, however, mean that these incidents must necessarily be accepted. In response to the need for law reform and general education to confront racism within the general public, Australian law reform and human rights bodies have sought to consult with the Muslim community to work out means of reducing this problem and ensuring 'racial vilification' is not allowed to occur.[58]

Today, unlike the early twentieth century, a number of anti-discrimination laws are in place at Commonwealth and State levels to protect all communities, including Muslims, from discrimination. Among the Commonwealth Acts in this regard are the *Equal Employment Opportunity (Commonwealth Authorities) Act* (1987), *Human Rights and Equal Opportunity Commission Act* (1986), *Racial Discrimination Act* (1975) and *Racial Hatred Act* (1995). These laws are complimented by State-based *Racial Vilification* legislation. While there is much cause for anxiety within the Muslim community in relation to the negative public responses to the 'war on terrorism' and Australia's involvement in the current occupation of Iraq, this legal and policy framework for inclusion and multiculturalism provides the fast growing Australian Muslim community with much to be optimistic about.

6

Middle Eastern Refugees in 'Fortress' Australia

Fethi Mansouri

This chapter focuses on the experience of refugees of Muslim and Arabic background, both in terms of current Federal Government immigration policy and in relation to the public perceptions that such policies have created. The Australian Government's introduction of 'deterrence' measures, such as temporary protection visas and off shore mandatory detention of asylum seekers in Pacific island nations, and its deliberate linking of its treatment of refugees to border protection and security threats, will be examined in the first half of the chapter. It will argue that this episode in Australia's long history of settling humanitarian entrants has undermined its reputation in the region, raised serious questions about its commitment to multiculturalism, and increased the sense of exclusion and denigration among members of Arabic and Muslim communities. This sense of anxiety about the direction of Australia's refugee policies targeted at Middle Eastern asylum seekers has been exacerbated by its willingness to join the US-led invasion of Iraq on what now appears to be false pretences.

The treatment of asylum seekers in contemporary Australia is not divorced from an historical context, nor is it detached from an increasingly nervous international environment. In fact, one of the most striking features of the international refugee regime over the last twenty-five years is the development of alternative forms of protection to those set out in the 1951 Refugee Convention. While these alternative forms provide protection against *refoulement*, they typically confer fewer rights than those granted to asylum seekers who gain Convention status.[1] Worse still, policies of deterrence have become a 'priority' for Western nations since the early 1980s with strict measures introduced for detecting, detaining, deporting and discouraging 'irregular' asylum-seekers.[2] Such punitive measures need popular support before being adopted. The popular support, in turn, is contingent on a negative representation of those asylum seekers who will be affected by the new regime.

The 1951 Refugee Convention, which as much as possible is supposed to regulate and standardise the treatment of asylum seekers and refugees, has 'always been at the mercy of political and economic considerations'.[3] In the case of the Australian Government's recent treatment of asylum seekers, political considerations seem to be the key factor dictating policy direction. In fact, the negative representations of asylum seekers from Middle Eastern countries which reached a climax during the so-called *'Tampa'* and 'children overboard' incidents, occurred shortly before the November 2001 election. Both events were influential in securing the Coalition's re-election. The first incident[4] involved a Norwegian freighter, the *Tampa*, which rescued 433 Afghan asylum seekers found in a sinking Indonesian ferry off the coast of Christmas Island in the Indian Ocean to the far north-west of Australia. Although the Island is Australian territory, it was then deemed to be outside the Australian 'migration zone'. On 27 August 2001, the *Tampa* crew, in response to the wishes of the asylum seekers and in line with maritime conventions, attempted to take them to Australian waters. However, the Australian Government refused the vessel entry into its maritime zone. Despite this refusal, the *Tampa* reached Australian waters on 29 August but was prevented from proceeding any further by the Australian Navy. The Government, maintaining its vow to ensure that the asylum seekers 'never set foot on Australian soil,' did not allow the asylum seekers to move from this sea-bound position until six days later when New Zealand, Nauru and Papua New Guinea agreed to process them.[5] Following this incident, the Australian Government made substantial legislative changes to its migration zone making it more difficult for future asylum seekers to enter Australian waters. It also cemented its processing arrangements with Pacific island nations resulting in what has become known as the 'Pacific Solution'.[6]

Fault Lines: Australia's Record on Asylum Seeker Policies

In 1954 Australia was one of the first countries to ratify the 1951 Refugee Convention. In 1973 it acceded to the 1967 Protocol thus committing itself to the principle of *non-refoulement*, that is, agreeing not to return asylum seekers to persecution. However unlike Canada, for example, Australia has not incorporated these international instruments into domestic law (the *Migration Act*), and thus it is not legally bound to provide protection.[7] Historically, it has been argued that there are clear factors that dominated Australia's thinking and actions.[8] On the surface these factors relate primarily to the fact that Australia wishes to adhere to the 1951 UN Convention and its 1967 Protocol in order to project a 'co-operative image' to the world community. More importantly, and during a period of economic expansion, Australia's active role in settling refugees can be seen as part of a broader migration policy that found in refugees young, active, educated migrants who would constitute a useful addition to the workforce. This is often referred to as the capitalist state imperative [9]

Changes announced in July 2004 by Immigration Minister Amanda Vanstone encouraging temporary protection visa (TPV) holders to apply for general migration visas are reminiscent of the capitalist state imperatives used by the Australian Government to exclude certain groups of refugees — often the old and the sick — from entering Australia in the past. Thus, one of the underlying motivations for previous Australian Governments accepting large numbers of refugees from Europe following the Second World War was the opportunity to increase the Australian population and workforce in a time of full employment and when traditional sources of migrants from Britain were insufficient to meet the growing demand for labour.[10] Until the 1970s the White Australia Policy still operated to effectively exclude refugees of colour, although prior to 1977, refugees were admitted under the same migration category as other migrants. The policy of selecting and admitting refugees under the same category as migrants, combined with the White Australia Policy, ensured only the healthy, young and educated with 'certain racial features' were selected for migration to Australia.[11] (See Chapters 4 and 5 for more detailed discussions on Arab and Muslim migration to Australia). The Howard Government's policies seem designed to exclude those TPV holders who do not meet the stringent standard migration criteria created to screen out those unlikely to be employable from gaining permanent residence in Australia.

The White Australia Policy was finally abolished in 1973 when the Whitlam Government announced that future immigration policy would not distinguish between migrants on the basis of race, colour or nationality, [12] a topic reviewed, from its ideological inception to its cessation by, Batrouney in Chapter 4. It was not until 1977 when the Fraser Government articulated a coherent refugee policy that asylum seekers could be admitted to Australia for humanitarian reasons irrespective of race, health, skills or their employability.[13] This distinguishing of refugees from other immigrants coincided with the arrival of 'boat people' fleeing the war in Vietnam.

From the 1970s, Australia experienced periods of high national unemployment and general immigration was reduced with a greater emphasis placed on family re-union, humanitarian and compassionate grounds.[14] The changing economy led to a need for more highly educated workers than before and successive immigration policies reflected this changing economic environment. The arrival in waves of asylum seekers by boat, mostly from Asia, quickly influenced the government to establish measures to regain their control over the immigration intake.

It is the relatively brief period from the mid-1970s to the end of the 1980s that Australia can accurately claim to have had a generous and liberal humanitarian program that accepted genuine refugees regardless of race, employability or how they entered Australia. Between 1945 and the 1991 Census, Australia had admitted more than 550,000 refugees and humanitarian cases, over a third of whom arrived between 1975 and 1991: 124,800 from Indochina, plus several thousand refugees fleeing conflict and political unrest in Asia, the Middle East, Central and South America, and Africa.[15] However during this period growing discontent in the community towards the increasing number of Asians[16] and 'economic' refugees emerged. In 1989 the *Migration Act* was overhauled to help 'curb the abuse of the immigration program by people seeking to come to Australia illegally.'[17] In 1991 the Port Hedland Immigration Reception and Processing Centre was opened and detained its first group of asylum seekers while their refugee status was determined.[18] Mandatory detention for all 'unlawful arrivals' was enacted under the *Migration Reform Act* 1992 by the Keating Government to deter further asylum seekers from coming to Australia.[19]

The 'temporary' nature of humanitarian protection visas for asylum seekers was first introduced by the Hawke/Keating Government in 1990 in response to the Chinese Government massacre of students at Tiananmen Square in 1989. Prime Minister Bob Hawke famously wept in public as he committed to protect Chinese nationals in Australia on student visas, issuing them with four year temporary protection visas. Hawke's decision was unpopular amongst his own party, the Liberal opposition and the Immigration Department. Around 20,000 Chinese nationals granted the four year temporary protection visa were eventually permitted to remain permanently in Australia. The policy was considered unsuccessful and quickly ended.

The conservative Howard Government came to power in 1996 following 13 years of Labor governance during which fundamental changes to the Australian economy and society were experienced: 'economic upheaval was accompanied by challenging debates in national identity: the Republic, Native Title, reconciliation, and high profile "official" multiculturalism.'[20] The lack of agreement and therefore closure on these debates put many of these policies in jeopardy.[21] The magnitude and rapidity of changes and new policy directions implemented by the Keating Government were opposed by many in rural and regional Australia who, by the 1996 federal election, were ripe for political exploitation.[22] The electorate was tired of Keating's 'big picture', 'elitist' politics that were seen to benefit minority groups such as Aborigines, women and ethnic groups at the expense of the majority.[23] The Liberal Party's slogan 'For all of Us' and its vision of a 'comfortable and relaxed' Australia appealed to the public. John Howard positioned himself so that he was able to tap into the national mood of discontent with Paul Keating's big picture focus that was seen to disregard more immediate personal issues such as interest rates and mortgages.[24]

In 1996 Pauline Hanson, elected to Federal Parliament for the first time, quickly gained notoriety and support for her message that 'the "Nation" was at peril, in danger of losing its identity, its unity, of being swamped and above all divided. In a time of profound economic change and increasing uncertainty, we witnessed in Hansonism the re-articulation of partially submerged discourses of cultural identity.'[25] In 1998 Hanson suggested granting temporary visas for all refugees and humanitarian places allocated by Australia annually.[26] Her articulation of fears for our national identity raised through issues from globalization to asylum seekers resonated with a large number of the Australian electorate and this did not go unnoticed by the Howard Government.

In September 1999 during the Kosovo War, the Howard Government offered to provide a temporary safe haven to around four thousand (predominantly Muslim) Kosovars under 'Operation Safe Haven'.[27] Two important precedents for Australia's humanitarian program were created during Operation Safe Haven: the first was the offering of temporary protection to people in genuine need (unlike the Chinese nationals in 1989, however, there was no prospect of the Kosovars remaining in Australia); and the second was the introduction of 're-integration' packages or financial inducements to return home.[28] Operation Safe

Haven was largely successful as by 2000 nearly all the refugees from Kosovo had returned home.

The War on 'Boat People'

From the late '90s, boats carrying asylum seekers fleeing violence and persecution in Iraq and Afghanistan started to arrive on Australia's northern shores. Thirty per cent of boat arrivals in 1999/2000 were Afghani, and 55 per cent were from Iraq, while the rest were predominantly Iranians, Palestinians and, to a lesser degree, Syrians and Kurds.[29] In response, the Coalition Government introduced the TPV in 1999 as part of a harsher policy aimed at deterring onshore asylum claims. Opinion polls from that time showed that the government had widespread support from the Australian electorate for this approach.[30]

Recent changes to the refugee policy in Australia may at best be described as an *ad hoc* series of harsh poll-driven measures, and at worst, as an excessively inhumane regime that seeks to punish genuine refugees for the mode of their arrival. This new approach to asylum seekers fleeing the turbulent political situation in the Middle East can best be understood in the context of local debates in Australia about national identity and border control.[31] In fact, in 1999, one year after Pauline Hanson's right-wing, populist One Nation party called for a regime of 'temporary' refuge to deal with the 'influx' of asylum seekers, the Federal Government produced Visa subclass 785, the 'Temporary Protection Visa' (TPV). In so doing, it overturned an erstwhile principle of refugee protection: that genuine refugees should not be penalized for their method of entry.[32] Previously described by then–Immigration Minister Phillip Ruddock as 'totally unacceptable and quite extreme,' the concept of temporary protection has subsequently been expanded as a punitive form of deterrence for would-be asylum seekers. In practice, the TPV has created exactly the type of uncertainty Ruddock predicted in 1998 when criticizing One Nation's 'highly unconscionable' immigration agenda.[33] Indeed, in one critical respect, the Federal Government has gone one step further than the anti-immigration hardliners of One Nation. By denying recognized refugees the right to family reunion, Ruddock's position became markedly more punitive than that of One Nation, which still appears to recognize that the obvious corollary of accepting 'a person … in need of protection' is that 'we must grant their wife or husband and dependent children residency also.'[34]

Given the magnitude of the refugee crisis globally, Australia's annual quota of 12,000 places — including both offshore and onshore applicants — is by no means excessively generous. The World Refugee Survey reports that:

> Australia hosted some 21,800 refugees and asylum seekers at the end of 2001. These include 7992 refugees resettled during the fiscal year 2000–2001 (which ended June 30); 5495 persons granted protection visas during the year (of which 974 were permanent and 4521 were temporary); 2703 persons remaining on temporary visas granted in previous years; applicants in 5385 pending asylum cases; and 180 persons with temporary safe haven visas.[35]

Incorporating unused admission places from the previous fiscal year, Australia allotted a total of 13,733 asylum places for allocation during the 2001–2002 year. In accordance with the recent policy of linking offshore (resettlement) and onshore (asylum) places in a single quota, Australia allocated 7992 places to applicants from outside Australia and 5741 places for those granted asylum in Australia. This artificial policy link has allowed the government to argue that 'unauthorized' onshore arrivals deny resettlement places to more 'deserving' offshore applicants. The Federal Government has been pushing the line that Australia is being swamped by cashed up 'illegal' migrants who are choosing Australia for 'lifestyle' reasons. The introduction of the TPV (for onshore applicants) was sold to the public as a necessary measure to stop the 'waves' of asylum seekers coming from the Middle East via Indonesia. These, asylum seekers most of whom have been found to be Convention refugees are routinely referred to by the various government agencies as 'illegal boat arrivals', an explicit and deliberate expression aimed at justifying their harsh and inhumane treatment at the various phases of the asylum process.

Border Protection Amendments and the Pacific Solution

The 2001 border protection changes were aimed at discouraging 'secondary movement' by eliminating the prospect of permanent protection to asylum seekers who spent seven nights in a third 'safe' transit country. Whilst this aspect of the 2001 changes was presented as a counter measure aimed at eliminating the 'pull factors' as the basis for asylum seeker movement, in reality it is another step towards ensuring that the Australian Government is able to screen potential refugees according to its own criteria and timetable. This goes against the spirit of the 1951 Convention which is built upon the 'internal arrangements of

Western societies, founded upon principles of individual rights, liberty and democratic tradition.'[36] Border controls, the government argues, are legitimate aspects of state sovereignty, yet in reality they are exclusionary deterrence measures which lead to *refoulement,* a breach of obligations toward the spirit of transnational justice embodied in the Convention.

Border protection became the major issue of the 2001 federal election. Following the *Tampa* incident and the Coalition Government's Pacific Solution a few weeks prior to the election, the 'children overboard' incident was reported in the media. Though the Coalition Government was returned for a third term, from the outset it was under pressure from allegations of misleading the Australian people with regard to the children overboard affair and providing poor political accountability. The government has also been under sustained pressure from its own Members of Parliament who are themselves under pressure from refugee advocates concerning the indefinite detention of refugees on the islands of Manus and Nauru, and the ongoing detention of children. Large populations of TPV holders within their electorates, many of whom make a valuable contribution to society also seek support from local MPs.

In August 2004, responding to these MPs and the criticisms in the national and international media over its treatment of asylum seekers, the Howard Government portrayed itself as being generous to TPV holders by allowing them to apply for a permanent migration visa. The catch was that the majority of TPV holders had little chance of meeting the criteria attached to permanent migration visas. Through applying the same criteria for general migration visas to TPVs the government is able to effectively exclude those TPV holders who are not healthy, employable or living in rural regions. It appears that for TPV holders there has been a blurring of the boundaries between humanitarian and migrant visas not dissimilar to the situation that existed prior to the 1970s.

The government is under no obligation to offer permanent protection to refugees unless this is seen to serve the 'national interest', be it international prestige or capitalist state imperatives. Refugees admitted following the Second World War were given permanent visas because the underlying rationale for their admittance to Australia was the need to increase the workforce. From the '70s, however, unemployment has plagued successive governments and the migration intake has changed to reflect the need for highly skilled labour. Refugees experience higher levels of unemployment than other migrants. The adoption of TPVs and the new changes announced by Senator Vanstone allowing TPVs to apply for regular migration visas reflect an underlying desire to accept only those humanitarian entrants that will not be a financial burden on society.

It is estimated that by mid-2005 all TPVs will have expired and, as the expiration of these visas results in holders having to apply for further protection, TPV holders will be left in a void until decisions are processed. Pending the outcome of the protection visa applications, they are permitted to remain in Australia temporarily. In January 2004 3960 TPVs had expired and, of the 660 decisions that had been finalised by mid-February 2004, 627 (88 per cent) were refused further protection. The remaining 33 applicants who were granted permanent protection, had arrived in Australia prior to the tightening of the law in September 2001.[37] A majority of those refused visa applications appealed to the Refugee Review Tribunal (RRT).

When in July 2004, the government announced that all TPV holders would have the opportunity to apply for permanent visas enthusiasm was soon tempered as, on closer examination of the details, it became evident that not all TPV holders would automatically qualify. All TPV holders wishing to remain in Australia would have to reapply for another visa and 'not all of them, of course, will get them,' Senator Vanstone admitted.[38] The 'devil was in the detail', as the announced regulatory changes gave temporary visa holders the right to apply for other non-humanitarian visas — such as family or spouse, employment, or student visas — however only some of these visas are permanent. For example, student visas are also temporary and, unlike humanitarian visas, do not commit the Australian Government to any protection obligations once the visa has expired. Consequently, since its introduction, there have been only a handful of TPV applicants applying for these non-protection visas.[39]

Equally stressful for TPV holders was the requirement that they go through the visa application process all over again, prolonging their deep sense of uncertainty. It was this aspect that prompted refugee advocate Marion Le to call it 'one of the cruellest things this government has done.'[40] Critics saw the announcement as being driven by the proximity of the 2004 federal election, and cynically called the changes 'ballot box compassion'[41] and 'temporary election visas'.[42] Mares noted that government rhetoric had changed, and the old Iraqi, Iranian and Afghan 'illegals' and 'queue jumpers' now made 'a significant contribution to the Australian community' and are 'contributing to the economies of regional Australia.'[43] He attributed this to pressure put on the government by influential rural and regional advocates who have benefited economically from the presence of TPV holders and 'have given TPV holders a voice in the corridors of power.' Indeed, Minister Vanstone was careful to confirm that the regulations would be 'framed in a way that clearly recognizes the contribution that many TPV holders are making in regional areas'[44] and would specifically include lower-skilled workers. She suggested this would be done by amending the skill requirements of the Regional Sponsored Migration Scheme to include people who had worked for their sponsor for 12 months.

This emphasis on work skills creates a new fiction that distinguishes between 'deserving' and 'undeserving' refugees.[45] It benefits the few who have been fortunate enough to secure long-term employment, but does not help the majority of TPV holders who are unemployed, self-employed, or in short-term insecure or casual employment. Ironically those genuine refugees on TPVs unable to qualify under general migration criteria to gain permanent residence in Australia are likely to be those most in need of humanitarian protection given that many are suffering from psychological illnesses and trauma that prevent them, for example, gaining employment.

The TPV policy itself is flawed, and rather than amending it, the simplest and most humane solution is to make the visas permanent.[46] What is needed is a 'genuine act of humanity, not a policy that will, yet again, prolong the agony of people who have suffered enough.'[47] The proposed changes represented a step in the right direction but did not fundamentally change the TPV, as many TPV holders, already found to be refugees, are still required to argue their case again and many will fail.

A return pending visa has been introduced for applicants whom the Australian Government has deemed to be 'no longer in need of protection'. This allows 18 months for rejected applicants to make arrangements to return home, and carries the same rights and restrictions as the TPV. This is undoubtedly a more humane alternative for rejected asylum seekers than (often forcible) removal or detention, which are the extant responses, and allows them to examine other alternatives.

From early 2004, the Immigration Minister has stated that the government is not encouraging the return to Iraq of the 3346 remaining Iraqi TPV holders in Australia, indicating that it was adhering the advice of the UNCHR.[48] Nevertheless, following the fall of Saddam Hussein's regime there were some refugees who sought to return to Iraq, possibly as many as 900.[49] This came despite the lack of basic services, such as housing, and the tenuous state of security in Iraq. For these returning

Iraqi refugees, however, 'the present horrors of detention in Australia outweighed whatever future fears they might have about the chaos and violence of occupied Iraq.'[50] By the end of 2003, the Department of Immigration and Multicultural and Ethnic Affairs (DIMIA) had facilitated the voluntary repatriation of 11 Iraqis from detention in Australia and 23 from Nauru[51] and in December 2004, Minister Vanstone was encouraging Iraqi asylum seekers who had failed in their applications for refugee status to 'return to their home country as quickly as possible.'[52] Considering that Iraqis are the single largest group of TPV holders in Australia, it was somewhat surprising that the government offered TPV holders a 'Reintegration Assistance Package', which provides financial grants and travel costs to those who volunteer to return to their home country. Encouraging Iraqis to return to Iraq has been clearly discouraged by the UNHCR, and acknowledged as dangerous by the Australian Government.[53]

Discursive Constructions of Middle Eastern Asylum Seekers

It has been argued that 'discourses are not about objects; they do not identify objects, they constitute them and in the practice of doing so conceal their own invention.'[54] This is clearly the case in the way the Australian Government constructed threats posed by asylum seekers to Australia's national security and identity. This negative discourse set the backdrop for asylum seekers to move from a humanitarian issue to a border protection issue. For this to occur, the government had to convince the general public of the threats posed by genuine asylum seekers arriving by boat. I argue here 'that rather than responding to a crisis, the Australian Government has generated the perception of a crisis in the Australian community.'[55] Manufacturing a crisis situation is crucial to ensuring popular support in order to secure the introduction of draconian policies. In fact, the number of asylum seekers reported during the 'crisis years (1999–2001) did not exceed 10,000; far smaller proportionally than most other Western countries and certainly not comparable to the numbers that developing countries such as Iran and Pakistan are accommodating (close to four million between them).

What is most striking about the asylum debate in Australia, however, is that the voices of Middle Eastern refugees themselves have rarely been heard.[56] This effective silencing of refugees and asylum seekers in Australia has been one of the more disturbing aspects of the debate as a whole as the individual human story was lost in the midst of legal and political arguments.[57] For several years now, the primary public labels employed to describe onshore asylum seekers have been 'queue-jumpers', 'cashed up immigrants' and 'illegals'.[58] The term 'queue-jumper' has been particularly prominent in public discourse; a term designed to suggest that onshore arrivals are undeserving, having taken a resettlement position from a more worthy (and certainly more grateful and compliant) 'offshore' refugee. Playing upon notions of fairness and orderliness, former Immigration Minister Ruddock even likened onshore asylum seekers to 'thieves' who 'steal' places from genuine refugees. Despite the absence of any real 'queue' in receiving countries such as Pakistan, Iran and Indonesia,[59] this language has been effective in depicting asylum seekers as a deviant group unworthy of protection.

These discourses of exclusion and denigration were reinforced throughout 2001–2002, when a systematic pattern of government misrepresentation sought to portray asylum seekers as serial child-abusers.[60] This was not limited to the most well-known and notorious case of the children overboard incident. Other episodes include the claim made by Liberal Senator George Brandis that 'a potential illegal immigrant [had] attempted to strangle a child.'[61] A subsequent Senate Inquiry found that navy witness statements reportedly relating to this alleged episode did not exist.[62] In another case of alleged child abuse it was claimed that adult Afghan detainees had forcibly sewn together children's lips during a hunger strike.[63] Separate investigations by the South Australian Government and the Human Rights and Equal Opportunity Commission, with the co-operation of Australian Correctional Management, however, found no evidence of parents encouraging children to engage in acts of self-harm.[64] This too was found to be an unsubstantiated allegation, but a pattern or regime of representation was now apparent. Under pressure, or to gain electoral mileage out of their tough stance, the government appeared quite willing to portray asylum seekers as an irresponsible and aberrant group, hostile to Australian standards of decency and parental responsibility, with little regard for their children's well-being or safety.

Meanwhile, Australia continued to be the only regime in the world where a mandatory detention policy applied to children, and continued to lock up young children in defiance of international treaty commitments on the rights of the child. Government rhetoric implicitly shifted the blame to the parents for putting their children in this situation. Despite a letter by Afghani detainees expressing their great offence at the baseless accusations of child abuse, and urging the Prime

Minister to set the record straight, the government refused to apologize.[65]

The *Tampa* and children overboard incidents described above became the 'central motifs' of the government's 2001 election campaign. Both issues involved the government as representative of the Australian nation and its clearly defined national identity against an 'other' that was Muslim and primarily Middle Eastern. This 'other' was first clearly established in the *Tampa* incident, when Howard declared as a central stance of the election campaign that 'we will decide who comes to the country, and the circumstances under which they come.'[66] Thus Middle Eastern, Muslim asylum seekers were established as a threat to the Australian nation, as indicated by the use of words such as 'floods' and 'waves' of onshore asylum seekers, when in reality the numbers of onshore asylum seekers were relatively small.[67] This is reminiscent of the pre-Federation fear and anxiety about the 'yellow peril' as captured powerfully in David Walker's *Anxious Nation*. More recently, Leach has argued that the government constructed and exaggerated particular representations of cultural difference as 'foreign' and threatening to the Australian nation.[68] For example, in referring to the parents who supposedly threw their children into the sea, Howard was quoted as saying 'I certainly don't want people like that coming to Australia.'[69] The government constructed an image of abhorrent parental behaviour framed by cultural practice, and inimical to Australian values of parental responsibility:

> The children overboard affair again presented Islam as an alien culture in which parents were so barbaric, so subhuman that they would endanger their children by throwing them into the sea to stop the Australian navy from doing its 'duty'.[70]

Moreover, the Coalition Government played a dangerous game of collapsing the distinctions between Middle Eastern, Muslim and terrorist by implication. In the fearful environment post-9/11, Howard declared that he could not rule out that some asylum seekers may be linked to global terror networks.[71] So the 'facile associative logic of racism'[72] attached itself to Muslim- and Arab-Australians in general, and to asylum seekers specifically, through the government establishing, or building upon, a particular discourse of Australian nationalism that excludes Muslims and Arabs. Once again Muslim asylum seekers, and by implication Muslim- and Arab-Australians as a cultural 'other', were dehumanized and Islam portrayed as threatening and dangerous to the

Australian nation and Anglo-Australian values. This cemented a hostility and distrust of Australians who may be associated with Islam, whether they are Muslim Australians, or mistakenly identified with Islam because they are of a certain ethnicity, particularly Arabic. These images were reinforced by shallow media coverage, as Pickering illustrates in her survey of refugee and asylum seeker issues in the *Sydney Morning Herald* and Brisbane *Courier–Mail*:

> Press coverage has focused on the deviant problem that asylum seekers and refugees represent to the robust Australian nation and the need for a strong state to keep out and control the menace. With few exceptions, reports on asylum seekers and refugees have not been interested in listening to the voices of asylum seekers, nor of home country conditions or conditions of flight. When alternative views are offered, they are usually presented as 'human interest stories' rather than 'hard' news.[73]

While Pauline Hanson was scorned for ignorance and racism when she suggested in 1996 that 'boat people' should be turned around and refugees sent home when their countries 'get better', both Liberal and Labor Parties have now become complicit in instituting punitive, inhumane measures in Australian law. Such changes signify that 'our leaders, from both major political groupings, are turning us into a nation of thugs.'[74] The question then is: why have these political leaders acted in such 'thuggish' ways and why do opinion polls suggest that they are acting in ways that are widely supported by the Australian people? One of the reasons Australians have acted so adversely to the arrival of asylum seekers is that they have a deep-seated fear of invasion and that this has been present since the arrival of the British in 1788.[75] Having seized Australia so easily, it was initially the Dutch and the French who were seen as the enemy and then later the Japanese, the Germans, the Indonesians, the Vietnamese and the Chinese, who each took their turn in providing the potential threat of invasion. There has, ironically, never been any real threat of invasion, with the Japanese in 1942 specifically rejecting the idea on the basis that it would require too many personnel, and that the 'national character' of Australians would mean they would 'resist to the end.'

Government rhetoric is starting to change: the old 'illegals' and 'queue jumpers' are now making '**a** significant contribution to the Australian community' and are 'contributing to the economies of regional

Australia.' This change can be attributed to pressure put on the government by members of its own backbench as well as influential rural and regional advocates who 'have given TPV holders a voice in the corridors of power.' The recent announcement to soften up the mandatory detention laws has also coincided with a higher approval rate for TPV cases finalized by DIMIA. As the latest figures published by the RRT show, between 1 July 2004 and 30 April 2005, more that 97 per cent of Iraqi and 89 per cent of Afghani TPV cases have been successful in their appeals to the Tribunal.[76]

Conclusion

It has been argued that this recent episode in the treatment of asylum seekers cannot be properly understood in isolation from the ethnic and cultural backgrounds of those involved.[77] The fact that most of the asylum seekers originated from Middle Eastern countries was seen as one of the main reasons for the public paranoia and the government's excessive punitive reaction. The government has argued that the harsh deterrence measures were justified because the so-called 'boat people' are essentially 'queue jumpers' who bypassed the available avenues offered through the resettlement program. Sadly, and following 9/11, there were even suggestions by government ministers that stopping the boats would help prevent the infiltration of potential terrorists. Strong rebuttals to all these arguments have been made by expert groups and even international agencies such as the UNHCR and Amnesty International. However, one crucial point that goes to the heart of this debate is the confusion between Australia's resettlement program which has a fixed annual intake of offshore applicants and its treatment of onshore asylum seekers.

The resettlement program is not a proper substitute for claiming asylum, a fact that has not been lost on all other countries signatory to the Convention. As some have noted, this is because Australia controls the selection process and the make up of the intake. In fact, 'preference goes to the educated rather than the skilled, the healthy rather than the disabled, the quiescent rather than the "troublesome".'[78] The most revealing aspect of Australia's radical asylum approach, in comparison to other countries, is that so few asylum seekers were needed to provoke it. 'Australia's historical fears about invasion from the populous nations to its North no doubt played a part in explaining the degree of controversy generated in 2001,'[79] but in reality, other Western countries such as the US, Germany and the UK receive on an annual basis tens of thousands of asylum seekers. While arguments for strong and effective control of the movement of people are valid, there should be a clear distinction between seemingly connected but quite separate issues such as terrorism and illegal people smuggling on the one hand, and the legitimate plight of asylum seekers on the other.

A question that has often been raised in the midst of this controversy is the apparent 'indifference' of the majority of Australians to the plight of asylum seekers from the Middle East. This indifference raises deep ethical questions about Australian society as a liberal democratic country. Perhaps, as some have noted, indifference is nothing more than 'a potent psychological defence'[80] against compassionate feelings which might otherwise overwhelm our detachment from the inhumane suffering of those who invoke our protection obligations under international humanitarian law.

One of the most paradoxical aspects of the asylum seeker debate in Australia has been that, while Australians pride themselves on having created one of the most successful models of a pluralistic and diverse society, they have also overwhelmingly shown themselves to be indifferent, if not outright antagonistic, towards the plight of asylum seekers. This apparent paradox can possibly be explained in terms of the arguments put forward by the government when justifying its harsh deterrence measures. The perception created is that refugee problems are essentially the product of bad governance or conflict stemming from the country of refugee origin alone. The assumption is that a liberal democratic state, such as Australia, has little or no role in creating refugee-producing conditions, and is acting in a charitable rather than a duty-bound role when accepting settlement of any pre-determined quota of Convention refugees.[81] Yet many of the situations which now produce forced migration result directly and indirectly from the foreign policies of Western countries which are now trying to exclude migrants.[82] A good case in point is the war in Afghanistan, and more recently Iraq, where the local conditions are not conducive to forcible repatriation of refugees. Western states have played major and minor roles in creating refugee-producing conditions — directly though foreign military intervention[83] and indirectly, through the global economic system which creates conditions of extreme hardship or conflict. As such, there are clear ethical, economic and legal obligations on countries such as Australia to ensure a responsible and humane approach to asylum seeker policies that transcends short-term political calculations.

7

AUSTRALIA AND GLOBALIZED ISLAM

Greg Barton

As a nation Australia has yet to really come to terms with Islam and Muslim society. Largely this is because it has never bothered to try; it did not feel that it needed to. For Australia, Islam has always been something 'out there' and 'other', a phenomenon far away, that has little to do with life in Australia. The events of recent years have produced a fresh interest in understanding Islam but there remains a persistent intellectual laziness that means that as Australians we are too easily seduced by simplistic explanations and mono-dimensional models. We are vulnerable to a sort of essentialist reductionism when it comes to our approach to Islam and the Muslim world, that vast belt of countries with Muslim majorities or large Muslim minorities stretching almost unbroken half way around the world from Morocco to Indonesia, from sub-Saharan Africa to southern Russia. If, in the past, we have managed to muddle through despite our ignorance there are two new developments that mean that is no longer acceptable. Firstly, there is the unpleasant reality that we have entered an age in which terror in the name of Islam is a lingering presence regularly provoking unease, misunderstanding and prejudice in all our dealings with the Middle East. Secondly, it is now clear that the forces of globalization, including the globalization of ideas, have so influenced the thinking and perception of Muslim's everywhere that our comfortably compartmentalized view of the Muslim worlds is now seriously inadequate.

Australia is hardly alone amongst Western nations in its ignorance of Islam but there are some specific factors that have shaped Australia's ambivalence. Australia today remains, in large measure, a product of its relatively recent Anglo-Saxon origins and its New World geographic isolation from the Old World. Only New Zealand is more remote. In the final quarter of the twentieth century new patterns of immigration and trade pushed Australia towards accepting, if not embracing, its antipodean position on the edge of Asia. Significant migration from the Middle East to Australia followed in the wake of the first wave of migration from Asia and, while Australia never felt connected to the Arab world in the way that it did to Southeast Asia, there was, for a while, a growing interest in the study of Arabic and Middle Eastern history and culture. There was even greater interest in Muslim Southeast Asia. For a time it seemed that classrooms and lecture theatres would drive an intellectual and attitudinal transformation of the Australian outlook, producing a generation of citizens linguistically and culturally at home in the region. Australia seemed finally to have awoken to the realization that its neighbourhood lay at one end of the Muslim world. Unfortunately, however, the 1990s saw a retreat from that nascent commitment to purposefully engaging with its neighbourhood.

Even as Australian interest in Asia and the Middle East waxed in the 1970s and '80s, awareness of the need to understand Islam and Muslim society lagged behind other interests. Islam continued to be seen as foreign and remote. It remained 'other' — either something strangely alien that should be feared, or bafflingly mysterious and exotic — but whatever Islam was, it was not part of our world, either conceptually or geographically.

Paradoxically, Islam was both essentialized and localized through a growing awareness that the familiar region to our immediate north was also Muslim. Asian Islam, however, was generally placed in a different category to Middle Eastern Islam. Australians, like most in the West, and perhaps in the Middle East as well, viewed the Islam of Asia, and of Indonesia and Malaysia in particular, as being generally less than 'true Islam'. This attitude had the dubious advantage of allowing those interested in Asian society to discount the central importance of Islam. Even when circumstances dictated that it was not possible to ignore Islam, these were construed as exceptions that proved the rule. The fact that the social, intellectual and political elites of Southeast Asia were much less likely to express religious conviction through regular prayer and fasting than a textbook understanding of Islam suggested should be the case, was generally seen as confirmation that their societies were not truly Muslim societies. And the fact that the more ostensible piety of the masses was generally married to seemingly un-Islamic local beliefs and practices — that is to say they did not fit with 'textbook Islam' — was seen as further proof that Southeast Asian Islam was a diluted version of Arab Islam.

Unfortunately, this rather simplistic view received significant scholarly support from two different directions. On the one hand, observers of religious life in poor, rural communities tended to present distinctive elements of folk Islam as being the product of *sui generis* local adaptation without recognizing that many 'Javanese' or 'Malay practices' were in fact widely spread across the Muslim world. Clifford Geertz,[1] for example, suggested that the practice of *selamatan* or *kenduri* was a Southeast Asian innovation, when similar rituals can be found in many Muslim societies. Even practices that were well known components of folk Islam from Morocco to Kazakhstan such as *ziarah* (pilgrimages to the tombs of saints) were presented as examples of local syncretism. This was largely because scholars of Asia tended to be less well informed about Islam in general, and folk Islam in particular, compared with scholars of the Arab world. On the other hand, academic writing about Islam in Southeast Asia tended to focus on urban, middle-class modernist expressions of Islam and relied upon informants who themselves were unfamiliar with, and critically disposed towards, traditionalist expressions of Islam.[2] As a result, the more scriptualist views of the modernists were presented as being inherently more Islamic.

If expert opinion was so frequently flawed, it is little wonder that the general public in Australia remained confused about Islam in the region and inclined to hold to simplistic stereotypes about Islam and Muslim society in both Southeast Asia and the Middle East. The result was not entirely negative, for it did tend to lessen anxiety about Islam in neighbouring societies and encourage Australians to travel and mix widely in the region. It did little, however, to promote a desire to learn more about Islam. Instead, it left many Australians with the mistaken view that Southeast Asian tolerance and openness was a product of Islam's absence, rather than its presence. Secondly, it tended to reinforce an opposite stereotype about Middle Eastern societies: their harsh traditions, severe patriarchies and narrow-mindedness, which were thought to be both common place and intrinsically Islamic.

As a result Australia's popular view of Islam and Muslim society, which was inclined towards reductionism and essentialism, remained. With reporting, even via quality media sources, tending to emphasize links between violence and Islam in the Middle East and ignoring Islam's contributions to society and politics in Asia, there seemed little likelihood that curiosity about Islam and Muslim society would increase. Moreover, as noted above, the 1990s saw a waning of a previously growing interest in Asia by both government and citizens in Australia just as the people of Southeast Asia were showing a heightened interest in understanding and practicing their faith.

Several extraordinary events in the first years of this new century, however, have invigorated Australians' interest in Islam. As an aid to identifying key themes in both the perception and substance of contemporary Islam this chapter will consider three recent developments that have challenged thinking about Islam in Australia.

The most significant factor remains the so-called 'new Pearl Harbour' experience of 11 September 2001, when al-Qaeda attacked America.[3] For Australians, however, an in some ways more disturbing event was the bombing in Bali on 12 October 2002, although it was very much smaller in scale. Suddenly al-Qaeda style terrorism was no longer just an external threat: New York is on the other side of the world but Bali, only partly for reasons of geography, feels almost like home ground. Two years after the Bali bombing a third, very different, kind of event occurred when on 26 December 2004, a series of massive tsunamis devastated coastal communities around the Indian Ocean, including Indonesia. Once the extent of the loss of life and property in the northern province of Aceh was realized, attention turned to this rather remote and unfamiliar corner of Indonesia and Australia became deeply engaged. This proved to be a very different sort of engagement with the Muslim world. Notwithstanding the obvious troubles caused by years of brutality between military and (non-Islamist) separatists, many Australians were pleasantly surprised to find that this supposedly 'fundamentalist' Muslim community was as 'normal' and tolerant as the rest of Indonesia.

9/11 — *Jihad* Goes Global

It is easy to be dismissive of the sometimes hysterical hype that followed that shocking morning in New York and Washington DC, and there is little doubt that claims that '9/11 changed the world' are, in many respects, spurious. But to argue that al-Qaeda's unprecedented attack on the American mainland, successfully targeting its financial/cultural and political/military seats of power, left the West unchanged is equally foolish. Overnight, a US administration with little appetite for international engagement, and a political culture accustomed to appeasing authoritarian regimes abroad in the name of national interest, was launched on a path of aggressive activism. Disinterest in the Muslim world and ignorance of Islam, even more entrenched in the US than Australia, was suddenly transformed into a passion for engagement in the Muslim world. This is not the place to critique American foreign policy in the wake of 9/11: suffice to say that conceptualizing the response as a 'war on terror' was scarcely less foolish than President Bush's momentary lapse into talk of a 'crusade'.

It is worth reflecting on how the 9/11 attacks affected Western thinking about Islam, how they impacted on Muslim societies around the world, and what they meant for Australia's thinking about the Middle East. That those horrific hours between 8:46 a.m., when the first 767 struck the North Tower of New York's World Trade Center and 10:28 a.m., when both towers had collapsed and the Pentagon had been struck by a third Boeing, represent some of the most poignant moments in modern history is difficult to deny. While the world has witnessed many worse tragedies in the last one hundred years — famines, pandemics, world wars, holocaust, brutal pogroms and unspeakable communal violence — none fire the imagination and stand out in our memory in quite the same way. Similarly, the shooting of John F. Kennedy, but one of the twentieth century's many assassinations, seared itself into the memories of a generation. The fact that these events were captured on film and broadcast live on radio — engaging many tens of millions of people around the world as witnesses — elevated them to a unique status. In the days that followed 9/11, the global pool of witnesses grew to unprecedented proportions as the hundreds of millions of people who had not seen the horror unfold live via satellite, saw the innumerable replays of airliners striking the Manhattan skyscrapers, two of the world's tallest office buildings, as they collapsed surreally into nothingness.

Evidence that the attacks were indeed the work of al-Qaeda steadily mounted in the weeks that followed and the ubiquitous images of the World Trade Center towers were soon joined by the ascetic-looking figure of Osama bin Laden. Backed by desolate rocky slopes, the mysterious millionaire-turned revolutionary appeared like a cross between an Old Testament prophet and Che Guevara. The world had a new image of an Islamic leader added to their stock of largely unfavourable impressions. For non-Muslim-Australians the association of Islam with bin Laden and 9/11 compounded a sense of despair about growing fundamentalism in the Muslim world, particularly in the Middle East. Thankfully, only a minority lapsed into outright Islamophobia but this minority seemed to dominate talk-back radio and tabloid reporting in Australia. For Australian Muslims, as for the vast majority of Muslims around the world, the association of Islam with al-Qaeda terrorism, created a double burden. They too were horrified and deeply saddened by what had happened on 9/11. They were doubly grieved that years of effort to promote an understanding of Islam as a religion of peace was undermined by a small band of extremists who had hijacked the name of Islam, claiming to speak for its 1.3 billion faithful.[4]

The chilling images and the storm of media coverage that followed were not accidental. The idea of crashing commercial airliners into iconic skyscrapers at the beginning of a New York workday had been carefully conceived to produce such a media spectacle. Al-Qaeda had hijacked the world's media just as surely as its terrorists had hijacked the airliners that became their cruise-missiles. It was an audacious plan to capture the attention of the world and provoke a response, and in the age of global media it succeeded as no act of terrorism had ever done before.

Muslims everywhere were grieved to see what had been done in, and to, the name of Islam but this was not al-Qaeda's concern. Al-Qaeda fully intended to provoke the disgust and anger of the world, and particularly of America. It wanted to push its terrible vision of Islam to centre-stage. It wanted to terrify the majority and impress a minority. The strategists and commanders at the tiny heart of this loose network of networks that had arisen out of the struggle of the *Mujahideen*, the holy warriors fighting the Soviets in Afghanistan had a darkly brilliant plan. They knew that most Muslims, who were enamoured of the West and its promise of progress and freedom, supported neither their vision nor their methods. They also knew that the great majority of the Muslim world was under the age of 27 and lived in societies burdened with crushing poverty that grew steadily worse with each passing year of their young lives. They were angry with their nations' authoritarian, corrupt regimes and with the Western support that kept them in power. While tens of millions of young men across the Muslim world were educated enough to escape poverty, they were nevertheless unable to find meaningful employment and purpose, leaving them burdened with what Thomas Friedman has aptly called 'a poverty of dignity'.[5] Al-Qaeda knew that it could leverage its limited resources to great effect by directly impressing some of these young men and simultaneously provoke the West into the sort of violent confrontation that would quickly turn ordinary Muslims' admiration of the West to anger and disillusionment.[6] And that is exactly what they did.

While the 9/11 attacks represent a significant turning point for *jihadi* Islamism's profile, their first truly global terrorist attack killing 2992 people, it was neither al-Qaeda's first attack against US interests nor its first attack on US soil. Al-Qaeda is believed to have contributed to the deaths of US soldiers in Somalia in October 1993 and to have been responsible for the June 1996 truck bomb that killed 19 Americans at their Khobar Towers barracks in Dhahran, Saudi Arabia. In August 1998 al-Qaeda's first successful large scale bombing campaign saw 224 people, mostly local staffers, killed in US embassy bombings in Kenya and Tanzania. Then in October 2000 a boat bomb was used to ram the USS Cole while it was docked in Aden, Yemen, causing the deaths of 17 US naval personnel. It appears also that the interception of an explosive-laden vehicle driven by an Algerian member of al-Qaeda at the US–Canada border in December 1999 foiled an attempt to stage a major attack in Seattle during millennium New Year celebrations. Somewhat overlooked in all of this is the fact that al-Qaeda's first attack on US soil, a vehicle bombing that resulted in the deaths of six people in New York, was carried out in February 1993 in the basement car park of the very complex that was razed to the ground by a very different kind of vehicle eight years later.[7]

Two of the masterminds of this unsuccessful 1993 attack, Khalid Sheikh Mohammed and Ramzi Youssef, also engineered failed plans to assassinate the Pope during his visits to Manila in 1995 and 1999. In 1994 the pair successfully trialled the use of small nitroglycerine bombs packed into contact lens solution bottles, difficult to detect during airport scanning, to blow up airliners. In December that year they planted a test bomb under a passenger's seat on a flight from Manila to Tokyo. It detonated mid-air as planned, killing one passenger and injuring 10 others, after the men had left the aircraft at an earlier stopover. Several weeks later an accident involving explosive material caused Youssef to flee his smoke-filled apartment, and the Philippines, narrowly avoiding arrest. Left behind was a laptop computer containing files of elaborate plans to plant larger bombs on 11 US-bound airliners that, over a 48 hour period, would detonate over the Pacific Ocean.[8]

It is tempting to think of the ambitious attacks of 9/11 as an attempt by al-Qaeda to launch itself onto the world scene, terrifying many but also impressing a few, and putting its stocks to the market in a kind of Initial Public Offering. But the above list of major known al-Qaeda operations makes it clear that the firm had been successfully in business for many years. In fact the network we now know as al-Qaeda coalesced in Afghanistan in the early 1990s out of a long-running initiative by foreign zealots to support the struggle of the Afghan *Mujahideen* against the Soviets. It exploited the opportunity afforded by the conflict to recruit, train and radicalize tens of thousands of foreign *Mujahideen* from

Saudi Arabia and the wider Arab world, Chechnya and Muslim Asia drawn to the high valleys of the Afghanistan–Pakistan border. Al-Qaeda emerged as a separate identity only after bin Laden and his fellow Saudis broke with the Saudi regime over the latter's willingness to allow US military forces to be stationed on Saudi soil following Iraq's invasion of Kuwait.[9]

The events of September 2001 marked a major watershed. The 9/11 attacks were not merely a milestone but a turning point, not just because of the way al-Qaeda captured the imagination of the entire globe by out-Hollywooding Hollywood with its audacious, telegenic strike on what in name as well as substance really is the centre for world trade. It was also a watershed year because after years of being ignored as a shadowy minor player by the US and its allies, al-Qaeda finally captured America's attention, galvanizing its collective psyche and provoking it into declaring war. Al-Qaeda succeeded in drawing America into military action in asymmetrical combat that both showcased its awful military capacity as the world's sole global superpower, but it also highlighted its weaknesses. First in Afghanistan and then Iraq, America was goaded inexorably into the sort of brutality that warfare with weapons of such indiscriminate power necessarily involves, and into making the sort of horrible mistakes and errors of judgment that the heat of battle inevitably brings. 2001 was a watershed point because al-Qaeda's attacks tipped America over the edge, embarking it on a series of campaigns that it would mostly win, from a limited military point of view, and often lose, from a public relations point of view. In all of this Australia proved a staunch and largely uncritical ally of the United States, tying its global stocks to those of America and as a consequence suffering with it the mounting hostility and disenchantment with America that swept across the Middle East in the wake of war in Iraq.

It is impossible yet to make a full assessment of what has been achieved in Afghanistan and Iraq. Such assessments will have to await the outcomes of post-conflict nation-building and their respective transitions to democracy. What is clear though is that America and its allies, including Australia, have, for the time-being at least, lost the confidence and good will of the Muslim world. Polling such as that done by the Pew Charitable Trust provides dramatic evidence of a reversal of sentiment towards the US across the Muslim world, beginning in 2002.[10] What is also clear is that al-Qaeda and related networks have negotiated an alliance in the field with Saddam loyalists who prepared well for a protracted, asymmetrical war of attrition with the US and its 'coalition of the willing'. In the short term this has given al-Qaeda and its allies a string of horribly successful guerrilla attacks, and terrorist acts against foreign forces and ordinary Iraqis. It has also drawn in fresh recruits to the cause and radicalized further cohorts of young men, such as occurred in Afghanistan. What this means for al-Qaeda in the long-term is uncertain, however, there can be little doubt that it has already contributed to a greater loss of life and quantum of suffering, most of all for the people of Iraq, than all of al-Qaeda's previous attacks combined.

While 2001 was an important turning point, it is only one in a series of turning points in recent history. Although not fully understood at the time, it is now clear that 1979 was also a defining year for two reasons. Firstly, in February 1979 the first true Islamic — or better, Islamist — revolution in history occurred in Iran. Although Islam, like Christianity, has a long political and military history, the idea of an Islamic revolution, borrowing heavily from Marxist theory, is a wholly modern idea. In the first half of the twentieth century several influential Islamic scholars had begun theorizing about the formation of a modern Islamic nation-state and by the middle of the century their ideas were married with those of revolutionary Marxism. But until 1979, the idea of treading the revolutionary path to create a theocratic state in which (a modern conception of) *Sharia*, or Islamic law, would be applied to all, by a few acting in the name of God, remained a utopian dream.

It was only after the Iranian revolution that the West really began to apply the 'F' word — fundamentalism — to Islam.[11] At official levels, its significance was played down as such a revolution, it was said, with considerable good reason, was very unlikely to occur anywhere else in the Muslim world. With rather less good reason, it was argued that the fact that Iran was a Shi'ah Muslim society, and that Shi'ah Islam has a very different concept of institutionalized clerical power to Sunni Islam, which comprises 80 per cent of the world's Muslims, meant that the revolution would have little impact on the broader Muslim world. In part this reasoning might well have been driven by a sense of embarrassment in the West, that it completely failed to foresee the revolution, having allowed Cold War paranoia and tunnel vision to endorse support for the brutal, authoritarian regime of the Shah. As it happened, Iran's successful Islamic revolution captured the imaginations of many young people across the world and the radical ideas of its chief architect, Ali Shariati, were read with interest by Sunni Muslims from Morocco to Indonesia hungry for new ideas.[12]

The second significant event of 1979 was the Soviet invasion of Afghanistan to prop-up an ailing puppet government. The West's obsessive Cold War logic again dictated that the Soviet invasion be interpreted as such a major threat to Western interests that it must be opposed by any means. Those means were the clandestine sponsoring, with the assistance of Pakistan's military intelligence agency ISI, of Afghani *Mujahideen* and their radical Islamist allies who flocked to the region in their thousands.[13]

The conflict in Afghanistan so over-extended and demoralized the Soviet military machine, and, after the manner of America's Vietnam War, so angered the Russian public, that it endangered the very health of the Soviet system. This was by no means the only fact contributing to the collapse of Soviet communism but it was certainly a significant factor.[14]

One decade later, in 1989, another watershed point was reached — *the* watershed point of the second half of the twentieth century. Under Mikhail Gorbachev *glasnost* and *perestroika* dramatically rewrote the rules of what was possible in the Soviet Union, triggering a popular rising in East Germany. By November that year, the Berlin Wall was demolished, followed by East European Communism as a whole. One year later the Soviet Union was dissolved and the Cold War was over. With the demise of the Soviet bogeyman, some in the West began positioning Islam as the new dark 'other', the West's new enemy. But for the most part euphoria about the 'end of history', to use the wildly optimistic phrase of Francis Fukuyama,[15] saw the West turning a collective blind eye to developments in Afghanistan and Pakistan. It was certainly preferable that the West not exchange the Communist bogeyman for an Islamist one; it would have been even better had it paused to consider the impact of its quickly forgotten involvement in the region, and taken responsibility for cleaning up the mess left in the wake of the Cold War. Instead, Afghans were left to fend for themselves under the anarchic barbarism of the Taliban.[16] With the Soviets driven out of Afghanistan many of the foreign *Mujahideen*, idealistic young men radicalized by a long and difficult campaign, trained and educated in Islamist camps, and profoundly bound together as brothers-in-arms, turned their attention outwards to a global project.[17]

Whereas the Islamic revolution in Iran was, by virtue of its success, a largely inward-looking concern, the *jihadi* Islamism that came out of the foreign *Mujahideen* in Afghanistan was very much a global affair. It built on the foundations of the reactionary interpretation of Islam promulgated around the poorer parts of the Muslim world by the zealous, close-minded missionaries of Saudi's Salafiyyah and Wahhabi movements[18] and articulated a radical Islamist vision of what scholars such as Olivier Roy have called globalized Islam.[19]

Embracing globalized Islam does not, however, require endorsement of al-Qaeda-style terrorist methods. Many who are attracted to this austere understanding of Islam, stripped of 14 centuries of Islamic learning and culture and opposed to post-Enlightenment liberalism in every form, are inclined to both admire the passion of *jihadi* Islamism and defend its ends, if not its means. Nevertheless, neither Salafism nor Roy's globalized Islam are the same as *jihadi* Islamism. It takes a particular set of circumstances to move someone from the essentially apolitical position of globalized Salafi fundamentalism to a point of willingness to embrace the revolutionary political message of *jihadi* Islamism, preparedness to swear allegiance to a *jihadi amir* (spiritual leader), and a conviction that initiating violence is justified as *jihad*.[20] In fact, while those who have merely dabbled with Salafi fundamentalism might be persuaded to go beyond Salaf quietism, most whom become deeply immersed in it are critical of *jihadi* beliefs and practices.[21]

Islamism and *Jihad*

Central to this entire issue are two distinctions: that made between Islamism and Islam, and between traditional understandings of *jihad* and modern *jihadi* Islamist understandings of *jihad*.[22] Islamism — the totalistic ideology derived by some from the imagery and ideals of Islam — remains little understood in the West. Although very much a product of the twentieth century, and composed of familiar twentieth-century elements, it appeared so alien and 'other' that it continued to be overlooked and misunderstood by the West until the very end of the century.

The word *jihad* literally means to 'struggle' or to 'strive' and throughout Islamic history has been associated with personal growth, good works in society, and with self-defence in just-war.[23] In the middle of the twentieth century, however, a rather different understanding of *jihad* was introduced in Egypt by Muslim Brotherhood intellectuals Hasan al-Banna and Syed Qutb. This *jihadi* understanding of *jihad* was the product of the union of the new Islamist thought of Rashid Rida in Egypt and Maududi in Pakistan, combined with the ideas of revolutionary Marxism.[24] A radically materialist understanding of Islam, *jihadi* Islamism argues that it falls to a faithful vanguard to give their lives to precipitating the revolution which will eventually usher in the utopia of a truly Islamic state in which no law but God's is recognized. Long ignored and overlooked by the West, despite the successful 1979 revolution in Iran and numerous outbreaks of ideologically driven violence in the Arab world and Muslim Asia, *jihadi* Islamism achieved an awful maturity via the *Mujahideen* struggle in Afghanistan which saw the emergence of such networks as al-Qaeda and Southeast Asia's Jemaah Islamiyah in the mid-1990s.

The almost total failure of the West to anticipate both the Iranian revolution in 1979 and the long-term consequences of sponsoring foreign *Mujahideen* in Afghanistan following the Soviet invasion that same year stand as stark reminders of Western ineptitude in this area. In hindsight Western colonial and postcolonial policies in the Muslim world throughout the course of the century were blithely sowing the seeds for later chaos.[25]

Policies began to change, but not nearly enough and not in all the right ways, after 11 September 2001, however, Islamism continues to be insufficiently understood. In the Arab world the relative absence of civil society and democratically accountable governments means that Islamism is apt to be dismissed as a desperate expression of political dissent. In Muslim Asia, despite the region representing the demographic majority of the Muslim world, Islam and Islamism remain little studied and widely misunderstood.

Given the sudden decline in positive sentiment towards the US across Asia over the last three years, the rise of Islamophobia in parts of Western society, and the simplistic rhetoric of the 'war on terror', it is hardly surprising that many progressive thinkers, both in Asia and the West, are reluctant to criticize any but the most extreme manifestations of Islamist radicalism. Indeed, many object to any implied conflation of political Islamism with *jihadi* Islamism and argue on liberal grounds, tacitly invoking the logic of cultural relativism, that those who claim to support pluralism should not single-out Islamism for criticism.

Many devout Muslim intellectuals and activists in Asia, not least those committed to defending the rights of women, however, are deeply troubled by the rise of Islamism in all its forms. They see Asia's Islamist parties, such as Pakistan's Jama'at-i-Islami, the Islamic Party of Malaysia (PAS), and Indonesia's Prosperous Justice Party (PKS), Crescent Moon and Star Party (PBB) as being guided by a deeply radical ideology that is at best prepared to accommodate democracy for utilitarian reasons, but remains at odds with the spirit of liberal democracy. In particular they are concerned that these parties seek to radically, if only incrementally, alter the constitutional and legislative character of the state in ways which are deeply detrimental to freedom of belief, expression, movement and association, especially for women and minority groups.[26]

In countering the charge that such concerns are merely the stuff of paranoia, prejudice and personality politics, they argue that creeping legislative 'reforms' in Pakistan and Malaysia (and currently under consideration in Indonesia) have already allowed a significant erosion of freedoms and rights in those societies. A more contentious claim is that a significant degree of synergy exists between political Islamists and *jihadi* Islamists, despite the former repudiating the violence of the latter, and the latter rejecting the former's accommodation of democracy.

Are either of the charges against the Islamists objectively defensible? How best should Islamism be understood? The development of a sound conceptual understanding of Islamism requires consideration of three different sorts of inquiry. Firstly, it is essential that attention be given to the history of ideas that has shaped Islamism. Islamism is not Islam, nevertheless it is, in certain respects, a religious movement and as such intellectual convictions and the ideas that shape them matter greatly. Secondly, it is important that Islamist movements are understood within an historical context. Without this there is no way of understanding the waxing and waning of Islamism as a social movement in response to changed social, economic and political circumstances. Finally, it is important to understand the varying social and political contexts to which Islamist movements across Asia currently relate. Just as an ahistorical approach blinds us to appreciating the dynamics shaping the movements' development, so too ignorance of specific local circumstances and their global connections prevents us from achieving anything more than a relatively superficial understanding of what is happening. Another way of perceiving the holistic and inter-disciplinary nature of Islamism is found in the arguments of Clifford Geertz and Bassam Tibi, that religion should be understood as both cultural and social systems.[27]

If Islamism is approached predominantly through the textual study of ideas and ideology, as both 'orientalist' scholars and some security experts have been inclined to do, an essentialist understanding emerges that inadequately explains and anticipates contemporary developments. On the other hand, an equally unsatisfactory understanding is produced if the seminal ideas of Islamism are overlooked in favour of consideration of only social factors, as some social scientists are inclined to do.

Ideas are very important to Islamism. Although Islamists might frequently be simply mistaken for fundamentalists (that is to say, having a socially conservative outlook but no desire for radical political change), and *vice versa*, Islamism is a social and political movement inspired by deep religious and intellectual convictions. Islamism is a response to the challenge of theodicy — it is an attempt to explain why God has permitted the prevalence of evil, in the form of social injustice (both locally and globally between the South and the North, and between the Muslim world and the West), moral turpitude, corrupt and dysfunctional political systems, and economic backwardness.

Islamism's answer to the sad state of the Muslim world is proclaimed as a religious one but is essentially a political one. It rejects any notion that Islam should be 'merely' a personal religion and argues for changes to the role and operation of state agencies and law in enforcing piety. The general backwardness of much of the Muslim world, and the moral failings of the entire modern world, are said to be rooted in the failure of mankind to submit to God's law. Broadly speaking, Islamism argues that the one panacea to the world's malaise is to be found in the application of *Sharia*, or Islamic law. Islamism's answer to theodicy is theocracy. Consequently, Islamism identifies secularism as being at the heart of the Muslim world's troubles and advocates the re-engagement of the state in personal morality.

Political Islamists are prepared to work through the political process to achieve their long-term aims. For this reason their contribution is often regarded as limited and benign. There are good reasons to support this position, not least of them being that since democracy, amongst other things, is intended to be an equitable means of regulating competing desires and opinions we ought to respect and defend the right of all political parties to participate in the process, so long as they respect the rules of the game. In an era in which we can expect many Muslim countries to make the transition to democracy this is not minor matter. Rather, we should expect that Islamist political parties, although minority elements in transitional Muslim democracies such Indonesia and Pakistan, will be a significant aspect of political life in the Muslim world for years to come. Moreover, given the globalizing forces at work in the Muslim world, it is inevitable that these parties, and the social movements that support them, will learn from each other and even collaborate transnationally on important issues.[28]

To the extent that these Islamist parties gain real political power and become responsible for the day-to-day burdens of government, there is reason to expect that, as appears to be the case in Turkey, they will moderate their views.[29] This dynamic, however, is very much dependent on the social movements that support and shape the character and outlook of these parties and this is, in turn, very much shaped by the prevailing political environment both domestically and internationally.

Given the fact that, by definition, Islamists have great faith in the power of law to change behaviour, it should also be expected that even as minority players Islamist parties will seek out strategic alliances that will afford them the opportunity to achieve incremental amendments to national laws through the legislature. They understand that laws, once passed through the legislature, are not easily repealed and that the cumulative effect of many small amendments can be considerable indeed. To be sure, the experience of Muslim nations such as Egypt, Pakistan and Malaysia has been that incremental change — a concession here, a compromise there — can result in a state implementing so many aspects of so-called *Sharia* provisions that it takes on many of the characteristics of an Islamic state without acknowledging that it is doing so.[30]

12 October 2002
Global *Jihad* is not just for the Middle East

It is this process of creeping 'Islamization' that concerns many progressive Muslim intellectuals and activists in Indonesia. For them the argument that Indonesian people and the Indonesian legislature will never allow Indonesia to become an Islamic state rings hollow. They point to the significant diminution of freedom of conscience, expression and association in neighbouring Malaysia as evidence that creeping Islamization through the legislature represents a concern that should not be lightly dismissed. They are particularly concerned about the small but highly effective Islamist political party Partai Keadilan Sejaterah (the Prosperous Justice Party – PKS) with its cadres of enthusiastic and well-organized students and young professionals. The fact that PKS achieved 7.3 per cent of the parliamentary vote in the April 2004 elections is reason enough to take it seriously.[31]

The success of the small Islamist parties in Indonesia's 1999 and 2004 elections, the first free and fair elections since 1955, was not seen as representing great cause for concern in either Indonesia or Australia. This is because Islamism has been a persistent element in Indonesian politics throughout its modern history and it is not at all clear from election results that support for Islamism has grown between 1955 and 2004.[32]

The development that really shocked Indonesians and their neighbours was the revelation that for years Indonesia had been home to a radical *jihadi* Islamist group, Jemaah Islamiyah (JI), with close ties to al-Qaeda.[33] These revelations came in the wake of the 12 October 2002 bombing of Paddy's Bar and the Sari Club in Denpasar Bali. Good police work led to the arrest of most members of the cell and the subsequent arrests of other JI members thwarted a number of further large-scale attacks from being carried out. Nevertheless, JI affiliates have continued to be active in outlying areas such as South and Central Sulawesi, and JI was able to conduct several more significant bombings, attacking Jakarta's Marriott Hotel in August 2003 and the Australian Embassy in September 2004.[34]

The substantial volumes of evidence that were produced by police investigations (which saw members of the Australian Federal Police working alongside their colleagues from the Indonesian Police in very fruitful co-operation) following the Bali bombings quickly established a startling picture of JI's historical development and close ties with al-Qaeda. In particular, evidence brought to light after the bombings confirmed most of the important details canvassed in several reports about JI written in the previous 12 months by Sidney Jones (and her colleagues at the International Crisis Group – ICG). But for many Indonesians the case against JI still remains unclear and disturbing levels of denial exist right up to Cabinet level in the Indonesian Government.[35]

For many people the evidence is both compelling and deeply disturbing. Even serious, seasoned foreign observers of Indonesia have found it difficult to accept the picture painted by earlier ICG reports. Suggestion that Indonesian extremists had strong links with al-Qaeda, and that hundreds had trained in al-Qaeda camps along the Afghanistan–Pakistan border, beggared belief. Indonesia Islam, it was said, was profoundly different to the Islam of Saudi Arabia's Salafi extremists, Egypt's Muslim Brotherhood and Pakistan's radical *Madrassahs*.

This view of Indonesian Islam is not, on the whole, wrong at all. It is true, in hindsight, that radical groups such as the Darul Islam (DII) movements that fought through the 1950s to establish small Islamic states in West Java and Southern Sulawesi were a more serious phenomenon than was sometimes thought.[36] In particular, it is now clear that even after these movements had long been closed down and suppressed, their networks remained remarkably intact, providing precursor elements for the emergence of the radical Islamist groups that eventually became Jemaah Islamiyah.[37] What the Bali bombing investigations have taught us is that even the most tolerant parts of the Islamic world are susceptible to the globalizing influence of radical Islamism.

It should have been clear all along that the basic cultural orientation of Indonesian society, even in pluralist, tolerant East Java, home of many of the Bali bombers, is no sure bulwark against globalization. It is also obvious now that globalization is not simply, or even primarily, about the westernization of the developing world. The familiar vectors of globalization — electronic communication, cheap printing and electronic reproduction, affordable and rapid transportation, trade and exchange, and the development of transnational networks — are just as effective in extending *jihadi* Islamist thought and culture as they are in promoting Western popular culture.[38]

Because one of the defining features of globalizing Islamism is the rejection of all cultural accretions accumulated in Muslim society since the golden years of the Prophet Muhammad and his companions, regional cultural differences are downplayed and local teachings and traditions discredited. In practice this remains more of an ideal than a reality, for even in al-Qaeda's training camps, Southeast Asians lived separately from their Arab and African brothers — basic cultural differences are not easily eradicated. Nevertheless, this emphasis on returning to the 'pure Islam' of the first years of the faith made it possible for converts to this new form of radicalism to turn their backs on the norms and practices of the communities in which they had grown up.

26 December 2004
Conservative Piety is not Fundamentalism

The Bali bombing opened the door to a series of unpleasant revelations about the extent to which our region has been influenced by globalizing forces that we had previously thought unviable. The post tsunami recovery effort in Aceh, however, provided some more happy insights into Muslim society. Aceh prides itself on being known as the Veranda of Mecca because of its early Islamization and long history of involvement in Muslim trade networks tying it to the Arab world two oceans away. Decades of separatist conflict involving unspeakable acts of brutality by both the Indonesian military and the Free Aceh Movement

(GAM) in this social conservative province have often produced the mistaken impression that Aceh's grievances are religious in nature.

The fact that the province's access to the outside world, and *vice versa*, was tightly regulated by the military meant that relatively few people had first-hand experience of life in Aceh. The tsunami that killed almost a quarter of a million people in Aceh on 26 December 2004, forced open the province to thousands of foreign aid workers, including Australian military personnel. Contact with the Acehnese revealed that, although Acehnese society could be said to be socially conservative, it was not fundamentalist. In particular, the Acehnese had little sympathy for *jihadi* Islamism or even for Saudi Salafism, and had little time for outsiders telling them that they had to turn away from their traditional, mystical, approach to Islam.

This is not to say that it is impossible that Aceh could go the way of the southern Philippines or southern Thailand and suffer the transmutation of local, ethno-nationalist, grievances into global *jihadi* ones. The fact that this has not so far occurred despite approaches from radical Islamist militia like Laskar Jihad is testament to the resilience of local Islamic culture. But if the post-tsunami rebuilding program goes sour or if the long-running local grievances are not attended to and a lasting peace is not achieved, global *jihadi* Islamism might indeed finally achieve a toe-hold in the province. It is significant that several of Indonesia's main *jihadi* militia such as Laskar Mujahidin (which has links with JI) and Front Pembela Islam, were active in the relief effort within days of the disaster as were hundreds of PKS activists.

Conclusion

The conservative, but tolerant nature of Muslim society in Aceh, for example, is indicative of traditional Islam as it is practiced by the majority of Muslims who continue to live in poor rural communities. Traditional rural Islam, with its strong emphasis on local traditions and folk-Islamic mysticism, remains the majority expression of Islam today, including Islam in the Middle East. Nevertheless, Muslim communities across the world today face strong globalizing forces and any serious attempt to understand Islam and Muslim society needs to consider these forces and the movements that they produce.

In the broad compass of history, Islam and globalization go together. Islam, like Christianity and Buddhism, was both a product of, and a vehicle for, globalization from its very inception. But the globalization of the present time is qualitatively and quantitatively different from its earlier waves. As noted, the Muslim world remains overwhelmingly rural, but that is rapidly changing and already cities of the Muslim world are witnessing rapid social change through global exposure and modernization. At the same time the demography of the Muslim world is strongly skewed to the young, with the majority of Muslims in the world today being under the age of 27. These young people have unprecedented access to education, globalized information and travel but live in societies where authoritarianism and social injustice are endemic. An increasing number are also living in Western democracies where political oppression is much less acute but questions of social justice, both at the local and at the global level, are often even more sharply observed. Increasingly they are turning to transnational Islam to provide answers to life's questions and a program of action in the struggle for change. Liberalism, Salafism, political Islamism and *jihadi* Islamism all represent different products of the globalization of Islam and Muslim society. Each one is important and each one needs to be understood at both the level of ideas and the level of social context and action.

While the commitment and sincerity of the Islamists is admirable, there is no escaping the fact that their theocratic response to theodicy drives an ultimately totalitarian agenda which is radically at odds with individual liberty. This does not mean there is no place for Islamist parties in a democratic system but it does mean that those who value the freedoms made possible by the separation of 'church' and state must be on guard against the incremental ratcheting forward of constraints on personal liberty, whether through quiet legislative changes or through noisy social movements in which a determined minority simultaneously claim to speak for a 'silent majority' and for God Himself.

As important as it is to understand the ideas driving Islamism Australia also needs to strive to make sense of the sociology of *jihadi* extremism and understand the social, political, psychological and religious forces that lead young men to find personal meaning in violent struggle in the name of Islam. The individual appeal of *jihadi* Islamism's radical certainty requires further study, as does the role of the state in contributing to, or breaking-down, the social conditions that enable *jihadi* groups to recruit and regenerate in overwhelmingly youthful and impoverished communities across Asia and the Middle East. Australia must also come to terms with the globalizing power of *jihadi* Islamism to exploit the failure of the state to overcome local problems, and leverage discontent associated with separatist grievances in areas such as Chechnya, the southern Philippines or southern Thailand, which transmute isolated regional ethno-nationalist disputes into networked battle-fronts in the Manichaean global *jihadi* struggle.

At the same time Australia needs to better understand the growth and development of Islamic liberalism. Islamic liberalism is an important mediator between Western liberalism and traditional Muslim society. But Islamic liberalism has not received anything like the scholarly and media attention that globalized Islamism, in all its hues — Salafi, political and *jihadi* — has. This is partly because the quiet growth of liberalism is not as news-worthy as the dramatic campaigns of Islamism, but also because Islamic liberalism is not as wide spread and as well developed across the Muslim world as is Islamism. This is not due to the essential characteristics of Islam but the prevailing political and social climate across much of the Muslim world, where civil society has been repressed, and patriarchal social conservatism tolerated or encouraged in order to protect the political status quo. The majority of Muslims around the world are likely to continue to experience the forces of globalization and modernization without expressly siding with either the liberals or the Islamists, but the equilibrium that is finally achieved depends very much upon the efficacy of both liberal and Islamist activism.

The pace of social change and the plethora of globalized ideas and movements means that understanding Islam and Muslim society is arguably more challenging today than it has ever been. But it is also more important than it has ever been before for Western nations, not least Australia, to engage with the Muslim world in a sophisticated and thoughtful fashion for mutual benefit and understanding. We need to pay more attention to Islam if we are to have any hope of understanding the Middle East and of being effective there.

Finally, Australia needs to also pay more attention to Islam and Muslim society at home. Olivier Roy argues cogently that the neofundamentalism of globalized Islam has particular appeal to alienated young Muslim men living in Europe. Circumstances for Muslim communities in Australia are markedly different than those in Europe and especially Roy's France. Nevertheless, his study should serve as a reminder to us in Australia of the importance of community. To the extent that those otherwise vulnerable to globalized Islam's siren call of certainty, purpose, dignity and belonging are purposefully integrated into their own communities and related to traditional sources of religious authority Australia should escape Europe's growing problem with religious extremism. But Australia should not lightly dismiss the problems of far-away Europe as not being of concern to it. In our globalized world today nowhere is far-away any more. In the world of ideas Australian youth are just as exposed as European youth. The difference lies in their relationships with their own communities and with broader Australian society. For those of us in a position to be of some influence this means we have to get the message out, through both tabloid and broadsheet media, that Australia needs stronger Muslim communities. Traditional religious leaders and their networks need to be strengthened and relations between religious communities built up. The apparent counter-intuitiveness of this message to many means that getting it understood and accepted will require protracted effort. We really do need to try harder.

8

THE ISRAEL–PALESTINE CONFLICT SINCE 9/11

Scott Burchill

The most concerning but widely predicted consequences of the 9/11 terrorist attacks on New York City and Washington were the opportunities the strikes and their aftermath afforded governments around the world to align their political struggles with domestic opponents as part of the 'war against terrorism'.

The best known examples were Russia with Chechen separatists, China with the Urgyr in the northwest of the country, Turkey and its Kurdish population, India with Muslim rebels in Kashmir, the Algerian Government and its political opposition, and Israel versus the Palestinians.

Israel opened its window of opportunity almost immediately after the 9/11 strikes by sending tanks into Palestinian towns such as Ramallah and Jenin for the first time, generally increasing its hold on the occupied territories. This was the chance for Prime Minister Ariel Sharon to settle some old scores with Yasser Arafat and the Palestinian population on the West Bank and Gaza. With occasional brief interludes, the violence has continued ever since.

In Australia, which has only a marginal interest in the Israel–Palestine dispute, the terrorist attacks on New York and Washington instigated a change in both rhetoric and policy by the Howard Government. Until 9/11 there was a pretence of even-handedness towards the dispute, even though in reality successive Australian governments had been strong supporters of the state of Israel and only belatedly acknowledged that Palestinians might have similar rights. After 9/11 much of the pretence of even-handedness was abandoned — arguably a victory for honesty in diplomacy — although the cost was an independent voice on the question. Since Al-Qaeda struck Washington and New York City, the position of the Australian Government towards the primary Middle East dispute has become virtually indistinguishable from Washington's.

Almost immediately after the attacks, the Australian Government began to accept the conflation of the defence of Israel with the so-called 'war on terror'. Attitudes changed as Canberra began to uncritically accept Washington's stand that it could be both Israel's strongest, most influential ally and a third party mediator in its dispute with the Palestinians. For example, Switzerland convened a meeting of the High Contracting Parties of the Fourth Geneva Convention on December 5, 2001 to discuss alleged Israeli violations of the Convention in its treatment of Palestinians in the West Bank and Gaza Strip. The Fourth Geneva Convention of 1949 (with additional Protocols), sometimes called the Convention on the Protection of Civilians in Time of War, is designed to guarantee special care and protection for civilians under wartime occupation, especially children.

The United States, Israel and Australia — in isolation from the international consensus — boycotted the meeting claiming that it was another attempt by anti-Israel forces to leverage international agreements that have no applicability to the occupied territories. In other words, Australia now considered the Israeli-occupied territories as a special case to which international law regarding the protection of civilians may not apply. It is difficult to imagine Australia boycotting such an important meeting before September 2001, or being so out of step with global opinion.

This chapter will focus on two key ingredients of Australian policy towards the Israel–Palestine conflict since the 9/11 attacks. The first is what the Howard Government means by an even-handed approach to the dispute and how this policy was influenced by the so called 'war against terror'.

The second is how a specific interpretation of the 2000 Camp David negotiations between Ehud Barak and Yasser Arafat, hosted by Bill Clinton, has been used to underwrite Canberra's policy settings in the Middle East.

Uneven-handedness

In the month after 9/11, John Howard eloquently summarized his Government's approach. According to the Prime Minister, 'it's even-handed. Yes we support a Palestinian homeland but there has to be an acceptance of, the unconditional acceptance of Israel to peacefully exist within secure and defensible boundaries.'[1]

There are a couple of important points to note about this formula which belie its initial apparent fairness.

First, there is support for a 'Palestinian homeland' but no mention of a Palestinian state or where it might be. It might be within a pre-existing state such as Jordan or somewhere in Africa.

Secondly, Australia's support for a 'Palestinian homeland' only comes after Israel's right to exist 'within secure and defensible boundaries' is unconditionally accepted by the Palestinians. Apart from the fact that no state within the international system acknowledges another's 'right to exist' because it is an unenforceable right (Australia does not acknowledge Israel's right to exist which is a very different claim to diplomatic recognition), it is clear from the Prime Minister that Israel's needs must be met first. There is no reference to 'secure and defensible' boundaries for Palestinians presumably because they are to get what's left over after Israel finally achieves internationally recognized boundaries. By definition this is not even-handed.

Perhaps this should not come as a surprise. Prime Minister Howard speaks 'as the leader of a government that has always been an unashamed and unapologetic friend of the State of Israel and the maintenance of the integrity of the State of Israel behind secure, internationally recognized borders has been a cornerstone of the foreign policy of many governments in Australia.'[2]

True enough, though no one has ever suggested he needed to apologize for his support for Israel and it is equally true that no Australian Government has ever given anything like equal support for the right of Palestinians to self-determination. On the right of Palestinians to resist the occupation of their lands — a right inscribed in international law including the Charter of the United Nations and the Universal Declaration of Human Rights — successive Australian Governments, including Mr. Howard's, have been all but silent. They have also been mute on related issues such as Israel's 'weapons of mass destruction' (WMD) and its disregard of UN General Assembly and Security Council resolutions. Nor is their any explanation for why Israel still does not have 'internationally recognized borders' over half a century after its establishment.

However, the best illustration of just how uneven the Howard Government's approach to the Israel–Palestine dispute has been can be found in its reaction to Palestinian suicide bombers, who emerged during the second intifada provoked by what President Clinton called Ariel Sharon's 'inflammatory escapade' to Temple Mount in September 2000.[3]

The Howard Government has not only been quick to publicly condemn each Palestinian suicide attack, it has also factored these attacks into a discourse which seeks to justify Israel's unwillingness to seriously negotiate a peace agreement with the Palestinians.

As Prime Minister Howard was preparing his case for war against Iraq in early 2003, he could not escape referring to the cause of much Arab hostility towards the West — Washington's support for Israel and its direct contribution to the repression of Palestinians via political support and credits for military procurements. In his Ministerial Statement to Parliament on Iraq in February, the Prime Minister asked: 'How can the Prime Minister of Israel be expected to do these things [negotiate with the Palestinian leadership] while ever the murderous pattern of suicide bombing continues to be inflicted on the Israelis?'[4] This came after an earlier expression of understanding for the devastating Israeli attacks in the occupied territories when the Prime Minister said 'I think there has been an over-reaction by Israel but the over-reaction is understandable given the nature of the attacks that were launched on Israel.'[5]

There are three points to note about these remarks which give a very clear picture of what the Howard Government means by even-handedness towards the Israel–Palestine conflict.

First, why Palestinian violence should end before Israeli violence is expected to terminate is never explained, principally because Israeli state terrorism is portrayed as responsive rather than proactive. Palestinian bombers are described as terrorists while Israel's attacks against Palestinian towns are defined as self-defence. Completely missing from Howard's account is any reference to the cause of Palestinian terrorism, namely thirty-seven years of brutal and humiliating occupation. For the Howard Government it is almost as if Palestinian suicide attacks suddenly fell out of the sky with no pre-history, provocation or context even worthy of mention. The occupation, if it actually exists, has apparently been characterized by Israeli non-violence. It is therefore best to commence the narrative of the conflict with the first suicide bombings after Sharon's provocative stroll in September 2000.

References to the occupation seem to be taboo. When asked to comment on the illegal Israeli settlements while visiting the region in May 2000, Howard said 'I'm not going to express a view on that.'[6] When referring to historical wrongs perpetrated against Palestinians in a speech in July 2003, the Prime Minister spoke of 'a sense of injustice' as if it were a debatable issue.[7] And perhaps most remarkable of all was Mr. Howard's suggestion that Palestinian claims for liberation constituted a 'convoluted argument about the alleged dispossession or prolonged disputes'.[8] The 'alleged dispossession' of Palestinians? One can only wonder how Mr. Howard explains the Palestinian refugee camps in Lebanon and Jordan, for example. The Australian Prime Minister has shown no reluctance to publicly condemn each instance of Palestinian resistance but has been conspicuously silent on the occupation which sparked them.

Secondly, Howard's argument is not an in-principle opposition to the use of violence *per se* because he has said that Israeli state terrorism is 'understandable.' In fact 'state terrorism' as a concept is missing from the lexicon of the Howard Government altogether unless it is in reference to official enemies such as Iraq under Saddam Hussein when it is freely deployed. Israeli missile strikes against Palestinian civilians are routinely 'understandable,' occasionally an 'over-reaction' or more often simply and conveniently ignored entirely. They are never described as a crime and little more than 'restraint' or 'moderation' is ever called for when publicity about them becomes too widespread to ignore.[9]

When questioned about the assassination of Hamas's spiritual leader Sheik Ahmed Yassin in March 2004, Foreign Minister Alexander Downer declared that 'we don't support targeted assassinations of this kind. But let's just keep it in sort of balance — there's a balance here.'[10] Where there clearly has not been a balance is in the comparative reactions of the Australian Government to suicide bombings and what are often politely referred to as Israeli 'incursions' into Gaza or the West Bank. The former regularly invoke a ministerial reaction, the latter infrequently and if so, always reluctantly. Canberra is somehow always able to understand Israeli terrorism but never Palestinian violence.

Thirdly, the Howard Government is effectively calling for a Palestinian surrender as a pre-requisite to negotiations. Whereas the occupation is to be considered as part of a negotiation process and withdrawal is not to be a pre-condition, the response to the occupation must stop before negotiations even begin. Is that even-handed? What incentive would the Israelis have to compromise? Such a back-down would almost certainly be politically suicidal for the weaker side.

There is no understanding and absolutely no sympathy from the Australian Government for the fact that only armed resistance has kept the cause of Palestinian nationalism alive. As the African National Congress discovered in South Africa, and countless others living under occupation in Indochina, North Africa and the sub continent have found, when peaceful avenues are blocked and extinction becomes a real possibility, armed struggle is regrettably the only last resort. How would the Palestinian cause have fared without violent struggle during the

1970s, for example, when many Israeli and US leaders denied the very existence of the Palestinian people?

Just as those resisting Western occupation in Iraq are branded terrorists, it has long been the fate of Palestinians struggling to liberate their own territory from occupation to be similarly branded. They are not expected to notice the source of the military hardware that kills them at a consistent rate of three to one, or the diplomatic backing for Israel in the West.

It should come as little surprise that when the opportunity for Ariel Sharon to align his struggle against the Palestinians with President Bush's new 'war against terror', he grasped it with both hands.

Blaming Arafat

The strategy is familiar and has been consistently applied.

By arguing that Yasser Arafat refused an Israeli offer of unprecedented generosity and concession at Camp David in July 2000 — with claims that he rejected anything between 80 per cent and 98 per cent of what he and his people wanted — it was possible to portray the Palestinian leader as the obstacle to peace in the Middle East rather than as a serious interlocutor with the Israelis. Arafat could be cast as the man who again missed an historic opportunity when Israeli Prime Minister Ehud Barak agreed to give him virtually everything he asked for in negotiations hosted by President Clinton in the last days of his second term in office.

This is the argument of the 'friends of Israel' from Greg Sheridan, Daniel Mandel and Colin Rubenstein in Australia, to *The New Republic*, *The New York Times* and *The Australian*, including its Middle East correspondents.

It remains the official attitude of the Australian Government and the regularly invoked explanation for what went wrong in 2001 and who is to blame for the subsequent violence.

According to Prime Minister John Howard, 'when Ehud Barak was the Prime Minister of Israel he offered in his peace settlement close to 90 per cent of the demands of the PLO'. Soon this became '80–90 per cent of what they asked for', and a few months later 'Barak's very magnanimous offer at Camp David [involved] offering Palestinians 90 per cent or more of what they wanted, including some involvement in Jerusalem'. By 2003 Howard was arguing that 'the great bulk of their (i.e. the Palestinians') demands were ultimately repudiated [in 2000]'.[11]

This position has become the Australian Government's standard line in almost all subsequent commentary on the spiralling violence that has ensued since the Barak Labour Government was removed from office and replaced by Ariel Sharon's Likud-led coalition. In summary, it is all Arafat's fault. He was offered a great deal — more than he could reasonably expect — and he foolishly knocked it back. Everything that has gone wrong since is a direct consequence of Arafat's failure to grasp Barak's magnanimous offer at Camp David.

This orthodoxy has been further strengthened by the publication of an insider's account of the negotiations hosted by Bill Clinton in the final months of his presidency. According to the foreign editor of *The Australian*, 'Dennis Ross, the chief US negotiator, recounts all this in irrefutable detail in his new book, *The Missing Peace*. The final Israeli offer included 96 per cent of the West Bank and Gaza, all the Arab neighbourhoods of East Jerusalem and some compensating territory from Israel proper for a sovereign Palestinian state.'[12] This is similar, though not identical, to Clinton's claim that Arafat was offered 91 per cent of the West Bank amongst other measures at Camp David, and later 'parameters' which recommended 94 per cent to 96 per cent of the West Bank plus additional negotiated arrangements on Jerusalem and other points of contention.[13]

If only Arafat had not missed this historic opportunity the settlers would have left peacefully, there would have been a Palestinian state and no need for the second intifada with its awful suicide bombings. Instead, he walked away from Barak's magnanimity and escalated the terror. The onus was now on the Palestinians to make greater concessions.

Given its prominence within the Howard Government's Middle East discourse, it is worth looking more closely at what Arafat was apparently offered by Barak — specifically what he subsequently rejected. A cursory review highlights an immediate problem with the argument. It is largely a fallacious version of history.

First, there were no specific proposals from either Israel (Barak) or the US (Clinton) at Camp David. Just 'ideas' and later 'parameters.' The US and Israel had no official position or definitive explanatory maps. Eventually some maps were published in Israel and by the highly authoritative *Report on Israeli Settlements* in the US, largely reconstructed from credible Israeli sources. All of the maps confirmed that the West Bank would be divided into four isolated cantons separated from the Gaza Strip, with its status left vague. Relevant maps can now be found and viewed.[14]

An examination of the maps reveals that 'Jerusalem' is vastly and illegally expanded, comprising 5.4 per cent of the entire West Bank and is not included in the percentage figure generously claimed by Israel's supporters.[15] There is a salient from the city to the east stretching virtually to Jericho, and including Ma'ale Adumim, a town established mainly by Rabin–Peres–Clinton–Barak to split the West Bank into two parts. There's another salient to the north, splitting the remaining sections also virtually in two. A small part of East Jerusalem, the centre of Palestinian life and the communications centre for the whole of the West Bank, is virtually cut off from all of them. Borders are under Israel's control, as are resources, most importantly water.

According to Robert Fisk, Jerusalem was to have remained the 'eternal and unified capital of Israel.' Arafat would only have received what Madeleine Albright called 'a sort of sovereignty' over the Haram al-Sharif mosque area and some Arab streets, while the Palestinian Parliament would have been below the city's eastern walls at Abu Dis and renamed Al-Quds. With the vastly extended and illegal Jerusalem municipality boundaries cutting deep into the West Bank, Jewish settlements like Ma'ale Adumim were not up for negotiation; nor were several other settlements. Nor was the 10-mile Israeli military buffer zone around the West Bank, nor the settlers' roads, which would razor through the Palestinian 'state'.[16] The Jordan Valley was to remain under Israeli control until some future unspecified date.

Discontiguous and encircled cantons, or more accurately *bantustans*, without borders with any country other than Israel; no agreement to dismantle or even stop illegal Israeli settlements on Arab lands; a refusal to return to the 1967 borders; retention of 'Israeli' bypass roads and adjacent lands which intersect the West Bank; no automatic right of return for refugees; and still Arafat failed to see the extraordinary generosity of the offer.

In truth, Arafat was offered about 46 per cent of the 22 per cent of Palestine (the West Bank) that was left after the establishment of the Israeli state. Or to put it more meaningfully, the Palestinian leader was being 'offered' by the occupying government about 12 per cent of the land from which the Palestinians were driven in 1948.

Unsurprisingly, Palestinians resented being told how much of their land Israel was 'generously' prepared to return to them. Camp David must have seemed like sitting down with the burglar and the police to be told by both how much of their stolen property they think should be returned. Generous 'concessions' indeed. Unsurprisingly, Arafat refused to commit political suicide by accepting such a humiliating and one-sided 'deal.' According to Noam Chomsky,

> the Camp David proposals divided the West Bank into virtually separated cantons, and could not possibly be accepted by any Palestinian leader. That is evident from a look at the maps that were easily available, but not in the NYT (*New York Times*), or apparently anywhere in the US mainstream, perhaps for that reason. After the collapse of these negotiations, Clinton recognized that Arafat's reservations made sense, as demonstrated by the famous "parameters", which, though vague, went much further towards a possible settlement … . Clinton gave his own version of the reaction to his "parameters" in a talk to the Israeli Policy Forum on January 7, 2001: "Both Prime Minister Barak and Chairman Arafat have now accepted these parameters as the basis for further efforts. Both have expressed some reservations."

> One can learn this from such obscure sources as the prestigious Harvard–MIT journal *International Security* (Fall 2003), along with the conclusion that "the Palestinian narrative of the 2000–01 peace talks is significantly more accurate than the Israeli narrative… ."

> After that, high-level Israeli–Palestinian negotiators proceed to take the Clinton parameters as "the basis for further efforts," and addressed their "reservations" at meetings in Taba through January. These produced a tentative agreement, meeting some of the Palestinian concerns — and thus again undermining the official story. Problems remained, but the Taba agreements went much further towards a possible settlement than anything that had preceded. The negotiations were called off by Barak, so their possible outcome is unknown. A detailed report by EU envoy Miguel Moratinos was accepted as accurate by both sides, and prominently reported in Israel.[17]

The new orthodoxy surrounding the Camp David negotiations and their aftermath falls apart on close scrutiny; however it has an important role to play in the West's explanation for why violence in the region continues and who is to blame. As Israeli scholar Tania Reinhart explains, 'the myth of generous Israeli offers at Camp David … is nothing but a fraud perpetrated by propaganda … at Camp David Barak was neither aiming for reconciliation nor genuinely attempting to move closer to an end of conflict.'[18]

The Howard Government's position on a settlement of the dispute subsequently became even more confused. In July 2004 Australia voted in the minority against the United Nations General Assembly resolution which referred the question of Israel's security/apartheid wall to the International Court of Justice (ICJ). Adopting Washington's position, Canberra claimed it was not appropriate to bring political disputes of this kind before the Court, though it is hard to see the ICJ ruling on anything other than political matters — its primary function.

Despite Canberra's refusal to even allow the legality of the wall to be judged, Foreign Minister Downer says that he 'would not want the barrier to become a de facto border and I have urged the Israeli Government to consider moving the barrier closer to the 1967 line.'[19] This follows an earlier claim that 'we support the green line being the border, the pre-1967 border, as the national border'.[20] Mr. Downer seems to be unaware that this position has been explicitly rejected by the Sharon Government and is inconsistent with Prime Minister Howard's claim that 'the basis of a settlement must be the Oslo accords.'[21]

Conclusion: The Role of Palestinian Leaders

The Palestinian leadership has always had a very specific role in the eyes of the Israeli and US political establishments. It has been to exert domestic control over the Palestinian population on behalf of Israel. The character or history of individuals such as Arafat has never mattered. Nor has their commitment to democratic processes or a willingness to wipe out corruption been key concerns. What has always been crucial was whether Palestinian leaders could assert their authority over the people in the interests of Israeli security and Washington's regional security interests.

The decision by Washington and Tel Aviv to ignore the only democratically-elected leader of the Palestinian people in the last two years of his life, together with President Bush's presumption that he alone can decide how much of the occupied territories Israel can expect to retain, are further indications of how one-sided Western approaches to the Israel–Palestine conflict have recently become. Canberra's ungenerous response to the death of Yasser Arafat on 11 November, 2004 suggests Australia no longer aspires to an independent foreign policy on the Middle East's most intractable dispute, and is content to echo Washington's uneven approach.[22]

It also seems to be the role prescribed and preferred by the Australian Government. Shortly before Yasser Arafat's death, Foreign Minister Downer outlined what was expected from his successors: 'In the end what we do need from the Palestinian authority is a greater degree of authority over their own people, a greater degree of strength in controlling security within the Palestinian territories'.[23] But will the population do as they are told by those who no longer pretend to be even-handed and have only a marginal interest in the conflict?

9

MILITARY INTERVENTION IN THE MIDDLE EAST

William Maley

In late 2001, the Australian Government dispatched troops to Afghanistan. Not since the Second Anglo–Afghan War had Australians served in this particular theatre of operations, and it marked a sharp change in Australia's approach to the Middle East, where since the end of the Second World War Australian deployments had been to support peace operations, most notably the Multinational Force of Observers in the Sinai.[1] However, the activities of Australian Special Air Service (SAS) soldiers in Afghanistan provided a foretaste of a further exercise, the supply of troops to support 'Operation Iraqi Freedom', launched in March 2003 by US President George W. Bush. While there was some superficial continuity of purpose underpinning this venture, in virtually all respects the Afghanistan and Iraq commitments differed dramatically, the one point of similarity being Australia's sympathy to the political priorities of the Bush Administration.

The geographical propinquity of Afghanistan and Iraq should not disguise the quite fundamental differences between the two cases. In the case of Afghanistan, the 11 September 2001 attacks provided a strong basis for international action (Operation Enduring Freedom), which had firm legal grounding. In the case of Iraq, international action (Operation Iraqi Freedom) was based on shaky legal grounds, and even shakier factual premises. In Afghanistan, the United Nations (UN) was involved in efforts to facilitate post-intervention political transition. In Iraq, the UN was systematically excluded from efforts to facilitate post-intervention political transition. Australia's involvement in Operation Iraqi Freedom was therefore of considerable symbolic significance. It saw Australia adopting a position which was at odds with those of virtually all its immediate neighbours, and with notably weak analytical foundations. Furthermore, the impact which Australia's stance might have on its relations with the Arab and Muslim worlds was not a significant factor in the government's thinking. Australian foreign policy is not what it used to be, and the aim of this chapter is to illuminate some of the key dimensions of these changes.

This chapter is divided into four sections. The first explores the character of Australia's post-war alliance with the US, and shows how it has passed through a number of distinct phases, shaped not just by the contours of regional and global politics, but also by the orientations of US and Australian leaders. The second examines Australia's involvement in Afghanistan after 2001, and demonstrates that this did not mark a departure from longstanding Australian policy settings. The third, which addresses the Australian involvement in Iraq, explains the ways in which it marked a radical departure from the rhetoric of 'good international citizenship' which had underpinned some of the foreign policy initiatives of the previous Australian Foreign Minister, Gareth Evans (now President of the International Crisis Group),[2] and reflected instead the lengths to which Australia was prepared to go to persuade the Bush Administration that Australia was a reliable and compliant ally. The fourth notes some of the implications of this shift for Australia's place in its region and the world, and some parallels with earlier episodes, most importantly the making of a quagmire in South Vietnam in the 1960s.

Australian Foreign Policy: Some Key Dimensions

Australian foreign policy has long been dominated by an aura of dependence. It is no surprise that Coral Bell chose *Dependent Ally* as the title for her study of Australian–American relations.[3] Nonetheless, until recently it has been a dependence within limits. This is in significant measure an outgrowth of Australia's origin as a European outpost in a remote part of the globe, from which Australian leaders looked to major powers elsewhere as guarantors of security in an unpredictable region. At the time of the First World War, which turned on Balkan rivalries and the European balance of power, Australia's participation had a near-automatic character, although there were local reasons for concern (notably a threat from German New Guinea). However, the Versailles Conference witnessed a certain amount of independent agitation by the gadfly Australian Prime Minister W.M. Hughes,[4] and the following two decades witnessed some erosion of the relationship with the UK, partly expressed formally through the *Statute of Westminster*, but partly occurring informally as tensions sharpened over issues relating to wool.[5] However, for Prime Minister Robert Menzies, it was unthinkable in 1939 that Canberra should not join London in its declaration of war on Germany following the Nazi invasion of Poland, and there is no reason to doubt that he enjoyed overwhelming popular support in Australia.

Menzies was driven in part by an awareness of the vulnerability of Australia's position in the 'Far East', which as he famously noted, was Australia's 'Near North'. However, by the time this was exposed by the fall of Singapore to the Japanese in early 1942, Menzies was no longer Prime Minister, and it was left to Prime Minister John Curtin, confronted with the collapse of Britain's position in the East, to orchestrate a shift of focus from London to Washington as ally of dominant salience in the region. In large part this reflected a bowing to strategic reality. The entry of the US into the Second World War following the bombing of Pearl Harbour effectively consigned to the US the key decisions on which the course of the war in the Pacific would depend. Curtin did what he could to see that Australian interests were taken into account, not least through the despatch of Sir Owen Dixon as Minister in Washington,[6] but Australia's condition of strategic dependence was not one that could be argued away, and there is little to suggest that either Curtin or Dixon ever thought it would be worth the effort.

On the contrary, Australia moved after the war to solidify its relations with the US. The context, of course, was twofold: the outbreak of the Cold War and a fear of its intrusion into Asia after the success of Mao's Chinese Communist Party in taking over the Chinese mainland in late 1949; and the outbreak of the Korean War in 1950. Formally, the alliance with the US was embodied in the ANZUS Treaty of 1951,[7] although the terms of the Treaty were not particularly demanding. At a deeper level, the alliance was grounded in the importance to Australia of what Robert Menzies, who had resumed as Prime Minister in December 1949, was to call 'great and powerful friends'. Indeed, it can easily be overlooked that in Menzies' second term, the relationship with Washington was to prove one of Australia's easier relationships to manage. The Eisenhower and Kennedy Administrations proved relatively undemanding, while the relationship with the UK, superficially bolstered at the symbolic level by successful royal tours in 1954 and 1963, became increasingly tense at the political level, especially over the issue of British entry into the European Economic Community.

One reason for this was that the ANZUS alliance was essentially concerned with classical security threats to the territorial integrity of the state, and formed part of a wider family of alliances — NATO, CENTO and SEATO — with particularly territorial ambit. Thus, Australia was not expected by the US to be a major actor in areas beyond the ambit of

SEATO and the ANZUS Treaty, and could focus on its own part of the world. In addition, the US, in the context of the Cold War, was not a 'rollback' but a 'status quo' power, much to the frustration of US anticommunists in the 1950s who denounced even such foreign policy patricians as Dean Acheson for being 'soft' on communist powers. Even the Vietnam War, where some Australian politicians were quite eager to deepen US involvement with a view to containing what were seen as dangerously destabilizing forces,[8] fell within this framework. The fall of Saigon in 1975 created a parallel thrust in Australian foreign policy, namely the cultivation by the Fraser Government (1975–1983) of China as a counterweight to the Soviet Union in Asia.[9] This was easily accommodated, however, as the US went through a period of post-Vietnam introspection, first under President Ford (1974–1977), and then under President Carter (1977–1981), who was also forced to deal with the backwash of the January 1979 Iranian revolution and the December 1979 invasion of Afghanistan. On this latter issue, Prime Minister Fraser took a position as strong as that of President Carter, but out of his own sense that the invasion represented a concrete strategic threat to world order, rather than out of any sense of obligation to back the US. 'World order' concerns were also central to the Hawke Government's decision to support action in 1991 to reverse Iraq's August 1990 invasion of Kuwait. That invasion had constituted an egregious violation of Article 2.4 of the Charter of the United Nations, and UN Security Council Resolution 678 had provided a solid basis for member states to take action under Chapter VII of the Charter.[10]

While the Vietnam commitment remains hotly debated, the broad pattern to which this narrative points is one in which Australia's actions in tandem with the US could be seen as justified either by calculations of interest — beyond the mere interest in maintaining the alliance — or by assessments of the requirements of world order. On occasion, Australian governments defied the wishes of the US, as the Hawke Government did under party pressure over the issue of MX missile tests during the Reagan Administration (1981–1989), and no great harm resulted.[11] The case of New Zealand, frozen out of the alliance by Washington after it blocked port visits by US naval vessels that might have been nuclear-armed, could be seen as staking out the limits of the leeway which an ally could enjoy, but arguably those limits were actually quite wide.

The nature of the relationship began to change in the last decade or so. First, the collapse of the Eastern Bloc and the end of the Cold War removed a key rationale for the old alliance structures. CENTO and

SEATO were wound up; then NATO became an alliance in search of a rationale. To some extent the same was true of ANZUS. This became sharply apparent in 1999 during the East Timor crisis. This was a matter of profound concern for the Howard Government, caught between the demands of Australian public opinion for a response to the massacres perpetrated in East Timor by pro-Jakarta militias, and an official position of accepting East Timor as part of Indonesia. The desired US pressure on Jakarta was initially not forthcoming from the Clinton Administration, which had reasons to value its relations with Indonesia as well as with Australia.[12] The fears which this episode triggered may have something to do with Canberra's embrace of Washington and its concerns in the period since: one of the lessons of 1999 drawn by the Howard Government seems to have been that the alliance needed to be revitalized. Second, non-state terror replaced state-to-state invasion as a salient security problem. The 9/11 attacks in the US, although causing far fewer US deaths than the annual road toll, prompted a reaction based on a potent mixture of fear and anger. Given the transnational character of terrorist groups, an implication for countries such as Australia was that contributions as an alliance partner might be demanded in theatres well beyond those which Australian defence planners might have contemplated, and where any threat to Australia or Australians might thitherto have been tenuous at best. Third, as Owen Harries has pointed out,[13] the result was that the US ceased to function as a status quo power. The implications of this shift for alliance relations were considerable: while status quo powers can be comfortable alliance partners, powers committed to changing the status quo have an unpredictable quality. Being allied to them can be the equivalent of bungy-jumping when one does not know the length of the rope.

Australia and Operation Enduring Freedom in Afghanistan

The initial signals which the Bush Administration transmitted were hardly globalist in character. Before his election in 2000, George W. Bush had seen surprisingly little of the world outside the US — indeed, he had probably travelled less than any other presidential candidate of the modern era — and during the campaign, his shaky grasp of foreign affairs issues was prominently on display; in one notorious episode, he proved unable to name the Prime Minister of India, a country of almost a billion people and one of the world's seven declared nuclear powers. Equally, Bush and his associates were critical of what they saw as the 'nation-building' activities of the Clinton Administration, activities which they painted as a misuse of the US military, and almost beneath the dignity of a great power.[14] All this changed in 2001 with the events of 9/11. Al-Qaeda's attacks on the World Trade Centre and the Pentagon thrust the US into a new kind of engagement with the wider world. It was not, of course, *entirely* novel. The Clinton Administration had been confronted with the problem of al-Qaeda and its leader Osama bin Laden at least since the bombing of US embassies in Kenya and Tanzania in 1998. (Barton provides a summary of the terrorist attacks against the US which have been attributed to al-Qaeda in Chapter 7.) However, the reaction of that Administration had been notably ineffectual, as was its approach to the Taliban movement in Afghanistan, which had hosted bin Laden almost from the moment of his return to Afghanistan from Sudan in 1996.[15] For the US, the 9/11 attacks constituted a psychological blow at least as powerful as the bombing of Pearl Harbour. However, unlike the Japanese attack of 7 December 1941, the September 2001 attacks were ambiguous as to their source. While specialists did not doubt for a moment that al-Qaeda was responsible,[16] it took a little while to gather the concrete evidence which established al-Qaeda's complicity; and the question of the responsibility of al-Qaeda's Taliban hosts was more complex again. But that said, there was little doubt that once the US produced evidence that established who was responsible, it would act and look to its allies for support. Indeed, its allies were forthright in lining up; the US's NATO partners took formal steps to invoke Article 5 of the April 1949 North Atlantic Treaty, and in France a newspaper published the famous phrase *Nous sommes tous Américains.*

Australia had taken little interest in Afghanistan. Diplomatic relations had been suspended following the Soviet invasion of Afghanistan, and after the collapse of the communist regime in April 1992, consular relations were established (with an Afghan Honorary Consul operating in Australia) but diplomatic relations were not. After the Taliban takeover in Kabul in September 1996, these consular relations remained in place, but the Afghan Consulate did not serve the Taliban, a situation which paralleled that at the UN, where Afghanistan's seat remained in the hands of the anti-Taliban Rabbani Government.[17] Nonetheless, the activities of the Taliban received little attention. When the Taliban entered Mazar-e Sharif and massacred large numbers of Afghans,[18] a press statement issued on 25 August 1998 by Australia's acting Minister for Foreign Affairs referred to the 'Unlawful Detention of Iranians in Afghanistan,' but said nothing about the Afghan victims. Furthermore, from late 1999 the arrival on Australian shores of boats carrying Afghans fleeing the oppression in their own country evoked little sympathy from Australian ministers, whose responses seemed more calculated to appease supporters of the racist One Nation party than to welcome the Taliban's victims.[19] Australia's involvement in Afghanistan was a product of sympathy for Americans, not Afghans. Prime Minister Howard, in an odd quirk of fate, happened to be in Washington DC on 11 September 2001,[20] and was plainly seized by the energy of the moment. Citing the terms of the ANZUS Treaty, Howard moved to line up with the Bush Administration, adopting its rhetoric of a 'war on terror', and committing Australia to support the Administration's actions. From this position there was little dissent within the political mainstream. The consequence was the deployment of a range of Australian forces to Afghanistan as part of the US-led Coalition, notably Special Air Service forces which engaged in direct combat operations. However, the scale of the deployment should not be exaggerated. Australian casualties were low (only one soldier, Sergeant Andrew Russell, was killed, in a mine blast), and significant forces were *not* committed either to the International Security Assistance Force (ISAF), which was deployed to Kabul in the aftermath of the overthrow of the Taliban, or to the Provincial Reconstruction Teams (PRTs) which a range of states (including New Zealand) supported outside Kabul as an alternative to ISAF, the wider deployment of which the US long resisted.[21]

In the case of Afghanistan, the legal case for action was strong. First, the UN Charter provides in Article 51 that 'Nothing in the present Charter shall impair the inherent right of individual or collective self-defence if an armed attack occurs against a member of the UN, until the Security Council has taken measures necessary to maintain international peace and security.' The article contains no reference to the source of the armed attack, but it would be perverse to limit it to state actors, since the result would be an open invitation to out-sourcing of violence, and 'creeping invasion'.[22] The Taliban, in other words, were a legitimate target.[23] Second, the Security Council proceeded to pass a number of resolutions in response to the 9/11 attacks, notably Resolution 1368 of 12 September 2001 and 1373 of 28 September 2001 which, without explicitly addressing the actions which the US Administration clearly proposed to take, expressed the strongest condemnation of the terrorist attackers, and solidarity with their victims. These resolutions formed the concluding parts of a series of resolutions, beginning with Resolution

1267 of 15 October 1999 and continuing through Resolution 1333 of 19 December 2000, by which the Security Council had brought pressure to bear on al-Qaeda's Taliban hosts following the August 1998 embassy bombings. Third, the official occupants of Afghanistan's UN seat raised no objections to the broad actions of the US and its allies, and it was clear that on the ground in Afghanistan, forces which supported the Rabbani Government accorded active rather than simply tacit or nominal support to the Coalition forces. Fourth, in the aftermath of the installation of the Afghanistan Interim Administration in December 2001, Coalition forces continued their actions against al-Qaeda and the Taliban with the approval of the widely-accepted new Afghan authorities. Far from flying in the face of the international community, the US and its allies acted with widespread, overwhelming support from the UN and its key member states, which would be difficult to explain if the action had been illegal.[24]

The strategic case for action in Afghanistan was also a strong one. The threat posed by al-Qaeda was not hypothetical or speculative: the lesson of 9/11 was that it was immediate and palpable (if any further lesson were necessary after the 1998 embassy bombings). Furthermore, the Taliban had provided Osama bin Laden with a secure operating environment, and the belief that through negotiations they might be induced to hand bin Laden over to the US was wishful thinking that ignored the powerful ties based on reciprocity and culture which bound the Taliban to their troublesome guest. The importance of adopting long-term strategies to deal with terrorism, a position on which most serious specialists were at one, did not obviate the need for short-term action to address al-Qaeda's specific threat. If al-Qaeda were left to fester, further attacks on a scale similar to those of 9/11 could have been expected to materialize. The credibility of the US and its allies was challenged by the attacks: anything less than a robust response would have sent the signal that the US could be attacked with impunity, which again would have invited further trouble. Furthermore, the prospects for a successful operation to deal with the Taliban were good. As well as becoming international pariahs as a result of their gender policies and their vandalistic approach to cultural treasures such as the Bamiyan Buddhas,[25] the Taliban had had little success in securing generalized normative support within Afghanistan, as the speed of their subsequent collapse was to demonstrate. The belief that Afghanistan was necessarily a graveyard for foreign forces was an oversimplification based on old precedents of dubious relevance. When the USSR invaded Afghanistan in December 1979, most of the country was not in crisis, and the bulk of the population united to resist the invaders; in 2001, by contrast, much of Afghanistan was in a state of ruin, the state had collapsed,[26] and the sustained attention of the wider world was exactly what many Afghans craved. There was also a determined anti-Taliban resistance with which Coalition forces could work, albeit one traumatized by the assassination of its key figure Ahmad Shah Massoud by al-Qaeda agents just two days before the attacks on the World Trade Centre and Pentagon.

In addition, the case for Australian participation was strong. As a founder member of the UN, Australia had an interest in ensuring that threats to international peace and security arising from the activities of transnational terrorist groups be addressed. As a formal ally of the US, which had fallen victim to direct attack, it had specific treaty obligations to meet, as well as wider obligations arising from its broader friendly relationship with Washington. It is also important to note that the dead and missing from the 9/11 attacks included a number of Australian citizens, some of them tourists, others employees of firms with offices located in the targeted buildings. Australians were therefore entitled to expect that their government would respond to the harm inflicted on their own kith and kin. And although it was unwise of Prime Minister Howard uncritically to adopt the ill-defined and open-ended vocabulary of 'war on terror', this had little or no bearing on the specifics of Australia's Afghanistan commitment. While Howard's approach to the war embodied the kind of bellicosity occasionally seen in political leaders who have missed the opportunity for active service, it is most unlikely that any alternative Prime Minister would have failed to act similarly.

The strength of the case for action with Australian support is not weakened by the subsequent course of events. There are indeed strong grounds upon which one can be critical of the handling of the Afghanistan situation by the US in the aftermath of the Taliban's overthrow. The US blocking of ISAF expansion, essentially with a view to conserving air-lift assets for use against Iraq, was a lamentable failure of judgment, which sent exactly the wrong signal to armed formations within Afghanistan and compromised the momentum of the process which the Bonn Agreement had triggered. The opium industry has taken off with a vengeance.[27] And the slow flow of resources to support reconstruction in Afghanistan disappointed the expectations which ordinary Afghans had been led to hold of the process — although after years of unfulfilled promises, their expectations may have been dampened by a useful degree of cynicism.[28] Australia's own withdrawal from Afghanistan displayed an indecent haste as well; by 2004, there was only one soldier left in the country, despite the specific request of the Afghan Transitional Administration that Australia maintain a commitment. These failings, however, were not an inevitable consequence of the decision to overthrow the Taliban by force; rather, they resulted from the drift of attention from Afghanistan which arose as the Bush Administration (with the Howard Government in tow) became increasingly — and some would say obsessively — preoccupied with Iraq.

Australia and Operation Iraqi Freedom

Operation Enduring Freedom was a war of necessity; Operation Iraqi Freedom was a war of choice, which Australia chose to join. Herein lies the central distinction between the two.

America's historical relationship with Iraq was a curious one. The Baathist regime of Saddam Hussein was brutally oppressive,[29] but during the 1980–1988 Iran–Iraq War, it received intelligence from US sources,[30] and support from US neo-conservatives.[31] A breach with Washington came only in 1990, when Iraq invaded Kuwait. Acting with the authority provided by Security Council Resolution 678 of 29 November 1990, a coalition of forces led by the US forced Iraqi forces to quit Kuwait.[32] Pursuant to Security Council Resolution 687 of 3 April 1991, Iraq was subjected to an exacting regime of sanctions designed to prevent it from developing weapons of mass destruction (WMD), and there were good grounds for believing that Iraq was effectively 'contained'.[33] Nonetheless, in a September 2002 address to the UN General Assembly, President Bush revived the issue of Iraq's weapons capability, and in response to pressure from the US, the Security Council put forward a set of further demands to the Iraqi Government in Resolution 1441.[34] What exactly motivated the US Administration remains a matter of some doubt, since different rationales were advanced at different times, and other relevant factors may have been left unstated. Genuine fear of Iraq, the influence of the right wing of the Israeli political spectrum and its supporters in Washington, a belief in the potential of democracy to bring change to the Greater Middle East, even unfinished Bush family business, could reasonably be cited. However, the Security Council divided on what course should be taken,[35] not least because of suspicion about the motives of neo-conservatives within the Bush Administration who were intent on attacking Iraq at any cost.[36] The French scholar Olivier Roy, one of the most penetrating observers of contemporary

Islam, argued that 'the rationale for the military campaign in Iraq was not that Iraq was the biggest threat but, on the contrary, that it was the weakest and hence the easiest to take care of. The invasion was largely aimed at demonstrating America's political will and commitment to go to war.'[37] It is hardly surprising that when US forces attacked Iraq in March 2003, they did so without further explicit Security Council authorization. In so acting, the US enjoyed very little support from the wider world, but one state which did line up with the Bush Administration was Australia.

Australia had little direct strategic interest in Iraq. In the name of 'good international citizenship', the Hawke Government had strongly supported Operations Desert Shield and Desert Storm in response to Iraq's invasion of Kuwait; and an Australian, Richard Butler, had served as Chairman of the United Nations Special Commission (UNSCOM) which, until Iraq ceased co-operation in December 1998, had monitored Iraq's compliance with its disarmament responsibilities. Human rights violations by Saddam's regime attracted occasional attention, but in practice the Howard Government detained unauthorized entrants fleeing persecution in Iraq with just as much aplomb as it showed in locking up Afghans fleeing the Taliban. In its public justifications, the government did not deny that its relationship with the United States played a role in shaping its position, but spokesmen maintained that its position was determined by fear of Iraq's weapons of mass destruction. Here, the government's public statements did not reflect the nuanced and equivocal character of the advice it received from key elements of the Australian Intelligence Community. To the public, the Prime Minister stated that 'The Australian Government knows that Iraq has chemical and biological weapons, and that Iraq wants to develop nuclear weapons,'[38] relying on material (now discredited) supplied by the US Administration and the British Government. However, even here it was selective, as a report to the Australian Parliament laconically concluded:

> Other significant intelligence not covered in the government presentations included an assessment in October 2002 that Iraq was only likely to use its WMD if the regime's survival was at stake and the view of the Joint Intelligence Committee of the UK, available at the beginning of February 2003, that war would increase the risk of terrorism and the passing of Iraq's WMD to terrorists.[39]

The government's less-than-frank approach to the issue suggests that while concerns about WMD were the ostensible reason for Australia's involvement in Iraq, the real reason was to please the Bush Administration, which was seriously isolated in its push for action. That the commitment was essentially political becomes even clearer when one notes how small a proportion of the Australian Defence Force (ADF) was actually deployed: in July 2004, Defence Minister Robert Hill candidly stated that 'we have a cap that we work within, which is a bit over 900,'[40] and Australia notably failed to contribute any personnel to the entity to provide security for the UN presence in Iraq for which the Security Council had solicited support in Resolution 1546 of 8 June 2004. Even with the deployment of a further 450 Australians to the Iraqi province of Al Muthanna, announced by Prime Minister Howard on 22 February 2005, the total number of Australians serving as part of 'Operation Catalyst' totalled less than 1500 (that is, less than 2.7 per cent of the permanent Australian Defence Force). For all the Prime Minister's 'We stand four-square to the Tempest' rhetoric, Australia's contribution to Iraq in purely military terms was notably small.

The Howard Government's decision to support the Bush Administration over Iraq set it at odds with the wider world in part because the legal case for action was extraordinarily weak. Iraq had not launched an 'armed attack' on anyone, and nor was there any credible evidence that an armed attack was imminent. This precluded reliance on Article 51 of the Charter. Furthermore, no explicit authorization for action against Iraq had been secured from the Security Council following President Bush's September 2002 speech. As a result, the Coalition partners were driven to a tortuous argument that action in Iraq in 2003 could actually be justified by reference to Security Council Resolution 678 of 1990 as well as Resolution 1441. The US produced its version of this argument only after the regime of Saddam had been overthrown,[41] but another version was put forward in a legal opinion produced by Prime Minister Howard on 18 March 2003 to try to justify Australia's position, an opinion which was written by two public servants (rather than the Solicitor-General), made no reference to any of the extensive literature on international law and the use of force by states, and totally ignored the drafting history of the resolutions it discussed. The weaknesses of the argument were manifest. Resolution 678 had used a standard formula to signal Security Council authorization: 'Acting under Chapter VII of the Charter,' it 'decides' that 'all necessary means' may be used to bring about a particular outcome. An early draft of Resolution

1441 had provided that a breach of its terms 'authorizes member states to use all necessary means to restore international peace and security in the area,' but in the face of opposition from a number of Security Council members, these words were omitted from the final text of the resolution: this drafting history makes it clear that it was not the intention of the Security Council at that point to authorize enforcement action. Furthermore, a draft resolution authorizing action tabled on 24 February 2003 and then in amended form on 7 March 2003 by the US, UK and Spain, was ultimately withdrawn by the sponsors when it became clear that there was no prospect of its being adopted. The resort to Resolution 678 had touches of the bizarre. While Resolution 678 authorized action 'to restore international peace and security in the area,' this could not realistically be read as providing an indefinite authorization for military force to be used, for the Security Council cannot embark on a general sub-delegation of its responsibilities under Articles 39 and 42 of the Charter:[42] to do so would violate the rule that a delegate cannot delegate (*delegatus non potest delegare*). All in all, the weakness of the legal case for action again pointed to alliance politics as being at the heart of Australia's position.

In contrast to the situation in Afghanistan, the strategic case for action in Iraq was weak. The basis for action was speculative at best, and proved to be hollow when the overthrow of Saddam Hussein's regime turned up no weapons of mass destruction at all.[43] Moreover the lack of proper planning for the aftermath of intervention was unforgivable.[44] The looting of the National Museum in Baghdad, a consequence of its omission from a fragmentary order tasking a particular unit to protect it as a site of significance, signalled very clearly that the Coalition forces were unprepared to discharge basic functions of maintaining order. Furthermore, the 'de-Baathization' process to eliminate vestigial elements of the old regime broke up the Iraqi army as a functioning institution.[45] On 2 July 2003 President Bush responded to threats to US forces in Iraq with the words 'bring 'em on'. His reckless wish was rapidly granted, and Iraq witnessed a serious upsurge in violent 'spoiler' behaviour.[46] This was especially marked following the US military thrust into Fallujah in April 2004, and the confrontation between L. Paul Bremer III's 'Coalition Provisional Authority' and the radical Shiite politician Muqtadar al-Sadr, whose family had an impeccable record of opposition to Saddam Hussein and drew support from some of the most marginalized elements of Iraqi society. By the formal (if not effective) conclusion of 'occupation' on 28 June 2004, not only were US forces suffering from the shame of the Abu Ghraib prison abuse scandal,[47] but it was far from clear that political order could be effectively reconstituted. As the year drew on, American soldiers continued to perish at the hands of insurgents, and Iraq increasingly resembled not an embryonic democracy, but — in Gertrude Himmelfarb's memorable phrase — the 'dark and bloody crossroads' where nationalism and religion meet.[48] The 30 January 2005 election to choose an 'Iraqi Transitional National Assembly' saw a turnout of 58 per cent despite a virtual lock-down of the country, suggesting that much remains to be done before Iraq can claim to have a legitimate and consolidated political order.[49]

The case for Australian participation was concomitantly weak. It was not part of a broad coalition, but of a quaint collection of states for the most part heavily dependent on US support, and contributing only small contingents. In a BBC interview on 1 January 2005, former British Foreign Secretary Douglas Hurd labelled them the 'Coalition of the Obedient'. Indeed, of the 32 states still in Iraq as of June 2004, more than a third were new states that had come into independent existence only in the 1990s and a further six were old Eastern European states that had long been subjected to various degrees of Soviet pressure. Not a single African, Middle Eastern, South Asian, or South American state was represented. The reasons why Australia's position was weak were several. First, while the intervention in Afghanistan offered good prospects of bettering the lives of ordinary Afghans, the argument in the Iraq case was deeply problematical. The Bush Administration was correct in highlighting the value of liberal democracy in the abstract, but showed little recognition of the difficulties of moving from one kind of order, the totalitarian variety, to another kind, the pluralistic. Often what immediately follows autocracy is not liberal democracy, but mayhem, which can leave *worse* off those who had developed effective coping-mechanisms for surviving under a dictator. A carefully designed epidemiological study pointed to sharply higher levels of mortality in the months following the intervention than in the months before.[50] Here, the problem lay not in poor decisions after the intervention, but in the very conception of what intervention with a relatively small ground-force could achieve. Australia in effect tied itself to the defective decision-making of its master. Second, Australia in following the US linked itself to a broader threat to world order. It opted not for policing, but for vigilantism. On occasion, vigilantes knock off some pretty nasty characters, but they are prone to get things wrong (as shown in the unforgettable 1943 film *The Ox-Bow Incident*), and rampant vigilantism tends rapidly to produce a life which is nasty, brutish and short. The key norms of the international system, embodied in the UN Charter, are worth protecting, and Australia in lining up with the Bush Administration walked away from them. But they are worth protecting not just because they provide a degree of order, but because they empower states by endowing their actions with legitimacy, providing a basis for socializing the costs of any failure.[51] This was overlooked by America and its allies, and it is why other states have felt no urge to ride to Washington's rescue as the situation in Iraq has unravelled.

Implications and Conclusions

As the preceding paragraphs suggest, Australia's Iraq commitment marked a sharp departure from the historical parameters of Australian foreign policy, in a way that the Afghanistan commitment did not. The sole point of continuity was fidelity to the US, and this indeed was also the sole basis of the commitment: had America not turned its attention to Iraq, Australia would not have done so. In this respect, the Iraq commitment differed markedly from Australia's commitment to South Vietnam, which was driven by more than just alliance politics. The Iraq commitment also involved Australia's going far out on a limb in support of the Bush Administration, and its willingness to isolate itself for the sake of the relationship with Washington was manifested once again in 2004 when Australia joined just the US, Israel, and three Pacific micro-states to oppose a UN General Assembly Resolution endorsing the Advisory Opinion of the International Court of Justice on the legality of the barrier wall built by Israel in territory occupied following the Six-Day War of 1967. Such actions, which Burchill analyses in detail in Chapter 8, raised questions not just about the bases of Australian foreign policy, but about whether it was meaningful to speak of an 'Australian' foreign policy at all, at least as far as the broad outlines of policy were concerned. In conclusion, therefore, it may be useful to reflect on what the costs and benefits of Australia's new approach might be.

First, if one accepts that the key rationale for Iraq was to solidify the relationship with the US, the question then arises what the benefits of this might be. It is clear that Prime Minister Howard succeeded in developing a warm relationship with President Bush, as reflected in the former's visit to the latter's ranch, and in the Bush visit to Canberra in October 2003. However, the benefit of such relations should not be exaggerated; in 2004, for example, they counted for nothing when

Australia sought to have sugar included in its Free Trade Agreement with the US.[52] The notion that supportive behaviour necessarily solidifies an alliance is also questionable, since this depends on particular assumptions about the approach to alliances of the parties to them. François Heisbourg, for one, has warned that the US may increasingly judge alliance partners not on the strength of what they have done in the past, but rather on the strength of what they are prepared to do in the future: 'The sheriff composes his posse and if you don't want to be part of the posse you will be punished.'[53] The US trashing of France over Iraq, notwithstanding France's strong support for the US after the 9/11 attacks, may be a sign of things to come. If this is the case, a middle power such as Australia may find itself under regular demand to re-establish its credentials. A difficult question to answer is how much damage Australia might suffer if it develops a reputation for being less-than-independent in its foreign policy. The methodological problem here is that of disentangling reactions to diminution of independence from reactions to the specifics of the policy settings which that diminution of independence may entail. But that said, reputation forms part of a state's 'soft power',[54] and a state which develops a reputation as a docile follower of some other runs the risk of finding its influence shrinking on questions which may be important to it, but unimportant to its patron. Furthermore, as Owen Harries has warned, great powers are prone to 'giving less weight to the views of those whose support can be taken for granted than to those whose support they wish to gain,'[55] and as a result, a reputation for pliability is not one from which any middle power is likely to benefit.

Second, and a further issue of interest to ordinary Australians, is the extent to which association with the policy positions of the Bush Administration may have increased their exposure to the risk of terrorist attack. The government's response to this has been to echo the Bush Administration's claim that 'they' threaten 'us' because of 'who we are and what we are.' The kindest comment one can make is that this claim is simplistic. While *some* enemies of the US and its allies may be motivated by a wholesale repudiation of Western values, there is every reason to believe that large numbers of potential recruits to terrorist groups are prompted by hostility to specific elements of US policy, most notably its seemingly uncritical support for right-wing Israeli politicians and residents of settlements illegally established in territories occupied by Israel after 1967.[56] If terrorist motivations are exclusively anti-Western, then Sweden should be as much at risk as the US — an obvious point, made by this writer in early 2004,[57] and by Osama bin Laden himself in a statement broadcast by the *Al-Jazeera* television network on the eve of the 2004 US Presidential election. An implication of this is that risks of terrorist attacks against Australians may have increased as a result of its support for US actions. Of course, it does not follow that a policy should be eschewed simply because it increases the danger of an attack against Australian interests. In certain circumstances, a compelling legal or moral obligation may require that a state commit itself to action which terrorists will not like: there is a strong argument that the measures taken to free Kuwait of Iraqi forces in 1991, to aid East Timor in 1999, and to overthrow the Taliban in 2001, fell squarely into that category. But where ordinary civilians will pay the price for politicians' mistakes, it pays to judge very carefully which circumstances require Australian commitments. There is very little to suggest that in the Iraq case, risks to ordinary Australians were appraised rather than ignored. Nor is there evidence that the government reflected at all seriously on the implications for Australia's reputation in the Arab world, even though it should have been obvious that graphic footage of casualties would be extensively disseminated.

Third, as the Australian Government responds to the failure of WMD to materialize with the argument that it is now necessary to 'stay the course' in Iraq lest terrorists claim a victory, it is wise to ponder the deeper implications of such an argument. In this writer's view, the whole argument should be approached with considerable caution. It is essentially a new version of the disastrous argument put forward in 1966 by President Lyndon B. Johnson and Secretary of State Dean Rusk to justify their position on the Vietnam War: that to disengage would create the appearance of a victory for the 'communists'. Ultimately, after much additional bloodshed, a different US Administration cut its losses and ran. If Iraq turns into a real quagmire — something over which Australia has no control — the same thing could happen there too. At most, the 'win for terrorists' argument should be but one of a number of considerations taken into account, and if the continued Western presence is handing a *strategic* advantage to extremists, the fact that a withdrawal might be interpreted by extremists as a *tactical* victory should not be a decisive barrier to that step. When one has dug oneself into a hole, it is a good idea at some point to stop digging.

In conclusion, there are clearly differences between the Vietnam War and the Iraq conflict, but there are alarming points of similarity as well, of which an inability on the part of intervening forces to appreciate the potency of nationalism is one. One pathology of great powers, fully on display in Vietnam, is the difficulty which their leaders face in coping with failure. The Vietnam War dragged on for years beyond the point where it was clear to informed observers that things had gone badly awry.[58] Uncritical allies of great powers run the risk of being sucked into the same whirlpools as their patrons. This danger is one which all Australian policy-makers would do well to bear in mind.

10

AUSTRALIA AND NORTH AFRICA:
THE MISSING LINK?

Benjamin MacQueen

This chapter will focus on the nascent, but prospectively valuable relationship between Australia and the Arab states of North Africa.[1] We shall see how the Australia–North Africa relationship has been hindered by a combination of distance, disinterest, and cultural apprehension, forces that can be addressed through renewed initiatives. In this, areas shall be highlighted where the association can take an important place in the broader relationship between Australia and the Middle East. Specifically, exploration of the significant areas of complementarity between Australia and North Africa, particularly in trade potential, shall be undertaken. This includes such elements as receptive markets for a variety of Australian exports, the potential for tourism and educational exchanges between the two regions, as well as an opportunity for Australia to overcome its cultural apprehension in fully engaging with the Arab world. Key areas of deficiency shall also be identified, in particular the lack of diplomatic exchange as well as the inappropriateness of the ideological grounding of current Australian foreign policy toward the region.

In exploration of these issues, this chapter will outline the foreign policy aims of the Howard Government as stated in the Department of Foreign Affairs and Trade (DFAT) initiative on 'Accessing Middle East Growth' of 2000, the Joint Standing Committee on Foreign Affairs and Trade 2001 report on 'Australia's Relationship with the Middle East,' and the Australian Government's foreign policy White Paper of 2003.[2] In particular, we shall see how the relationship between Australia and North Africa has only marginally benefited from renewed initiatives in trade and business with the Middle East while political, social, and cultural exchanges have been neglected. In this, the Australia–North Africa relationship is likely to remain one-dimensional and only partially, even superficially, beneficial without a diversification and deepening of links.

The strengthening of such links, it is argued, can have a profound impact on Australia, North Africa, and the relationship between Australia and the states of the broader Middle East.

Existing Relationships
Distance, Disinterest, and Cultural Apprehension

The relationship between Australia and North Africa has been minor. Outside the areas of trade in primary products, each of the respective partners has a minimal impact on and presence in each other's region. However, as Australia seeks to boost its presence in the Arab world in the realms of economic, political, and cultural relations, North Africa provides a fertile ground in which both parties can benefit from a newly forged relationship. In order for this to be pursued, there needs to be a marked change in the basis of the approach to promoting links between Australia and North Africa to overcome the impacts of distance, disinterest, and cultural apprehension.

The foreign policy of the Howard Government, particularly in relation to the Middle East, has been guided by the principle of economic functionalism, with a heavy focus on the importance of bilateral relationships as well as tempered by the cloud of cultural apprehension. Within this primarily economic relationship, trade and business exchanges form the core, functional element, through which stronger associations and greater co-operation can develop.[3] Such an orientation echoes earlier themes of Liberal governments in Australia and their emphasis on realism and attraction to pragmatic approaches such as functionalism. As Dalrymple contends, conservative governments in Australia have traditionally followed a realist perspective in their foreign policy formation, as opposed to the idealist orientation of their left wing colleagues.[4] Such realist philosophy emphasizes the importance of bilateral, rather than multilateral relationships as well as a focus on 'common interests' rather than an idealist vision as the basis for foreign policy.

The Howard Government's realist and functionalist orientations to foreign policy have become increasingly apparent since their election in 1996, and particularly since the events of 11 September 2001. A focus, almost exclusively, on foreign policy as reflective of the 'national interest' encapsulates the direction of Australia's external relations.[5] Such an understanding of the 'national interest' has excluded any discussion of the importance of cross-cultural exchange, focusing almost primarily on economics and security as the defining logic of Australian foreign policy.

An examination of the foreign policy priorities of the Howard Government, expressed particularly in the 2003 DFAT White Paper, bears this out.

It is here that one can witness, most starkly, the cultural apprehension which tempers the Howard Government's foreign policy vis-à-vis the Arab Middle East and North Africa. The idea of cultural apprehension refers to the 'civilizational' undertones of Australian (as well as US) foreign policy, particularly since 9/11. This is referential to the concept of 'civilizational' difference and confrontation as outlined by Huntington and his questionable, but highly influential thesis on a potential 'clash of civilizations'.[6]

The framing of the so-called 'war on terror' as a confrontation between 'the West' and the 'Islamic world' and the targeting of Arab and Islamic states and communities in this 'war' has perpetuated a view of Western leaders perceiving themselves as part of the same civilizational/cultural realm. Such a Huntingtonesque view sees the binding of these communities over apprehension toward other cultural 'blocs' (for instance, 'Confucian', Latin American, or Islamic).[7]

Apart from the more overt displays of this (namely the 2003 US invasion of Iraq of which Australia was an active participant, which Burchill and Maley discuss in chapters 8 and 9), the impacts of such apprehension can be more subtle, even insidious. Primarily, it is the anxiety with which the Australian Government, influenced by US foreign policy and the civilizational clash thesis, approaches the Middle East, and the Arab–Islamic world more particularly. This is most notably seen in the expressions of Australian foreign policy priorities in relation to the Middle East and North Africa through the various DFAT white papers.

As outlined in the 2003 DFAT White Paper, Australian foreign policy is directed by the twin principles of 'security and prosperity', stemming from realist and functionalist orientations.[8] These are seen as interrelated themes centered on a 'basic human needs' perspective of the sources of insecurity.[9] That is, insecurity stems from the deprivation of 'basic needs' such as 'food, clothing, and shelter'.[10] Security can be gained through the promotion of economic prosperity globally in which these basic human needs can be met. Essentially, this means that economic reform is seen as the best engine of political freedoms and security. This is revealing in that it exposes the reasons why priority is placed on the economic relationships Australia has internationally, and why cross-cultural understanding is often neglected in such an environment.

In terms of specific policy direction, bilateral channels are central to this process for the Australian Government. Bilateralism is seen to set the benchmark for further multilateral co-operation.[11] Indeed, multilateralism has often been derided by the Australian Government as an inefficient means to achieve 'national interests', echoing the influence of realist perceptions over Australian foreign policy formation. The focus on bilateral links is an expression of the Australian Government seeking to pursue what it defines as 'national interests' based on 'developing functional affinities with countries and groups of countries' with which Australia shares 'specific interests'.[12] This is not to say that the Australian Government has foregone the use of multilateral channels. Indeed, it has been consistently active in the WTO, with co-operation in this organization forming an important element of the existing Australia–Middle East relationship. However, its relationship vis-à-vis the UN preceding the 2003 invasion and occupation of Iraq reflects such a contemptuous view of this predominant multilateral organization.

Such a policy direction corresponds to the focus of Australian foreign policy in the 'eastern' Arab states.[13] In particular, focus has been on emphasizing commercial links in order to foster further co-operation. Economic diversification and trade liberalization, it is argued, are the tools from which such dynamism can be developed. Efforts toward cross-cultural understanding have been articulated as an adjunct to this process, not as a central component of the process of integration.

The Australian policy approach to North Africa has been a combination of this structured tactic and the *ad hoc* method Australia has taken in its relationships with Africa.[14] Indeed, whilst successive Australian governments have nominally included the North African states within any policy initiative dealing with the Middle East, the influence and impact of such initiatives has been slight. Reasons for this are not overtly apparent. However, one may speculate that Australian inability and reluctance to engage in any meaningful way with the Arab states of North Africa has been a blend of distance, disinterest, and cultural apprehension. This latter factor is crucial, and one that needs to be countered by new directions in Australia's policy orientation and engagement with the Arab world.

In this, the Australian Government needs to be motivated by principles other than strict economic functionalism in order to move toward establishing a deeper relationship with North Africa. In particular, following the stated aims of the government in terms of promoting human rights and political pluralism as an honest, independent, and constructive international participant has the potential to sow the seeds of important cross-cultural exchange between Australia and North Africa as well as Australia and the wider Arab region.[15] Such priorities are paramount in the current international environment where Australia, as a prominent player in the invasion and occupation of Iraq, is seen as somewhat of an adjunct to the foreign policy direction of the United States.

Comments by the Secretary-General of the Arab League, Amr Moussa, reflect the antagonism with which Australia's activities in the Middle East and North Africa are increasingly viewed. Speaking to Qatari-based news agency *Al-Jazeera* in reference to the possibility of Australian-supported intervention in Sudan in the wake of the invasion and occupation of Iraq, Dr Moussa asked 'why this antagonistic policy by Australia against the Arabs? They should get off our back and leave us alone.'[16] Such comments are deeply worrying in that they reflect a squandering of a previously mutually-affable relationship between Australia and the Arab states. Australia's consistent pro-Israeli voting record in the UN has also deepened such resentments, most starkly seen when Australia, as one of only six states (including the US, Israel, Palau and the Marshall Islands) voted against the motion condemning the Israeli 'security fence' in the UN General Assembly.[17]

Such transformation need not be a radical departure from the stated aims of the Australian Government. Indeed, the promotion of the principles of 'good governance,' highlighted as a key area for Australian foreign and trade policy, should take prominence. This is not to discount the vast potential, and complementarity, for Australian–North African trade. However, the current fragile trade relationship is not an adequate basis for promoting a deep and diverse relationship. Instead, Australia can have a positive impact not only in North Africa but in terms of enhancing its broader regional image if it is more definitively guided by ideas conducive to supporting 'the rule of law, respect for human rights and development of sustainable policies and institutions.'[18] Encouragement toward these goals need not be undertaken in a paternalistic, interventionist-style manner, but instead through mutual understanding and cross-cultural exchange.

Current Status of the Australia–North Africa Relationship: Trade, Security, and Cultural Exchange

Trade

The existing Australia–North Africa relationship is essentially a trade relationship. This trade and economic interaction, whilst it is the basis of the association, is characterized by a lack of depth and diversity. Such a lack of diversity is seen through the vast bulk of economic interaction being based on the exchange of primary products. The balance of the trading relationship is heavily weighted in favor of Australian exports to North Africa (AUD\$ 73 million in 2003 — see fig. 1) where reciprocal trade to Australia lags behind (AUD\$ 34 million in 2003 — see fig. 2).[19] Within this, there has been an imbalance in terms of the weighting of trade between Australia and specific North African states (see fig. 3). For instance, Australian exports reached AUD\$ 52 million to Algeria in 2003, whilst the value of exports did not surpass AUD\$ 20 million to Tunisia, Libya and Morocco combined.[20] In terms of exports to Australia, Moroccan products (mainly fertilizers[21]) far outpaced exports from other North African states.[22]

Australian companies are active in the extraction of hydrocarbons (oil and natural gas) from North Africa, particularly Algeria and Libya. Australian companies have benefited from the privatization of the Algerian hydrocarbon industry during and after the 1990s and the opening of the Libyan market after the lifting of UN sanctions in September 2003.[23] BHP–Billiton and Woodside Petroleum are the key Australian players in the North African energy market. In Algeria, BHP–Billiton has a large investment in the ROD Integrated Development project in which it has a 36 per cent share in a joint venture with the Algerian state oil company SONATRACH.[24] In addition, BHP–Billiton is engaged with Woodside Petroleum, SONATRACH, and the Japanese Teikoku Oil in the Ohanet oil and gas project in south-eastern Algeria.[25] In Libya, Woodside have signed an AUD\$ 140 million contract with the Libyan National Oil Company in the wake of the lifting of UN sanctions.[26] While these represent significant developments, particularly the opening of an Australian diplomatic post in Libya to accommodate the potential growing trade relationship, they are only a partial step toward forging a deep and diverse relationship.

Such one-dimensional trade figures can be contrasted with the dynamic nature of trade between Australia and other Arab states, particularly in relation to the states of the Persian/Arabian Gulf.[27] Up to the 1990s, Australian trade with the Gulf States mirrored similar trends to those of the Australia–North Africa relationship (both in terms of content and scale of trade). However, since the 1990s, trade with the Gulf States has diversified markedly, with a dramatic increase in the export of elaborately transformed manufactures (ETMs), particularly automobiles, to the Gulf and the growth of Australian investment in the burgeoning service sector of the Gulf economies.[28] Increased interest and investment in alternative areas of co-operation has fostered a progressively more diverse relationship, particularly in the areas of technological, educational, and cultural exchange.[29] Admittedly, the Australia–Middle East relationship has a long way to go in terms of fully realizing its potential in these areas. However, such progress is impressive when placed in contrast to the Australia–North Africa relationship, one that is marked by a lack of diversity. This has seen the Australia–North Africa relationship stagnate, and even recede, over recent years.

This comparison bears further insight in that the trends taken advantage of by Australia in its trade relationship with the Gulf States (particularly growing populations and gradual trade liberalization) are also exhibited in North Africa.[30] In particular, the rapid population growth and the increased prominence of 'new middle classes' is an important development for the Australian economic relationship with the Middle East. It is these groups which have generated demand for a wider variety of Australian products, as well as provided for the possibility for tourism and other business opportunities between Australia and the Middle East. However, this is not reflected in the Australia–North Africa relationship. It is important to note that the general economic downturn in North Africa threatens the further growth of such middle classes, thus it is in Australia's interest to promote economic growth as well as political and social reforms in order to promote the basis of a favorable relationship.[31] In addition, the growth of middle classes is an important element of the security environment within states such as those in North Africa, thus it is also in Australia's interest to help foster the development of civil society and pluralistic politics in these states. Such developments are in line with the stated aims of the Australian Government's 'good governance' platform.[32]

Security

Australian involvement in the security issues facing the states of North Africa has been non-existent since the deployment of Australian troops in the Second World War. The closest the Australian military has come to direct involvement in North African security issues has been the shaded co-operation given to Israel, France and Great Britain by Australia during the 1956 Suez Crisis and the participation of Australian forces in the Multi-National Force of Observers (MFO) who oversaw the return of the Sinai Peninsula to Egypt following the 1979 Camp David agreement.[33] However, the patterns of Australian involvement in the broader security issues of the region have framed the way in which Australia and Australian motivation in the region are perceived. In particular, the intimate co-operation between Australia and the United States' led 'coalition of the willing' in the 2003 invasion and occupation of Iraq has mitigated the success of the burgeoning trade relationships Australia has formed in the region without pursuing unilateral military intervention.

Such an effect can be seen in the trends of trade between the two regions. Whilst it may be premature to draw such conclusions, one can notice a slowing of the relationship since 2003 (see figs. 1, 2 & 3). For instance, Australian imports from North Africa fell from AUD$ 86 million in 2002 to AUD$ 36 million in 2003. Even more markedly, Australian exports to North Africa fell from AUD$ 257 million in 2002 to just AUD$ 74 million in 2003.[34] From this, and from comments such as those by leading figures like Dr Amr Moussa outlined above, one can assert that the security activity of Australia in the broader region has important ramifications for Australia's role in North Africa. Thus, it is essential that Australia is guided less by the foreign policy of the United States, viewed less than favorably in the Arab world, to one directed more by notions of promoting good governance and prosperity in the region.

Direct involvement in the security issues of the region is not in Australia's interests nor is it a feasible proposition, both in terms of logistics and in terms of fostering a mutually-beneficial relationship. However, constructive engagement with both the states and societies of North Africa can have the positive impact of promoting a stronger pluralist political culture in the region. In this, cross-cultural exchange needs to be promoted and fostered as a key avenue of interaction between Australia and North Africa.

As indicated earlier, this need not be a departure from the stated direction of Australian foreign policy. Indeed, the Australian Government sees the development of 'good governance', defined as 'sound policies, mature institutions and accountable systems,' as essential for Australian security and prosperity.[35] The promotion of respect for human rights is also an integral part of this program, as it is for the Australian aid program, a matter taken up by Mansouri and Sankari in Chapter 11. Rather than viewing political reform solely as a bi-product of economic prosperity, Australia can actively encourage the strengthening of civil society in North Africa as a vehicle through which to encourage political stability in the region.

Civil society is active and vibrant in North Africa, although it does face difficulties when it is seen to directly confront the political status quo. The Arab states of North Africa possess some of the most pluralistic and dynamic political environments in the region. However, this is often tempered by arbitrary, and often severe, repression on the part of political elites. For instance, Algeria has witnessed a brutal civil war over the past 15 years, claiming close to 150,000 lives.[36] However, this state also possesses some of the most open media and civil society institutions regionally. In addition, a variety of political parties, from Trotskyist to moderate Islamist, compete for political representation within the parliament.[37] This is tempered by the presence of political and military elites who have jealously guarded their pre-eminent positions within the Algerian political structure since 1962. The tension that exists between an increasingly politically active and conscious population and elites is a central dynamic in the perpetuation of insecurity in the region. Thus, it is in the interests of all states, including Australia, to promote the principles of 'good governance' in these states as a way of addressing such tension.

As with other foreign policy issues, such activity is directed through bilateral channels.[38] However, this presents a major problem for the achievement of these goals due to the lack of mechanisms to promote such bilateral co-operation and assistance in the face of deficient diplomatic exchange. This is a crucial area of deficiency between the regions, one out of line with the bilateral focus of the Australian Government. In this, it is incumbent on the governments of both regions to either establish adequate diplomatic exchange or to move to operate through multilateral channels to achieve its stated objectives.

Cultural Exchange

Areas of cultural exchange between Australia and North Africa, again, have been minimal. One can recognize increases in such exchange, particularly through migration. However, we must be careful not to overstate the modest migration rate from North Africa to Australia. In 2001, some 8918 people Australia-wide identified themselves as being born in North Africa out of a total of 213,940 (slightly over four per cent) migrants to Australia from Arab states.[39] Whilst this is a diminutive figure, it still provides a kernel from which cross-cultural awareness may be able to grow.

Cultural exchange, more than other areas, has been the victim of a lack of interest on the part of both the Australian and North African Governments, seen in the deficiency of diplomatic exchange. The lack of such institutional supports to promote cultural exchange has spilled over to other areas, including education and tourism. The issue of inadequate diplomatic representation is important as such official channels are essential for the facilitation of interaction on a variety of levels, including the provision of visas as well as facilitating business exchange.

In terms of the Australian diplomatic presence in North Africa, Australia maintained an embassy in Algeria until April 1991, providing a hub through which political, economic, and cultural exchange could be channeled. However, with the closing of this embassy, along with the absence of diplomatic representation in other North African states, successive Australian governments have chosen to ignore a potentially valuable relationship. Again, this can be contrasted with the situation in the Gulf where Australia not only maintains thorough diplomatic representation (indeed, Australia opened an Embassy in Kuwait in late 2004), but also has provided for streamlined visa arrangements as well as an ease of access, particularly through the direct air links between the region and Australian cities.[40]

Diplomatic representation of North African states in Australia is similarly deficient. Tunisia maintains a consulate in both Melbourne and Sydney, however, the Melbourne consulate has only honorary status whilst the Sydney consulate only received upgraded status in 2004. The opening of a Libyan embassy in Australia is a possibility in the wake of the establishment of an Australian post in Tripoli, however, this is tenuous.[41]

Future Prospects

Given the apparent barriers facing the development of the Australia–North Africa relationship, it is difficult to rationalize the absence of institutional supports to promote the association in the future. Indeed, the exchange of diplomatic representation is a necessity in this endeavor, along with the broadening of other institutional supports to promote economic and cultural interaction. The activity of non-government forces, particularly educational institutions, business, as well as interpersonal exchange is central in this, particularly in the wake of Australia's changed perception in the Middle East and North Africa following the invasion of Iraq in 2003.

The atmosphere in which Australia engages with the Middle East and North Africa has changed dramatically since its involvement in the 2003 invasion and occupation of Iraq. Despite its efforts at establishing an economically-based relationship, leading to further integration and co-operation, Australian activities are increasingly viewed with skepticism regarding possible unspoken intentions. This is a crucial problem in that misperception of intentions has been a central dynamic in the perpetuation of global security concerns since the end of the Cold War.[42] In order to counter this, Australia must broaden its efforts toward cross-cultural understanding in the region. The core of such strategies includes the expansion of diplomatic representation and of educational and business exchanges, trade diversification, cultural exchange as well as tourism. Such activity is essential in North Africa as the political, social, and economic problems faced by these states are symptomatic of factors that often give rise to crucial global security concerns.[43]

There are several ways of approaching this. Firstly, as we have already explored, governments in Australia and North Africa must be encouraged to increase their level of diplomatic exchange, particularly through formal representation in one another's states. Encouraging diplomatic exchange is important in that it would provide official channels through which further economic and cultural exchange may take place. An important step towards this has been the opening of an Australian diplomatic post in Libya accompanying the lifting of UN sanctions and the growth of Australian investment in the Libyan hydrocarbon sector. However, the expansion of such 'official' connections must not be an isolated process. Indeed, far from operating according to a model of functional co-operation, both regions must seek to broaden cultural exchange initially as a way of facilitating greater economic and political exchange.

It is in this area where 'grass-roots' exchange becomes crucial for deepening the Australia–North Africa relationship. It is important to examine the specific areas of economic and cultural exchange where such developments can take place. 'Mid-level' exchange through business is a crucial element in the process of forging a deeper relationship. Australian business has been one of the few areas active in North Africa and provides a useful platform from which to promote further interaction. However, 'grass-roots' interaction is the central area where the relationship can generate true momentum. Educational exchanges can form an important element in this, particularly as Australian tertiary institutions are well-equipped to accommodate students from North Africa. The promotion of tourism both to and from North Africa is also an important step in raising cultural awareness and understanding. The combination of this intellectual and physical interaction, complementing an existing economic relationship, can help overcome the difficulties of distance, disinterest, and cultural apprehension.

Fostering a New Relationship through
Trade Diversification and Cultural Exchange

The central concern in the future business, trade, and economic prospects for the Australia–North Africa relationship is diversification. This is an issue that mirrors similar, although less pressing, concerns for the broader Australia–Middle East relationship. Trade liberalization is an important step in this process, one that does not pose too much of a concern with the WTO membership of Morocco and Tunisia and the prospective membership of Algeria and Libya.[44] However, trade liberalization will only have a partial impact in an environment of a one-dimensional trade relationship. Thus, it is important to identify areas in which the relationship can be enhanced. In this, lessons can be learned from similar trends in the expanding economic relationship between Australia and the Middle East. Of particular importance are business contacts and agents, as well as identification of areas of trade enhancement, namely in the area of ETMs, simply transformed manufactures (STMs), services, and investment.

Business links between Australia and North Africa run through the two main Australian business interests in the region, BHP–Billiton and Woodside. As outlined above, these two companies have substantial regional investments, primarily in Algeria and Libya. As such, they must be at the vanguard of any drive to diversify the economic relationship between Australia and North Africa. Efforts toward diversification, involving these two major players, may include cross-promotion of Australian products through the important business contacts established by BHP–Billiton and Woodside. The use of contacts, or business agents, is a crucial method of any business relationship in the Middle East.[45] Thus, these two companies can facilitate a broader level of interaction through these agencies. In addition, these business links can help the area of cultural exchange by promoting the study of Arabic language and culture at the tertiary level through the provision of scholarship programs. Education in these areas will benefit these companies' ability to do business in the region as well as add depth to the overall connections between the regions.

Australia is well placed to expand its trade in ETMs with North Africa, particularly in the automobile and telecommunications industries. The market for Australian automotive products is potentially the most dynamic, particularly in light of the booming automotive trade between Australia and the Gulf in recent years.[46] The rapid growth of the middle classes in North Africa (as in the Gulf), along with similar climatic and geographic conditions make Australian exports potentially more marketable than similar products from Europe or North America. Telecommunications products may also benefit from similar factors, with the growth in such trade with the Gulf region based on the ability of Australian industries to cater for particular geographic circumstances and population patterns.

Algeria provides a useful example here. Its geographic and demographic composition is similar to that of Australia, with marked population density in coastal, temperate areas combined with a large, sparsely populated interior. The expertise of Australian industry in catering for these types of environments stands them in good stead to provide services and products appropriate for the North African market.

The export of simply transformed manufactures (STMs) is an underdeveloped area in the trade relationship between Australia and North Africa. However, lessons can be learned from the Australia–Iran relationship that may help boost trade with North Africa. In particular, STM exports are compatible with states that have an existing industrial basis, such as Algeria, and to a lesser extent, Morocco and Tunisia. The export STMs (such as iron, agricultural products, etc.) may complement the existing industrial infrastructure, as happens with Australian exports to Iran. However, this is contingent on the reform of these largely inefficient industries.[47] In addition, the export of STMs from North Africa to Australia can also be enhanced in a similar way.

Services and investment provide another area where the Australia–North Africa trade relationship can be enhanced and diversified. These industries provide great potential and are central to not only improving the economic relationship but, crucially, the cultural and political relationships also. Education is a key area in terms of expanding cultural and economic links. Australian universities are well placed to include intakes of students from North African states as well as to engage in academic exchange programs. This corresponds to the broader initiatives of Australian educational engagement with the Middle East.[48]

However, there are difficulties here, linked to the inadequacies of Australian diplomatic representation in the region. Tertiary students from North Africa looking to access Australian universities have to operate through the Australian Embassy in Cairo. This provides a significant logistical impediment to the expansion of educational links. Such impediments can be seen in the numbers of North African tertiary students studying in Australia compared to those traveling to the US or Canada. North African students in Australian universities number no more than 100 in total whilst their numbers exceed 5000 in both the United States and Canada.[49] Indeed, Australian students looking to either study or research in North Africa must operate through embassies offshore (for instance, the Moroccan embassy in Jakarta) which has proven a time-consuming process, discouraging many from pursuing this.

Outside the realm of education, tourism and the enhancement of air and freight links are crucial for creating connections between Australia and North Africa. There is a highly efficient existing infrastructure of transportation, particularly air links, between Australia and the Gulf region. Such infrastructure can be expanded and integrated into a regional network of connections between Australian and North African destinations. This can be complemented by the establishment of broader diplomatic representation both in Australia and North Africa, as well as a streamlining of visa processes as has happened between Australia and many Gulf states.

Expanded diplomatic representation and institutional supports for business, education, and tourism are two key areas that must be promoted in any initiative to enhance the Australia and North Africa relationship. Institutional supports, aimed at enhancing and coordinating trade and cultural exchange between Australia and the Middle East, currently exist. In particular, the Council for Australian–Arab Relations (CAAR), the Australia–Arab Chamber of Commerce and Industry (AACCI), the Australian Arabic Communities Council (AACC), as well as the Australian Arabic Council (AAC) all have mandates to deal with relations between Australia and all Arab states.[50] However, most activities have been limited to interaction with those states in the Arab east. This is understandable considering the proportion of migration, tourism and trade, which have been heavily weighted in favor of these states. However, this should not preclude the expansion of these institutional supports to accommodate deeper relationships with the states of North Africa.

The importance of establishing diplomatic exchange between Australia and North Africa as a key first step in fostering the relationship cannot be overstated. Creating an ease of movement and access between the two areas requires official channels to facilitate the granting of visas, similar to the processes established in the Gulf. Despite the geographic distance between the two regions, the infrastructure is present to minimize the impact of this. As we have already seen, given the complementarity in terms of trade potential, the lack of these official diplomatic supports appears highly counterproductive, an expression of the unfortunate disinterest with which both regions view the relationship.

Such disinterest interacts with the issue of cultural apprehension to compound this associational void. Thus, the enhancing of official contacts must be complemented by the raising of cultural awareness through educational and other exchanges. Again, official institutional support through diplomatic representation is essential for this, as it can facilitate an ease of movement between the two regions. However, this must be complemented by the promotion of cross-regional education opportunities as well as tourism in both Australia and North Africa.

Conclusion

If we are to speak of promoting the Australia–North Africa relationship, then we must deal with the issues of distance, disinterest, and cultural apprehension. These elements are central to understanding why the relationship between these two regions remains stagnant. In order to deal with such contingencies, Australia needs to alter its priorities in terms of foreign policy orientations. In particular, acknowledgment of the inappropriateness of slavishly following the doctrine of economic functionalism as the key to all relationships is central. Recognizing the need to promote cross-cultural exchange as not merely an adjunct, but as an equal partner to economic co-operation is crucially important. This can help address not only the flagging Australia–North Africa relationship but also the cultural apprehension that pervades both sides of the relationship between Australia and the Middle East.

Primarily, Australia and the states of North Africa need to expand diplomatic representation. This is the key element that will facilitate the logistical requirements assisting expansion in other realms. Business and trade diversification, educational links, and cultural exchange are the necessary byproducts that will stem from this. Education and cultural exchange are particularly crucial elements that are needed to counter the damaging influence of cultural apprehension that appears to influence Australian foreign policy not only in North Africa, but also in the Middle East.

As stated, this need not be a radical departure from the affirmed aims of the Australian Government's foreign policy priorities. Australia can play a valuable, perhaps unique role in acting as a genuinely interested, compassionate, and concerned international citizen in helping the nascent, but highly dynamic civil society institutions in North Africa form the core of greater political pluralism in North Africa.

However, the potential limits of such a relationship must also be recognized. Australia will always seek to be closer to the 'eastern' rather than the 'western' Arab world due to geographic proximity as well as the stronger existing relationship. Despite this, ignoring the deficiencies of the existing relationship between Australia and North Africa deprives the two regions of a potentially rewarding friendship, not only in terms of economics, but crucially in terms of cross-cultural understanding.

11

ECONOMIC INTERESTS AND THE HUMAN RIGHTS CHALLENGE

Fethi Mansouri and Jamal Sankari

The fact that Australia, like America, has neither a colonial past in the Middle East, nor 'a long-standing cultural attention to Islam,'[1] makes its current discursive characterization of the region and its diverse culture rather 'abstract' and 'second-hand'. Indeed, Australia's perception of and interaction with the Middle East seems increasingly connected to external factors, most notably the US alliance. This chapter deals with the nature of Australia's interests in, and engagement with, the Middle East by focussing on the historically dominant theme of trade and highlighting the crucial but missing link, namely, the region's current debate on political reforms and human rights application. This dimension of the relationship — in the current international political context — is crucial because as some have argued 'realizing human rights is tantamount to achieving global justice'[2] though the ongoing debate about the dichotomy of universal rights versus local cultural values still poses a significant conceptual obstacle yet to be resolved. Recent research has already suggested a 'direct correlation between economic performance and the degree of democracy,'[3] a problematic claim that is nevertheless difficult to reject outright.

As this book was in its final editorial stages before going to print, the news about the Australian Wheat Board (AWB) secret payments to Saddam Hussein's regime started to emerge and quickly developed into an international scandal rarely seen in Australia's recent diplomatic history[4]. What this 'scandal' reveals is that the AWB was willing to deliberately breach UN sanctions against Iraq in order to secure trade contracts. In fact, inquiries set up at the request of the UN named the AWB 'as the worst example of a company paying kickbacks to Saddam Hussein's regime under the discredited oil-for-food program'[5]. Though the government has argued that it had no knowledge of the conduct of the AWB's officials, this incident highlights the need for a more consistent and transparent approach to trade negotiations that does not ignore international obligations. It also illustrates that linking trade policy to wider socio-political objectives especially human rights would ensure an effective foreign policy agenda that reflects Australia's attachment to the universality of human rights.

The chapter starts by outlining some trends in the economic relationship between Australia and key Middle Eastern states and the importance of linking economic interests to wider socio-political objectives. It aims to place the economic bilateral relationship within its broader social and political contexts arguing that Australia's widening of its strategic sphere of engagement with the region by incorporating a consistent position on human rights issues would be strategically beneficial in the long term. The discussion is set out in two parts: the first reflects on the scope and nature of Australia's current economic relationships with the Middle East, and the second explores its approaches and responses (or lack of) to local political issues such as human rights debates at both the government and non-government levels.

Given that Australia's present involvement in the Middle East has come to be driven by its military alliance with the US, it is worth reflecting on current strategic thinking in the US on key economic and political imperatives[*] in the region. In the wake of 9/11, US Trade Representative Robert B. Zoellick indicated that to fight terrorism there needs to be 'prosperity and democracy throughout the world,'[6] but more urgently in the Middle East. This agenda, reflected in the idea of a Middle East Free Trade Area, is driven by an assumption that 'stagnant growth, [and] falling income' in the region would likely lead to 'political tension and rising appeal for religious extremists.'[7] Similar concerns were articulated in the 9/11 Commission Report which included a recommendation for 'a comprehensive US strategy to counter terrorism [which] should include economic policies that encourage development, more open societies and opportunities for people to improve the lives of their families and to enhance the prospects for their children's future.'[8] Therefore, bringing local political issues such as democratization and human rights within the ambit of economic engagement can position Australia's foreign policy in the Middle East region within a wider international framework that increasingly emphasises the interconnectedness of economic policies and long-term political stability.

In the case of Australia, there are additional reasons for linking human rights to foreign policy objectives in the Middle East, including the desirable outcomes of improved human rights practice and intra-state stability. Another compelling reason is that an 'Australian concern for regional human rights infringements lends weight to an "honest broker" self-image [that] can only lead to a strengthening of longer-term regional relations'[9]. The linking of the human rights question to the perceived national interest embodied in the trade relationship can potentially be anchored in the fact that Australia has consistently argued for a 'universality' of human rights that 'transcend[s] international political boundaries.'[10] The claim of the universality of human rights has been dismissed 'because it is allegedly western, elitist and interventionist' [11] and in the long term might bring about the standardization of other cultures. Notwithstanding the conceptual merit of this argument, even a minimalist approach to promoting human rights in the Middle East might be conducive to nurturing human agency and dignity, two necessary conditions that would transcend cultural relativism. We will begin by analysing Australia's emphasis on the trade agenda in its relationships with key players in the Middle East and show that even within this narrowly defined trade agenda, the local cultural and social variables have been predominantly ignored.

Trends in the Economic Relationship between Australia and the Middle East

The Middle East is 'an economically diverse region that includes countries with a common heritage, at various stages of economic development, and with vastly different natural resource endowments.'[12] However, Australia's trade policy towards the region has failed to engage with this diversity and the significant changes which have occurred in Middle Eastern economies in recent decades. It appears that the Australian trade approach to the Middle East at the level of government policy and company practice continues to make crucial strategic choices in something of a research vacuum. This region receives little academic attention in Australia, apart from the rather standard policy briefings produced by DFAT (the Department of Foreign Affairs and Trade) and related bodies such as Austrade.

International business research acknowledges the importance of socio-cultural understanding as a basis for effective economic engagement. Trade negotiations and market entry strategies are highly complex processes and are often affected by a host of local factors, such as political risk, investment risk, host government requirements and the expectations of foreign companies. Consideration of these elements in trade relationships can powerfully influence market entry and expansion decisions, and the choice of appropriate communication strategies and modes. However, as crucial as these factors are, a missing link remains: that is, a more sophisticated cultural understanding of the region in order to better understand the key issues influencing outcomes in economic interactions with specific countries. In fact, the impact of a proper appreciation of socio-cultural differences on the success of international business operations has been evidenced in many empirical studies[13] which have shown that having a deep understanding of local culture is a strategic advantage in particular in the context of the Middle East.

Arguably, such understanding has been lacking from Australia's trade policies towards the Middle East. Much of the scant work undertaken in the area of Australia's trade relationship with the Middle East was initiated by the Federal Government in the 1990s and was driven by concerns about trade balances. It was only in the late 1990s that Australian trade policy began to acknowledge the importance of the rapidly developing Middle Eastern markets and its increasing diversity beyond energy exports. In 2000, DFAT published *Accessing Middle East Growth: Business Opportunities in the Arabian Peninsula and Iran* which acknowledged the increasing diversification of Middle Eastern economies and the potential for a diverse range of Australian businesses, including the services and manufacturing sectors, to capitalise on these developments.

While this belated policy recognition of the economic diversity of the Middle East should be welcomed, government policy, as reflected in official reports, continues to suffer from a lack of socio-cultural understanding. Official departmental reports aimed at promoting particular products in specific target countries may present a useful amount of factual information, but they fail to provide any analysis of the nature of commercial transactions in the Middle East and the critical role of cultural variables which, if properly investigated and understood, may assist Australian organizations to identify emerging opportunities in the region. In the current world climate, as Barton so clearly demonstrates in Chapter 7 in regards to Australia's relationship with Indonesia, a greater understanding of the Middle East and its traditions is vital. Increased trade with Middle Eastern nations will bring about closer contact with Australian government departments and, equally, with commercial entities in this country.

Given that trade often sets the tone of a nation's overall engagement with a country or region, Australia's trade relationship with the Middle East continues to reflect an unsophisticated understanding. For example, despite significant regional economic growth across the Middle East, two-way trade remains small and continues to be dominated by resource-based products.

In 2000 the Federal Government appointed a Senate Inquiry Committee to prepare a comprehensive review of Australia's relationship with the Middle East. A report on the Committee's findings was published in August 2001, and among its key conclusions was the fact that in trade terms, the Middle East is more important to Australia than *vice versa*. This conclusion is based on the fact that in 1999, the Middle East consumed 4.7 per cent of Australia's total exports, while Australia received only 0.7 per cent of the Middle East's total exports. Though economically this makes for positive trade account figures, it is arguably the case that in the long term and from a political point of view such a structural imbalance would not be in Australia's own interests. This is because trade agreements are increasingly built on two-way relationships that enable both parties a level of access to each other's markets and capital. It is within such contexts that overall trade volumes and market share can consistently increase. The fact is, however, that Australia's exports in 2000 to the 14 countries of the Middle East covered in the Senate Inquiry were comparatively small, totalling AUD $5.6 billion — the same figure as Australia's exports to Taiwan. In this context the Middle East region represented only 5.1 per cent of Australia's total exports. This figure has fluctuated over the past two decades between a high of 8.2 per cent in 1982 to a low of 2.5 per cent in 1995.[14]

During the 1990s, Australia's aggregate exports to the Arab Peninsula and Iran rose 11 per cent annually, reaching AUD $3.4 billion. In 2003, Australia's exports to the Middle East region were worth AUD $5.2 billion having tumbled to just over AUD $2 billion on the eve of the 1991 Gulf War.[15] According to the Australian Chamber of Commerce and Industry (ACCI), Australia's trade relationship with the Middle East is not in good shape. The general conclusion from its work on the Middle East is that Australia's trade performance — in terms of market share — has deteriorated significantly because of what is referred to as an 'increasing mismatch.'[16] This 'increasing mismatch' is believed to be the result of a growing proportion of Middle East imports devoted to sophisticated manufactured products whereas Australia's exports to the region are still dominated by primary products.

In its submission to the Joint Standing Committee on Foreign Affairs, Defence and Trade, the Australia Arab Chamber of Commerce and Industry (AACCI) pointed out that Australia's overall share of Middle East imports is poor. AACCI argues that in order to understand how well Australia is doing one needs to consider market share rather than total dollar figures. Market share shows how Australia has performed in relation to other suppliers, rather than simply looking at Australia's exports and how they have moved from one year to the next.

Furthermore, Australia's trade relationship with the Middle East continues to be dominated by primary products, despite what has been described by the Joint Standing Committee on Foreign Affairs, Defence and Trade as 'outstanding opportunities' in service sectors such as engineering and consulting, healthcare and pharmaceutical services, education and training, tourism and tourism training, agribusiness, ICT products and services and financial services.[17] Bilateral trade figures with Middle Eastern states, which vary quite significantly from state to state, indicate a very limited range of products or resources exchanged. Bilateral trade with the UAE in 2004 amounted to AUD $392 million, $234 million of which was passenger motor vehicles and $46 million was meat. Imports amounted to $876 million, with crude petroleum the major component amounting to AUD $799 million of this figure and $42 million in liquefied propane and butane.[18] By contrast, in 2004, trade with Jordan — which is almost on a par with the UAE in terms of economic openness[19] — totalled AUD $95 million, $74 million of which was live meat exports. Australia, on the other hand, Australia imported just AUD $1 million of fertilizers from Jordan.[20]

Of particular concern is the failure of Australian trade to diversify into elaborately transformed manufactures and service sectors. While Australia rightfully trumpets the successful export of automobiles to the Middle East, such success continues to be the exception to the rule. Its sluggishness in relation to trade diversification is reflected in the fact that Australia currently attracts less than one per cent of students from the Middle East who undertake higher education courses overseas.

While Australia recognises that it needs to diversify its exports to the Middle East it has yet to develop a sophisticated understanding of exactly what the Middle East is beyond the notion of a region of oil producing states (with which it does have well established, if limited, trade relationships). This is perhaps surprising given the historical relationship between Australia and the Middle East and the very strong grounds which already exist for building a better relationship.

Economically, 'there are significant prospects for increasing two-way trade and investment'[21] between the two regions. In fact, at the most fundamental level, and on a number of grounds, the focus on trade links between Australia and the Middle East makes good sense given their similar environmental attributes and the complementarity of the resources sectors in both regions. Moreover, the Middle East, in spite of the obvious difficulties following the events of 9/11, is still expected to be potentially among the fastest-growing destinations for Australian exports beyond 2002.[22]

Yet, if Australia continues to approach its trade relationship with the Middle East as a one-dimensional issue of market access, it is difficult to imagine how a broader if not deeper connection can be built. Arguably, one of the most effective ways to build a more sophisticated overall engagement with the region (amongst other things), would be to engage local governments and non-government actors on the issue of good governance and human rights as foundations for better socio-cultural understanding. Not only will this approach engender a more stable political environment that is conducive to constructive foreign relations, but it would also reflect the current political obligation on the Australian Government following its participation in the military operations in Afghanistan and Iraq. In the current international climate, human rights promotion will arguably provide a bridge between Australia's twin national interest priorities: the economy and security.[23] The former has been the dominant theme in this relationship while the latter has taken on an added weight since the events of 9/11 and the ensuing 'war on terror'. Perhaps if there is any positive effect to be gained from 9/11 and the subsequent military incursions in the region it is surely the necessity to engage with Middle Eastern states as more than just potential markets and energy sources. Australia, as a member of the 'coalition of the willing' has embarked on a mission of regime change and, consequently, nation-building in Iraq, even if not originally intended. It is within this context that a new emphasis on human rights institutions, civil society and political reforms should be formulated and pursued.

Broadening the Foreign Policy Agenda

As a liberal secular democracy and a religiously pluralist, multicultural society, Australia has — notwithstanding the much-publicized *Tampa* incident and the mandatory detention of asylum seekers (matters which are detailed in Chapters 4 and 5 of this volume) — an impressive record in promoting human rights, particularly through its aid program. As such it certainly has the potential to play a significant role, commensurate with its resources and capabilities, in assisting in the emergence of stable and vibrant civil societies, and the establishment of transparent and representative governments in the Middle East.

The current spotlight on the Middle East and the discourse on democratization and political reforms which manifested most vividly in 'people power' in Lebanon, the holding of general elections in Iraq, as well as municipal elections in the Palestinian Territories and Saudi Arabia, has brought to the fore a new set of dynamics in the region, engendering conditions that may be conducive to greater participation for liberal democratic countries such as Australia. Indeed, given the importance of human rights in contributing to regional development, political stability and economic prosperity, Australia could position itself favourably to add impetus to this current momentum by making human rights, and the enhancement of the institutions of civil society, a fundamental component of an integrated, holistic foreign policy. This would encourage a multifaceted relationship with the Middle East, inclusive of trade, finance, education and aid. Its somewhat inconsistent and at times segmented foreign policy would, however, need to develop a better-defined and systematic framework in order to support a sustainable political economy of human rights in the Middle East. Consequently, preserving and securing Australia's interests in the Middle East would entail a re-ordering of its foreign policy priorities there, bringing human rights within its ambit as a basis for promoting its long-term strategic interests.

Although there is a strong case for the inclusion of a human rights agenda in Australian trade and foreign policy toward the Middle East, the effectiveness or otherwise of such a human rights-based engagement would depend largely on the approach that the appropriate Australian Government agencies adopt and pursue. It can be argued that a sophisticated and strategic relationship with the Middle East ought not only be underpinned by the observance of human rights principles, but that such an engagement needs to embody an agenda that is, and is clearly perceived to be, culturally sensitive and receptive to the dynamic intellectual and cultural currents in the Middle East. In order to prevent its human rights-integrated trade from being undercut by critics and sceptics pointing to what is seen to be a national-centrically driven and self-righteously propelled agenda, it is necessary that Australian Government policy-makers avoid being informed by preconceived essentialist views of the Middle East, as found in orientalist discourse on the region.[24] Too often Middle East political regimes are characterized as inherently authoritarian; its society fractured and backward; its culture as anti-western and exclusive; its religion prone to violence and hatred.[25] Doubtlessly, a detailed critique of the Western portrayal of Middle Eastern societies, politics and cultures is beyond the scope of this chapter. Suffice to briefly point out the political ramifications of such Western constructs for our inquiry, in particular the consequential implication that democracy, accountability and the rule of law are concepts that are supposedly alien to, and incompatible with, Islamic political cultures in the Middle East. There needs to be wider awareness and deeper appreciation in government circles of both the diversity and dynamism of largely Muslim Middle Eastern societies, as well as the evolving multifarious intellectual and political Muslim discourses in the region. One theme that has featured prominently in current scholarly research studies and in political and intellectual debates is the application of human rights and democracy. The animated debates, vigorous discussions and ever-growing literature on these seminal issues, together with the variant points of view with regard to Islam's position on human rights and democracy, are indicative of the variety of readings of these issues as expounded by intellectuals and religious scholars of different ideological hues. This is reflective of the dynamic and mutative character of contemporary Islamic intellectual and political thought.[26]

Therefore, for the integration of human rights in Australia's foreign and trade relations with the Middle East to have the desired tangible impact on the region, it is vital that a re-ordered engagement be seen to be inclusive of and sensitive to the particularistic sensibilities and cultural values of the people of the region. There are genuine mass-based reform movements, and burgeoning civil society groups that have spearheaded the drive for political openness and pluralism in the region.[27] The challenge for Western governments, in general, and that of Australia in particular, is to formulate and pursue a prudent and well-tailored strategy; one that finely balances, on the one hand, the national strategic interests of Australia with the agenda of regional governments, and the needs and aspirations of local citizenry, on the other. Such equilibrium is vital if a genuine multi-faceted engagement is to be successfully pursued.[28]

There is a cogent view, as articulated by some contemporary Muslim intellectuals, such as An-Na'im, that violations or non-observance of human rights principles stem largely from 'a lack or weakness of cultural legitimacy of international standards' in the Middle East.[29] Given the significance of the cultural factor in determining the extent to which human rights standards are understood and accepted, then as a corollary any serious and effective approach by a western government to enhance the standards of human rights observance necessitates a genuine and thoughtful attempt to understand the nature and influence of culture and religion in Middle Eastern societies. Thus, it is vital that the active support of influential religious and cultural groups in the Middle East is enlisted prior to any kind of foreign involvement.

It has long been acknowledged by the international development community that human rights promotion can support the democratic process in the Middle East and contribute to the long-term development of the region. Given the oft-stated nexus between democracy and human rights, there is compelling reason to believe that the democratic reform of the Middle East would, in the long-term, contribute substantially to the reduction of intra-state tension and inter-state conflict in that volatile and vitally important region. The United Nations Human Development Programme (UNDP) recently recognised the urgent need for an acceleration of democratic reforms in the Arab world 'with specific proposals for new regional human rights institutions, robust and freely elected legislatures, and truly independent judiciaries.'[30]

Australia's Involvement in the Development of Human Rights
Espousing the view that human rights are intrinsically intertwined with global peace and security, the pioneer Western states, including Australia, regarded human rights as universally acceptable standards to uphold justice and mitigate the effects of oppression.[31] International law recognizes four categories of human rights: civil, political, socio-cultural and economic. Human rights advocates affirm that all four categories are inherent, inalienable and universal.[32] Ever since its pivotal involvement in the drafting of the Universal Declaration of Human Rights and its leading role in the UN General Assembly's adoption of the Declaration in 1948, Australia has been instrumental, as recently argued by Irene Khan, Secretary General of Amnesty International, in developing international law, including key treaties and important global institutions such as the International Criminal Court.[33] Australia is a party to six key UN human rights international treaties:

the International Covenant on Economic, Social and Cultural Rights, the International Covenant on Civil and Political Rights, the Convention on the Elimination of All Forms of Racial

Discrimination, the Convention on the Elimination of All Forms of Discrimination Against Women, the Convention against Torture, and the Convention on the Rights of the Child.[34]

However, due to concerns over compliance procedures, Australia has been a late signatory to these agreements. Furthermore, there have been discrepancies and anomalies in Australia's implementation of these treaties. The fact that it has not fully complied with the criteria that uphold those treaties, can perhaps explain the Foreign Minister Alexander Downer's statement that 'Australian policy, therefore, does not presume to hold other nations to standards that we do not apply to ourselves.'[35] Yet, this view is evidently at odds with the official Australian position on human rights which articulates the case for their universal application as a priority that transcends the political boundaries of nation-states. The implication of this official line is that Australia rejects the view that human rights issues constitute an 'internal matter' of any sovereign state.[36] Despite this, Australia's 'behaviour in international human rights forums,' its controversial approach to asylum seekers, including the issue of indefinite mandatory detention as outlined by Mansouri in Chapter 6, and its resistance to UN calls for transparency and accountability through compliance with the wishes of international monitoring agencies, has seriously compromised its status as a 'good international citizen'.[37] Given that Australia consistently promotes democracy and the rule of law, on the regional and world stages, and readily denounces regimes which have an abysmal human rights record, there is a growing perception of double standards and hypocrisy.[38] Thus, when the Australian Government says that it wants to make the treaty body regime more 'efficient and effective' and to ensure that it has a focus on gross violations of human rights, what it actually means is 'hands off Australia', that the state is the sole arbiter of particular issues, and that its views override the stipulations of those of the treaty bodies.[39] In other words, the Australian Government resorts to national sovereignty as a defence to allegations against Australia of human rights abuses.[40]

Despite Australia's questionable commitment to human rights in relation to its treatment of refugees and asylum seekers, promotion of human rights, including through the incorporation of good governance norms in its development assistance programs, has for some time been a central component of the Australian Government's aid program.[41] The government regards human rights as an integral part of Australia's foreign policy,[42] and that the 'real basis for a sustained improvement in human rights' needed to be through domestic institutional reform initiated from within.[43] For the purpose of promoting and strengthening institution building as an effective means of realizing 'good governance and the observance of human rights,' the Australian Government has contributed considerable funds to its development co-operation programs.[44] To illustrate the scope of Australia's contribution in regard to human rights, Downer cited the cases of Australian-sponsored human rights programs in Southeast and East Asia. Indeed, Australia has had success in founding and funding two key human rights institutions in this region: the Indonesian Human Rights Commission, established by the Keating Labor Government in 1993, and the Asia–Pacific Forum of National Human Rights Institutions by the Howard Government in 1996.[45] In light of Australia's juridical expertise and experience in human rights institution building and training in Southeast Asia and the Southwest Pacific region, it can be plausibly argued that it has the potential to play an important role in buttressing human rights institutions in the Middle East. Furthermore, given Australia's role in the occupation of Iraq, it can now be said that Australia has an obligation to participate in the promotion of good governance and human rights as areas in which Australia is well placed to make a strong contribution. After all 'good governance sound policies, mature institutions and accountable systems-is a basic condition for stability and prosperity in all countries. Open, accountable and transparent institutions and sustainable policies help deliver security, respect for human rights and economic development.'[46]

Yet remarkably, despite its strategic importance in regard to global security and stability, and despite the region's extensive commercial links and communal ties to Australia, the Middle East does not loom large in official policy documents as a region where Australia needs to promote human rights institutions with a view to engendering vibrant civil societies. Although claims about the centrality of human rights to foreign policy objectives are evident in Australia's attitude and overall approach to international treaties and agreements, Australia has pursued trade and economic liberalization agreements that seem to demote human rights agendas as secondary to the country's 'national interest'.

Human Rights and the National Interest

Australia, in common with other Western countries whose foreign policies are guided by a realist worldview that subordinates international law and morality to overarching strategic, economic and security concerns, invokes international human rights pragmatically as 'an instrument of foreign policy, and then only in [an *ad hoc*] and opportunistic manner.'[47]

The label 'national interest is a subjective understanding of the common good of society — one that is more compelling and enduring than short-term preferences or sectional demands — to which all foreign policy must ultimately be oriented.'[48] Indeed, 'for Australia, as for most states, the national interest has invariably been identified as a combination of national security plus national prosperity, with the occasional dash of national values.'[49] How does Australia's position on human rights and trade compare with those of the Western powers, such as the US and the EU? The US position is that where there is a conflict between national security and economic and strategic interests on the one hand, and the promotion of human rights in foreign policy on the other, it tends to disconnect human rights observance from bilateral and multilateral agreements.[50] By contrast, the EU has made human rights an indispensable component of international relations by coupling their implementation with trade. The prominence of human rights in EU foreign policy is perhaps best illustrated by the workings of the European Court on Human Rights and the European Court of Justice.[51]

In addition to Australia's increased regional obligations as an occupier in Iraq, there are compelling national interest grounds for deeper human rights engagement with the Middle East. Unquestionably, human rights are inextricably linked to national peace and international security. Observance of human rights inhibits mass refugee flows, contributes to a lessening of tension or reduction of hostility in inter-state relations, and helps in ameliorating the conditions of poverty and inequality, which contribute to social unrest and political violence.[52]

Human Rights and Democratization

Although the two concepts of human rights and democracy are concomitant, they are not synonymous. Subscribing to a minimalist definition of human rights as the right to life, some theorists advance the somewhat contentious view that although democracy and human rights are, in general, mutually independent, the latter may help bring about the former.[53] The approach of the Howard Government on this issue has been to promote simultaneously transparent representative governance and human rights, with a pronounced focus on Australia's immediate region.[54]

An emphasis on supporting and promoting democracy in the Middle East certainly appears to have the support of Australians, with 52 per cent responding 'yes' to the Lowy Institute's 2005 Poll when asked: 'Should Australia play an active role in efforts to promote democracy in the Middle East?'.[55] The fact is that democratically elected governments are less prone to wage war against each other, as evidenced by the course of inter-state relations in Europe since the end of the Second World War. For Australia, a politically stable and an economically integrated Middle East would contribute to global security and enhance the prospects for much increased investment and bi-lateral trade.

As has been argued by Foreign Minister Downer , Australia's 'approach to human rights is a characteristically practical one: to bring real improvements and a 'fair go' to the lives of individuals. We pursue this in a number of ways, including through constructive dialogue, focused technical assistance activities, and the building of institutions which can play a major role in strengthening of the rule of law and civil society.'[56] Indeed, Australia has strong credentials regarding the promotion of human rights through its development assistance programs and Australia was widely applauded, for example, in its capacity building programs in East Timor which included a strong human rights dimension, notably regarding the development of East Timor's judicial system. Through its aid schemes to countries such as Papua New Guinea, East Timor and Fiji, the government has enabled the training of judges and magistrates with a view to invigorating the democratic processes and electoral commissions of those countries.[57]

While it is understandable that the focus of Australia's aid program is on its immediate region (and increasingly so given its recent commitments in PNG and the Solomon Islands), conspicuously absent from this statement on human rights in government foreign policy are the geographically distant but increasingly important trading countries in the Middle East.

Given the potential correlation between democratic reform in the Middle East and long-term regional stability, it can be argued that it is in Australia's national interest to adopt a similar approach to the one currently pursued in Southeast Asia and the south west Pacific; an approach that is conducive to the advancement of human rights and the strengthening of accountable and transparent government institutions. Similarly, there is a need to engage more closely with governments and NGOs (both secular and Islamist) in the Middle East region with a view to expediting the pace of reform and positively influencing its direction.

Australia's experience in other regions is surely transferable to the Middle East context as it played an instrumental role in establishing such human rights institutions in the Asia–Pacific region. As argued earlier in this chapter, despite the strategic and economic importance of the Middle East as potentially one of Australia's fastest export markets, human rights have been conspicuously absent from government trade policy toward the region. Where human rights are a recurring theme in government policy it is in relation to development aid and training schemes. This approach is perhaps best exemplified by Australian official and private sector involvement in Iraq and the Palestinian territories of Gaza and the West Bank.

According to a report by AusAID, Australia has provided AUD $11 million to the UN Development Group Iraq Trust Fund to help in the improvement of 'governance, civil society, electoral assistance and support for refugees.'[58] A much larger financial commitment, however, would be required if Australia were to seriously commit to the development of those key sectors. Until December 2004, the Australian Government had pledged over AUD $126 million to Iraq, the bulk of which was designated for agricultural assistance and the reconstruction of infrastructure.[59] Of the total $126 million that Australia has assigned to Iraq, the Government earmarked $6 million as financial support to the UN and Iraqi preparations for the January 2005 elections, heralded as a milestone in its transition to democracy. In addition, part of that financial pledge was reserved for assisting human rights investigations to be undertaken by the newly formed Iraqi Special Tribunal.[60] In May 2005, the Federal Government announced that additional funding to the amount of AUD $45 million over two years would be provided to assist in the development of democratic government institutions, agriculture and trade reform.[61]

In a recent report on Iraq, Amnesty International targeted the following spheres as key areas in need of reform to ensure the protection of human rights in post-Saddam Iraq. It recommends a comprehensive legal review to be undertaken by a future Iraqi Government to ensure that: its laws conform to international human rights standards; inhuman or degrading punishments are terminated; an independent judiciary is set up to review and reform the criminal justice system; and to protect rights to freedom of expression, assembly and association. Another major area recommended by Amnesty is human rights education and awareness raising, funded by the international community.[62]

Australia is well positioned to provide significant technical assistance in relation to all of these areas, most notably in reforming Iraq's judicial and penal legal systems because it has the relevant expertise in that sphere in its long-established and highly reputed legal system, its independent judiciary, and its modern penal system. It is certainly able to send a commission of experts in penal and international law to review, in conjunction with Iraqi and international jurists, Iraq's legal system and oversee the process of reform.

Similarly, Australia's police force has gained recognition for its role in training and organizing the law enforcement agencies in developing countries in its region, namely East Timor and Papua New Guinea. Australia's Federal Police could also play a critical role in helping to restructure Iraq's embryonic, but beleaguered police force into an efficient and accountable law enforcement agency. In the context of promoting a human rights sensitive law and order enforcement, a number of areas must be addressed, such as raids on homes, searches of private premises, arrest of suspects, detention without charge, torture and ill-treatment of detainees, and the use of disproportionate force.[63] Iraq's police force could undergo a human rights training program in order to ensure that detainees have rights of access to families, lawyers and judges, and that there are mechanisms in place to ensure the proper treatment of detainees, before they are brought to court to face charges.

Crucial to the long-term success of a systematic human rights regime in Iraq is the establishment and maintenance of a vibrant civil society, where there is genuine freedom for the media, political parties and associations, syndicates and clubs, trade and professional unions and pressure groups. Specifically, Australia could contribute to those areas where it has a reputable record, namely: freedom of information, parliamentary protection of rights, equal opportunity law, privacy laws, freedom of expression, right of assembly, press laws, and the status of minorities.

The Palestinians of Gaza, the West Bank and Jerusalem, are another example of the need for better Australian regional engagement on human rights issues. In common with the citizens of Iraq, who voted in national democratic elections in January 2005, the Palestinians of the West Bank and Gaza participated in municipal elections, which took place in three phases, beginning in December 2004 and ending in May 2005. Like the Iraqis, the Palestinians have chosen the path of political reform and democracy, and in its January 2006 elections it delivered a surprise to the West by opting for Hamas, ousting Yasser Arafat's Fatah party. Palestine's democratisation has so far given rise to embryonic institutions that are predicated, in light of the volatility of the security and political situation in the occupied territories, on fragile foundations, which will be tested as Hamas transforms itself from a movement of resistance into an instrument of governance. Given the pivotal importance of Palestine–Israel to regional stability and global security, it is in Australia's national, strategic and economic interest to play a more constructive role in buttressing these nascent democratic institutions by leading the international community on the integral issue of human rights promotion. In its report, entitled 'Australian Development Co-operation in the Middle East Strategy for 2004–2006', AusAID views the reaching of a lasting Palestinian–Israeli peace settlement as serving Australia's national interest. A peaceful and stable Middle East, the report adds, would strengthen global security and enhance 'Australian trade and investment opportunities.'[64] Crucially, what is missing from the AusAID report, however, is the issue of human rights. It can be argued that Australia's national interest would be best preserved and advanced through a consistent and comprehensive adoption of a human rights approach to trade links, investment schemes and diplomacy in relation to the Palestinian Territories. An integrated human rights — trade approach in Australia's foreign policy would complement and reinforce existing development aid programs and peace-building efforts.

In the Palestinian Territories Australia has, for many years, consistently earmarked up to half of its annual financial allocations as humanitarian aid through the United Nations Relief and Works Agency (Versailles) and, to a lesser extent, via other multilateral agencies such as the World Food Programme (WFP), the United Nations Children's Fund (UNICEF), the International Committee of the Red Cross (ICRC), and Australian NGOs.[65] In comparison with other Western donors, Australia's net contribution is quite negligible. For example, in 2003–2004, AUD $11.1 million worth of aid flowed to the territories from Australia a figure that increased marginally in 2004–2005 to AUD $12 million.[66] In contrast, Canada, a Western donor with similar population size and GDP to that of Australia, annually contributes financial humanitarian assistance and developmental aid to Palestinians of the West Bank and Gaza to the amount of CAD $25 million.[67] In June 2005, the Canadian Government pledged that its annual aid to the Palestinians will increase by $12 million to a total of $37 million, with the possibility of a further increase depending on 'progress and reforms'.[68]

Promoting Human Rights as a
Basis for Effective Middle Eastern Engagement

There is a serious disconnection between, on the one hand, Australia's economic and trade interests, and, on the other, its foreign and security policy interests in the Middle East. This chapter began by considering Australia's outdated view of the Middle East economy which has informed its regional trade policy, whereby the region is seen essentially as an oil economy and market for Australian primary produce. The chapter then argued that the promotion of human rights in the Middle East should be central to efforts of the international community to promote regional peace, stability and ultimately, prosperity. It was noted that not only does Australia have an obligation to promote human rights in the region as an occupier in Iraq, but it has a national interest to do so, and, furthermore, is well qualified in the area. Closing the circle, this section will highlight the potential role that deeper human rights engagement with the Middle East could play in fostering a more sophisticated understanding of Middle East societies and cultures leading ultimately to a better, more sustainable basis for deeper trade engagement with the region.

It is common for proponents of trade liberalization to draw connections between trade and human rights. The argument is that human rights and political reforms inevitably follow economic and trade liberalization. While even a cursory analysis of the *actual* relationship between trade liberalization and human rights indicates that this is by no means true (consider, for example, Western trade with China), it may be that effective human rights engagement could provide a basis for subsequent trade liberalization.

The Australian Regional Dialogue on Human Rights (ARDHR) was set up by the Australian Government to advance human rights in Asia through co-operative dialogue with senior government officials, with a view to addressing human rights in a number of countries with which Australia has trading ties. Currently Australia engages in annual dialogue with important countries in Asia such as China, and Vietnam. Since 2002 the Australian Government has been engaging in dialogue with one Middle East country, Iran. Although relatively recent, in comparison with China, the dialogue with Iran has resulted in significant progress. A delegation from Iran's Islamic Human Rights Commission embarked on a visit to Australia in 2003 to examine the functions and mechanics of the Australian Human Rights and Equal Opportunity Commission.[69] In comparison with Australia's approach to dialogue to facilitate full implementation of human rights principles, the EU has, since 2002, followed a consistent policy founded on the principle of conditionality, one that predicates negotiated trade agreement in progress on a number of salient political reforms, notably human rights.[70]

Thus, in view of the increasingly important bi-lateral trade relations between Australia and other states in the region, there is a solid basis for expanding the ARDHR initiative to encompass such key trading countries as Saudi Arabia, Israel, the UAE, Egypt and Iraq. It logically follows that an expanded and strengthened ARDHR would contribute significantly towards the building of a much more durable relationship between Australia and its trading partners in the Middle East.[71]

Since the early 1990s the Human Rights Council of Australia (HRCA), a private sector NGO founded in 1978, has developed a close working relationship with DFAT, with the aim of promoting human rights through the provision of government sponsored aid programs. This was viewed as an effective means of promoting human rights in developing countries. In 1998, the HRCA launched a report entitled 'The Rights Way to Development: A human rights approach to development assistance.' The report argues the case for integrating Australia's development aid policy into the international human rights framework.[72] Among the key recommendations of the report were:

1. Human rights and development must be integrated and systemized;
2. Aid priorities should not depend on donor country interests;
3. Priorities for assistance should be determined by donor human rights obligations and recipient human rights entitlements;
4. The human rights approach involves consultation with the recipient country or agencies; and
5. Greater transparency, accessible information on human rights and aid, and a 'willingness to change.[73]

In order to lay out the mechanics for the implementation of human rights – contextualized development aid, the Council also published 'The Rights of Way Development Manual' in 1998. The Manual underscored the importance of directly linking development aid to the realization of civil and political rights.[74] This is consistent with Australia's historical preference for constructive dialogue in pursuing foreign policy objectives in particular when these relate to political and social matters.

The expansion of Australian human rights initiatives beyond their current regional emphasis, which does not encompass the Middle East in any significant manner, would complement its rather modest contributions towards aid in Iraq. In the case of the Palestinian Territories, the UN, US, EU and Australia have underscored the importance of linking political democratic reform of the Palestinian National Authority to progress in the Palestine–Israel peace process. Notwithstanding this shortcoming of linking the Peace Process to internal political issues, the Australian government and relevant NGOs need to take a more active role in strengthening the 'rule of law' as a crucial step in the process of establishing a democratic and stable Palestinian state.[75]

Conclusion

'Human rights are universal principles, but, inspiring as those principles are, none implement themselves. Good governance, effective institutions, adequate material resources and international support are usually what make the difference between noble aspirations and effective realization.'[76] This is especially the case in the Middle East where political and institutional deficiencies still hinder the implementation of human rights. Yet, despite the increasing strategic and economic value of the Middle East to Australia the current overall focus remains narrow.

As outlined at the beginning of this chapter, if Australia is to successfully improve its overall economic relationships with the Middle East, it will first need to develop an understanding of the key cultural and environmental factors that characterise the Middle East.[77] Language constraints and hostile media divert attention, while stereotypes support the view that the Middle East exports oil and is otherwise not actively involved in international trade. In fact, the diversity of imports by Middle Eastern economies has increased significantly as real incomes have risen and the threat of inter-state conflict has subsided.

Should current policies identify mechanisms for increasing economic interactions between Australia and the Middle East, new areas such as tourism, education and cultural ties would make for a more dynamic exchange. The development of a set of policies aimed at promoting overall links between Australia and the Middle East, and the identification of key cultural and political attributes of Middle Eastern societies, will support a more mutually-rewarding engagement.

Taking the Australian Government's acknowledgement of the importance of human rights principles as a basis for regional peace and stability, this chapter proceeded to argue that this country's concerns for human rights violations ought to be evidenced in its foreign and trade policies towards the Middle East. The fact that the Australian Government's upholding of the universality and indivisibility of human rights has not translated into practice with respect to its bi-lateral trade relations with Middle Eastern states underscore the limited dimensions of its human rights engagement with the region.

Whilst the Australian Government has on a number of occasions affirmed its position on the necessity of linking developmental aid to observance of international human rights by the recipient countries, and is committed to the realization of social, economic, legal and political rights, its foreign policy has neither been equivocal nor consistent on the issue of linking trade to human rights. With the current process of political reform underway at various speeds through this vitally important region, and given the growing economic volume and investment value of the Middle East — particularly in light of the recent resumption of live sheep shipments to the Gulf, and the landmark negotiations on a Free Trade Agreement with the UAE — the time is ripe for the maturation of the Australia–Middle East engagement.

CONTRIBUTORS

Greg Barton is Associate Professor in Politics at Deakin University. His research has focused on Islam, civil society and politics in Indonesia and Malaysia, including the emergence of radical Islamism in Southeast Asia. Greg has published extensively in this area and is regularly asked to comment on related matters in the Australian and international media. He has a broad interest in religion and modernity and has recently started comparative research in Turkey. His publications include *Abdurrahman Wahid, Muslim Democrat, Indonesian President: a view from the inside* (UNSW Press and University of Hawai'i Press 2002) and *Indonesia's Struggle: Jemaah Islamiyah and the Soul of Islam* (UNSW Press 2004 and Singapore University Press 2005). He is currently working on two books: *Islamic Liberalism in Indonesia*; and: *Islam's Other Nation: a fresh look at Indonesia*.

Trevor Batrouney is a sociologist and historian who has written extensively on the migration and settlement of Lebanese in Australia. His several books include *Kurdish immigration and settlement in Australia* (Australian Government Publishing Service 1995), *Selected African communities in Melbourne: their characteristics and settlement needs* (Australian Government Publishing Service 1991) and *The Lebanese in Australia* (AE Press 1985) plus numerous papers and chapters on immigrant groups and issues. He has held the positions of Assistant Director of the Bureau of Immigration Research and Research Manager at the Australian Institute of Family Studies. He is currently an Adjunct Professor at RMIT University.

Scott Burchill is Senior Lecturer in International Relations in the School of International and Political Studies at Deakin University. Before joining Deakin University in 1990 he was a Political Officer in the Department of Foreign Affairs and Trade (Indochina and Europe desks) in Canberra. He has also taught at the University of Melbourne, Monash University and the University of Tasmania. He is the author of *The National Interest in Theories of International Relations* (Palgrave Macmillan, London 2005) and co-author of *Theories of International Relations* (3rd ed Palgrave Macmillan, London 2005).

David Lowe is Associate Professor in History at Deakin University's Faculty of Arts. He has published on Australia's involvement in wars, including the Cold War, and on aspects of its overseas policies during the 1940s and 1950s. David joined Deakin University from Cambridge in 1991, and from 1993 to 1995 was Monash Lecturer in Australian Politics at the Menzies Centre for Australian Studies, University of London. In 1999 he published the book, *Menzies and the 'Great World Struggle: Australia's Cold war 1948–1954* (UNSW Press); and in 2003 co-authored, with Joan Beaumont and Chris Waters, *Ministers, Mandarins and Diplomats: Australian foreign policy-making, 1941–69* (Melbourne University Press). His current research and writing spans several themes: parliamentary debates and Australian foreign policy; the history of Australian involvement in the Colombo Plan; and the life of the late Sir Percy Spender, Australian Minister for External Affairs.

Benjamin MacQueen is a PhD candidate and lecturer in Middle Eastern Studies at the Department of Arabic and Middle Eastern Studies, Deakin University. His doctoral dissertation focuses on civil war and conflict resolution in Lebanon and Algeria. His research interests include government and politics in North Africa and the Middle East, conflict and conflict resolution, foreign policy in North Africa and the Middle East, culture and critical theory in Arab-Islamic societies, civil society, democratization and political reform.

William Maley is Professor and Director of the Asia–Pacific College of Diplomacy at the Australian National University, and has served as a Visiting Professor at the Russian Diplomatic Academy, a Visiting Fellow at the Centre for the Study of Public Policy at the University of Strathclyde, and a Visiting Research Fellow in the Refugee Studies Programme at Oxford University. He is author of *The Afghanistan Wars* (Palgrave Macmillan, New York 2002); editor of *Fundamentalism Reborn? Afghanistan and the Taliban* (New York University Press 1998, 2001) and co-editor of *From Civil Strife to Civil Society: Civil and Military Responsibilities in Disrupted States* (United Nations University Press, Tokyo 2003).

Fethi Mansouri is Associate Professor in Middle Eastern Studies at Deakin University's School of International and Political Studies where he teaches history, cultures and ideologies of the contemporary Middle East. He is Project Group Chair of Deakin's Institute for Citizenship and Globalisation, Deputy Director of its Centre for Citizenship and Human

Rights (CCHR) and founding Convenor of the Refugee Studies Group. His research interests cut across Middle Eastern studies with specific reference to the settlement of Muslim migrants in the West and applied linguistics with focus on multicultural education and bilingualism. His recent projects on the Arab-Muslim Diaspora in Australia include: the settlement patterns of Middle Eastern asylum seekers and refugees; cultural diversity in secondary education and capacity building among ethno-specific community organizations. He has published extensively in these areas and recently authored (with Michael Leach) *Lives in Limbo* (UNSW Press 2004), a study into the social, economic and psychological impacts of the temporary protection visa regime.

Abdullah Saeed is Sultan of Oman Professor of Arab and Islamic Studies and the Director of the Centre for the Study of Contemporary Islam at the University of Melbourne. In 1992, he completed his PhD in Islamic Studies at the University of Melbourne. His research interests include modern Qur'anic hermeneutics, Islam and modernity, religious pluralism and human rights, Islamic law reform, Islamic finance, and Islam in Australia. His major publications include *Approaches to Qur'an in Contemporary Indonesia* (edited, OUP 2005), *Interpreting the Qur'an: Towards a Contemporary Approach* (OUP 2005), *Freedom of Religion, Apostasy and Islam* (co-authored, Ashgate Publishing 2004), *Islam in Australia* (Allen & Unwin 2003), *Muslim Communities in Australia* (co-edited, UNSW Press 2001) and *Islamic Banking and Interest* (E.J. Brill 1996).

Jamal Sankari completed his BA Honours in History from the University of Western Australia, Perth. He obtained his MA (in Social Sciences) from Curtin University in Perth, and his PhD (in Political Sciences) from the University of Melbourne. He teaches Middle Eastern Politics in the School of International and Political Studies, Faculty of Arts, Deakin University. He is the author, most recently, of *Fadlallah: The Making of a Radical Shi`ite Leader* (Saqi Books 2005). His research interests include modern Islamic thought, contemporary Islamism, and human rights and democracy in the Middle East.

David Walker is Professor of Australian Studies at Deakin University. He previously taught at Auckland University and the University of New South Wales. In 1997/98 he held the Monash Chair of Australian Studies at Georgetown University, Washington, DC and is currently a Fellow of the Academy of Social Sciences of Australia. He has published widely in

Australian social and cultural history, has extensive experience in the development of Australian Studies programs in Indonesia, PR China and Japan, and has written extensively on Australian representations of Asia. His recent publications include *Anxious Nation: Australia and the Rise of Asia, 1850–1939* (University of Queensland Press 1999), for which he won the Ernest Scott Prize for History in 2001, and co-edited, with Laksiri Jayasuriya and Jan Gothard, *Legacies of White Australia: Race, Culture and Nation* (University of Western Australia Press 2003).

Sally Percival Wood is a Researcher at the Centre for Citizenship and Human Rights at Deakin University, where she is currently assisting with a project investigating the social, cultural and educational experiences of Arab-Muslim secondary school students in Melbourne, and the efficacy of Australia's current multicultural educational policies. She is also writing and researching, with Associate Professor Purushottama Bilimoria, on personal (customary) laws in India with a focus on Muslim women under both *Sharia* and secular laws for a forthcoming book. Sally recently spent time in India where she took part in research on public and mental health for a chapter in a forthcoming volume *Indian Ethics* to be published by Ashgate Publishing (U.K. 2006).

NOTES

Notes

1   L. McIntyre. 'Introduction'. In *Australia and the Middle East: Papers and Documents*, edited by J. Knight and G. Patz, 1–3. Canberra: the Canberra Branch of the Australian Institute of International Affairs, 1976: 1.
2   A. Mohammadi. *Islam Encountering Globalization*. London: Routledge Curzon, 2002: ix.
3   R. Falk. *Human Rights Horizons: The Pursuit of Justice in a Globalizing World*. London: Routledge, 2000: 150.
4   Falk, *Human Rights Horizons*, 147.

Chapter One

1   J. Knight and G. Patz, eds. *Australia and the Middle East: Papers and Documents*. Canberra: the Canberra Branch of the Australian Institute of International Affairs, 1976.
2   Knight and Patz, *Australia and the Middle East*, 4.
3   Knight and Patz, *Australia and the Middle East*, 5.
4   Knight and Patz, *Australia and the Middle East*, 11.
5   David Walker. 'Cultural Change and the Response to Asia: 1945 to the Present.' In *Australia and Asia*, edited by Mark McGillivray and Gary Smith, 11–27. Melbourne: Oxford University Press, 1997.
6   Australia announced in May 2004 that it would open a diplomatic mission in Libya, which is counted as one of the Maghrib states, albeit a significantly wealthier one than the others mentioned here. See DFAT (Department of Foreign Affairs and Trade), Joint media release by the Minister for Foreign Affairs Alexander Downer and the Minister for Trade Mark Vaile. 'Australia to Open Diplomatic Mission in Libya.' 21 May 2004. http://www.foreignminister.gov.au/releases/2004/joint_open_libya_missio n.html
7   See the DFAT publications, *Doing Business with Qatar, Doing Business with Saudi Arabia*, and *Doing Business with United Arab Emirates*, March 2005.
8   DFAT, *Doing Business with United Arab Emirates*, 19.
9   DIMIA (Department of Immigration and Multicultural and Indigenous Affairs), Fact Sheet 82. Immigration Detention, 14 October 2004. http://www.dimia.gov.au/facts/82detention.htm
10 Barry York. 'Australia and Refugees, 1901–2002: An Annotated Chronology Based on Official Sources.' Canberra: Parliamentary Library, Parliament of Australia, 2003. http://www.aph.gov.au/library/pubs/online/Refugees_s3.htm
11 Comparatively, in 2001 43 per cent of New Zealanders and 25 per cent of Americans thought that refugees arriving by boat should be put back to sea.

'Refugees Not Welcome Australians Say.' Roy Morgan Research. 25 September 2001. http://www.roymorgan.com/news/polls/2001/3446/

12   AusAID (Australian Government Aid Program) 'Australian Development Co-operation Strategy in the Middle East: 2004–2006.' (nd) http://www.ausaid.gov.au/publications/pdf/me_strat_0406.pdf and 'Country Programs — Middle East.' 11 May 2005. http://www.ausaid.gov.au/country/country.cfm?CountryId=98411310

13   AusAID. 'Country Programs — Iraq.' 11 May 2005. http://www.ausaid.gov.au/country/country.cfm?CountryId=54777444

14   AusAID. 'Country Programs — Indonesia', 10 February 2005. http://www.ausaid.gov.au/country/country.cfm?CountryId=30 and DFAT, Joint Media Release. 'Australia Indonesia Partnership for Reconstruction and Development — Inaugural Joint Commission Meeting.' 17 March 2005. http://www.foreignminister.gov.au/releases/2005/jointpr170305_aus-ind.html

15   AusAID. 'Country Programs — Papua New Guinea.' Estimate Total Aid 2005. http://www.ausaid.gov.au/country/papua.cfm

16   An exception is Knight and Patz, *Australia and the Middle East.*

17   Written by V. Chirol and quoted in Thomas Scheffer. '"Fertile Crescent", "Orient", "Middle East": The Changing Mental Maps of Southwest Asia.' *European Review of History*, Vol.10 No.2 (2005): 253–72, see 264–5.

18   See Scheffer, '"Fertile Crescent", "Orient", "Middle East".'

19   Scheffer. '"Fertile Crescent", "Orient", "Middle East",' 271.

20   Scheffer. '"Fertile Crescent", "Orient", "Middle East",' 270.

21   In 1993 Shimon Peres, Israel's former Minister for Foreign Affairs, set out his proposal for the way forward in the Middle East after the Gulf War in his book *The New Middle East*, New York: Holt, 1993.

22   Robert Manne with David Corlett. 'Sending Them Home: Refugees and the new politics of indifference.' *Quarterly Essay.* Issue 13, 2004: 61.

23   Manne with Corlett, 'Sending Them Home,' 60.

24   Manne with Corlett, 'Sending Them Home,' 73.

25   Interim Justice Minister Hashim al-Shibli quoted in 'Iraq urges Australia to keep refugees.' *Al-Jazeera.* 31 December 2003. http://english.aljazeera.net

26   'The Lowy Institute Poll 2005 Data Book,' 6.

27   S.P. Seth. 'What sort of self-image do Australians seek?' *Khaleej Times.* 9 April 2002. http://www.khleejtimes.co.ae/ktarchive/090402/editor.htm

28   'Iraq urges Australia to keep refugees.' *Al-Jazeera.* 31 December 2003. http://english.aljazeera.net

29   This term was coined by Robert Manne. See Manne with Corlett, 'Sending The Home.'

30   From the 'Overview' of the Commission on the Intelligence Capabilities of the United States Regarding Weapons of Mass Destruction's 'Report to the President.' 31 March 2005. http://www.wmd.gov/report/overview_fm.pdf

31   From the Australian Government's Inquiry into Australian Intelligence Agencies. *Report of the Inquiry into Australian Intelligence Agencies.* http://www.pmc.gov.au/publications/intelligence_inquiry/

32 Inquiry into Australian Intelligence Agencies. *Report of the Inquiry into Australian Intelligence Agencies*, 'Summary of Findings and Recommendations,' 15.

33 Andrew Wilkie, 'A lack of intelligence.' Sydney *Morning Herald*. 31 May 2003. http://www.smh.com.au/articles/2003/05/30/1054177726543.html

34 'PM admits public doesn't support Iraq decision.' *The Age*. 15 March 2005.

35 'Australia in the World' Address by the Prime Minister, The Hon John Howard MP, to the Lowy Institute for International Policy. 31 March 2005: 7.

36 John Howard, 'Australia in the World.'

37 'Camels, Cars and Currencies — Australian Exporters and the Middle East.' Australian Trade Commission, 2004. http://www.austrade.gov.au/corporate/

38 The UAE has also entered FTA negotiation with the US during March 2005. 'UAE, Australia to negotiate a free trade agreement.' *Khaleej Times*. 15 March 2005.

39 AUD $584m for the 2003–2004 financial year.

40 AUD $271m for the same period.

41 DFAT. United Arab Emirates Fact Sheet at http://www.dfat.gov.au/geo/uae/

42 AUD $1036m per annum for the financial year 2003–2004.

43 AUD $600m, made up of crude and refined petroleum, and liquefied propane and butane.

44 Tim Harcourt. 'The Middle East — A Mecca for our Exports.' Australian Trade Commission, 2005. http://www.austrade.gov.au/corporate/

45 See DFAT, 'Country, Economy and Regional Information' fact sheets for details at http://www.dfat.gov.au/geo/

46 'Riots spur soul-searching in Australia: Nation examines its racial, religious, cultural identity'. *Washington Post*. 25 December 2005.

47 'Race riots turn Sydney's suburbs into battleground'. *The Guardian*. 12 December 2005.

48 'Howard wrong on racism, poll finds'. *The Age*. 20 December 2005.

Chapter Two

1 Edward Said. *Orientalism: Western Conceptions of the Orient*. London: Penguin, 1995. For art and the orient, including Australian painters, see Roger Benjamin, ed. *Orientalism: Delacroix to Klee*. Sydney: Art Gallery of New South Wales, 1997.

2 The history of these threats is examined in David Walker, *Anxious Nation: Australia and the Rise of Asia, 1850–1939*, Brisbane: University of Queensland Press, 1999 and Walker, 'Survivalist Anxieties: Australian Responses to Asia, 1890s to the Present.' *Australian Historical Studies*, Vol.34 (120) (October 2002).

3 Arthur Diosy. *The New Far East*. London: Cassell and Company Ltd, 1904: 327–39.

4 J.F. Raffaelli. 'A Picture by Emperor William.' *Harper's Weekly*, 22 January

1898: 76.

5   'Guy Newell Boothby', in Bede Nairn and Geoffrey Serle, eds. *Australian Dictionary of Biography.* Vol.7: 1891–1939, A-Ch, Melbourne: Melbourne University Press, 1979.

6   Albert Dorrington. *The Radium Terrors: A Mystery Story.* New York: W.R. Caldwell & Co., 1910.

7   See the first of the Fu Manchu novels published in 1913, *The Mystery of Dr Fu Manchu*, 19.

8   'Mr. Rudyard Kipling: An Interesting Interview.' *The Age*, 13 November 1891.

9   Cited in Cyril Pearl. *Morrison of Peking*, Ringwood: Penguin, 1970: 213.

10   Charles H. Pearson. *National Life and Character: A Forecast.* London: Macmillan & Co., 1893.

11   Homer Lea. *The Valor of Ignorance.* New York: Harper & Brothers Publishers, 1909; and Lea. *The Day of the Saxon.* New York: Harper & Brothers Publishers, 1912.

12   For an elaboration of this theme see David Walker, 'Shooting Mabel: Warrior Masculinity and Asian Invasion,' *History Australia*, 2005, forthcoming.

13   For an overview see James Jupp. 'Afghans.' In *The Australian People: An Encyclopedia of the Nation, Its People and Their Origins*, edited by James Jupp, 164–5. Cambridge: Cambridge University Press, 2001.

14   Christine Stevens. *Tin Mosques & Ghantowns: A History of Afghan Cameleers in Australia.* Melbourne: Oxford University Press, 1989. See also Cigler, Michael. *The Afghans in Australia.* Blackburn: Australasian Educa Press, 1986.

15   Stevens, *Tin Mosques & Ghantowns*, 144.

16   Stevens, *Tin Mosques & Ghantowns*, 148.

17   Stevens, *Tin Mosques & Ghantowns*, 148–50.

18   Rata [T.R. Roydhouse], *The Coloured Conquest.* Sydney: New South Wales Bookstall Company, 1903.

19   See 'Lebanese' in Jupp, *The Australian People*, 554–8.

20   For an overview of the versatile Chinese see Eric Rolls. *Sojourners: The epic story of China's centuries-old relationship with Australia.* Brisbane: University of Queensland Press, 1992. Morrison provides a familiar late nineteenth view of Chinese adaptability and tenacity in George Ernest Morrison. *An Australian in China.* Oxford: Oxford University Press, 1985, 223–4.

21   See 'Turks' in Jupp, *The Australian People*, 709–10.

22   Rev. J.J. Malone. *The Purple East: Notes of Travel.* Melbourne: W.P. Linehan, 1911: 138–9.

23   Richard White. 'Sun, Sand and Syphilis: Australian Soldiers and the Orient, Egypt 1914', *Australian Cultural History*, no.9, 1990: 56.

24   White. 'Sun, Sand and Syphilis', 54. Among many accounts of the Australians in the Middle East see H.S. Gullett and Chas Barrett. eds. *Australia in Palestine.* Sydney: Angus & Robertson, 1919.

25   Walker, *Anxious Nation*, 185–7.

26   Randolph Bedford. *Explorations in Civilization.* Sydney: Angus & Robertson,

1914[?].

27   David, Edgeworth. 'A Wilderness: Australia's Arid Centre.' *Sydney Morning Herald*, 13 August 1924: 12.

28   Brian Elliott. *The Landscape of Australian Poetry*. Melbourne: F.W. Cheshire, 1967.

29   M.H. Ellis *Express to Hindustan: An Account of a Motor-Car Journey from London to Delhi*. London: John Lane the Bodley Head Limited, 1929; Florence M. Taylor. *A Pot-Pourri of Eastern Australia with Comparisons and Reflections*. Sydney: Building Publishing Co. Ltd., 1935.

30   H.W. Ponder. *Java Pageant: a description of one of the world's richest, most beautiful, yet little known islands of the world*. London: Seeley Service & Co., 1934: 116–20; and Ponder *Javanese Panorama: a further account of the world's richest island with some intimate pictures of life among the people of its lesser known regions*. London: Seeley Service & Co., nd.

31   Paul McGuire. *Westward the Course: The New World of Oceania*. Melbourne: Leighton House, 1946: 266.

32   Eric Lambert. *The Twenty Thousand Thieves*, Melbourne: Newport, 1951: 19.

33   Lambert. *The Twenty Thousand Thieves*, 27–8.

34   Lambert. *The Twenty Thousand Thieves*, 81.

35   Frank Clune. *To the Isles of Spice*. Sydney: Angus and Robertson, 1948: 212.

36   Clune. *To the Isles of Spice*, 320.

37   Frank Clune. *Tobruk to Turkey: With the Army of the Nile*. Sydney: Angus and Robertson, 1943: 27.

38   Clune. *Tobruk to Turkey*, 79.

39   Clune. *Tobruk to Turkey*, 125.

40   Clune. *Tobruk to Turkey*, 126.

41   For comment on Hindus and the prediction about Muslim India, Frank Clune to P.R. Stephensen, 17 January 1945, P. R. Stephensen Papers, 1905–1965, 62 (127), item 1, ML MSS 1284, Mitchell Library, Sydney.

42   For Clune on Jinnah, see Frank Clune. *Song of India*, Sydney: Invincible Press, 1946: Chapter 13.

43   Buddhism and Islam are linked as 'competing non-communist influences' in a Working Paper titled 'Cold War — Outline Notes' prepared for a conference on Cold War Planning, Department of External Affairs, 20 December 1954, Series A7936/2, Item B/4/2 Part1, National Archives of Australia (NAA); J. Plimsoll to posts in Asia, 'Buddhism in Asia', 25 January 1955, Series A 1838/283, Item TS383/1/1/1 Part1, NAA; C.T. Moodie to Secretary, Department of External Affairs, 18 May 1955, 'Buddhism in Burma', Series A 1838/283, Item 563/10/2/ Part1, NAA.

44   For Australian responses to the Bandung conference see David Walker, 'Nervous Outsiders: Australia and the 1955 Asia–Africa Conference in Bandung', *Australian Historical Studies*, April 2005, forthcoming.

45   W.R. Crocker. *The Racial Factor in International Relations*. Canberra: Australian National University, 1956: 4.

46   Crocker. *The Racial Factor in International Relations*, 30.

47   Crocker. *The Racial Factor in International Relations*, 34.

Chapter Three

1   D. Campbell. *Writing Security: United States Foreign Policy and the Politics of Identity*. Minneapolis: University of Minnesota Press, 1992, especially 23–34 and 61–104.

2   The term 'orientalist' here is used with the meaning provided by Edward Said in his pioneering book, *Orientalism*,. It refers to the Western determination to define the Orient, and thereby extend control over the Orient, through labels and characteristics that were generally negative, and contrasted neatly with positive Western-Christian attributes. Said focused particularly on European imperialists and the Middle East.

3   M. Templeton. *Ties of Blood and Empire: New Zealand's Involvement in the Middle East Defence and the Suez Crisis 1947–57*. Auckland NZ: Auckland University Press, 1994.

4   See generally, R. Thompson. *Australian Imperialism in the Pacific: The Expansionist Era 1820–1920*. Melbourne: Melbourne University Press, 1980.

5   *Daily Telegraph* (Sydney), 7 January 1914, in G. Greenwood and Charles Grimshaw, eds. *Documents on Australian International Affairs 1901–1918*. West Melbourne: Nelson, 1977: 212.

6   See Chapter 2.

7   Shortly after the New South Wales offer to send a small force had been accepted, Victoria also offered a contingent, but this was declined by the British Government.

8   The best account is K.S. Inglis. *The Rehearsal: Australians at War in the Sudan 1885*. McMahons's Point: Rigby, 1985.

9   For a recent Australian account, see Les Carlyon. *Gallipoli*. Sydney: Macmillan, 2001, and for a British account, see Michael Hickey. *Gallipoli*. London: John Murray, 1995.

10 See Joan Beaumont. 'Australia's War.' In *Australia's War 1914–18*, edited by Joan Beaumont, 8–14. St Leonards: Allen & Unwin, 1995.

11 Beaumont, 'Australia's War,' 26–7.

12 Joan Beaumont. 'Europe and the Middle East.' In *Australia's War 1939–45*, edited by Joan Beaumont, 9–12. St Leonards: Allen and Unwin, 1996.

13 Beaumont, 'Europe and the Middle East,' 12–14.

14 For a sample of the respective positions see: Carl Bridge. 'Poland to Pearl Harbor.' In *Munich to Vietnam: Australia's Relations with Britain and the United States since the 1930*, edited by Carl Bridge, 38–51. Melbourne: Melbourne University Press, 1991: 38–51; and David Day. *The Politics of War*. Pymble: Harper Collins, 2003.

15 David Lowe. *Menzies and the 'Great World Struggle': Australia's Cold War, 1948–1954*. Kensington: UNSW Press, 1999: 29–30 and 43–4.

16 Brigadier Rourke's Notes of Council of Defence Meeting, CRS AA1971/216, Australian Archives, Canberra (AA).

17 Rourke, Notes of Council of Defence Meeting.

18 Rourke, Notes of Council of Defence Meeting, 80–99 and 128–51.

19 Rowell memo for McBride, 28 February 1952. 'Citizen Military Forces — Survey', CRS A5954 item 2291/4 (AA).

20 See Lowe, *Menzies and the 'Great World Struggle.'*

21 See Akira Iriye. 'The International Order.' In *The Columbia History of the Twentieth Century*, edited by Richard W. Bullit, 229–47. New York: Columbia University Press, 1998.

22 Inglis, *The Rehearsal.*

23 The first references were to the Little Boy *at* Manly, but Hopkins and other cartoonists increasingly came to prefer *of* Manly.

24 Inglis, *The Rehearsal*, 63–71, and Robert Crawford. 'A Slow Coming of Age: Advertising and the Little Boy from Manly in the Twentieth Century.' *Journal of Australian Studies*, March 2001: 126–43

25 Inglis, *The Rehearsal*, 157–63.

26 White, 'Sun, Sand and Syphilis,' 50.

27 White, 'Sun, Sand and Syphilis.'

28 C.E.W. Bean. *What to Know in Egypt: A Guide for Australian Soldiers*, 1915, extracted in *On the War-path: An Anthology of Australian Military Travel*, edited by Robin Gerster and Peter Pierce, 85–88. Melbourne: Melbourne University Press, 2004.

29 For published examples see, Hector Dinning. *By-Ways on Service: Notes from an Australian Journal*, 1918, in *On the War-Path*, 87–96; and Henry Gullett. *The Australian Imperial Force in Sinai and Palestine 1914–1918*, 1923, in *On the War-Path*, 100–102; and see also White, 'Sun, Sand and Syphilis,' 49–64.

30 White, 'Sun, Sand and Syphilis,' 61.

31 For further discussion see Joan Beaumont. 'The Anzac legend.' In Beaumont (ed.), *Australia's War 1914–1918*, 161–5.

32 Quoted in Robin Gerster. *Big-Noting: The Heroic Theme in Australian War Writing*. Melbourne: Melbourne University Press, 1987: 208.

33 Lawson Glassop. *We Were the Rats*. Sydney: Angus and Robertson, 1944: 127–32; and see David Walker. 'The Writer's War' in Beaumont, *Australia's War 1939–45*, 136–61.

34 W. J. Hudson. *Blind Loyalty: Australia and the Suez Crisis*. Melbourne: Melbourne University Press, 1989: 7.

35 Said, *Orientalism*, 31–42.

36 Menzies' trip diary, 1950, Menzies Papers, MS4936, Series 13, National Library of Australia.

37 According to Australian Ambassador in Washington, Percy Spender — quoted in Hudson, *Blind Loyalty*, 96.

38 For further discussion on this point, see Lowe, *Menzies and the 'Great World Struggle'*, 179–84.

39 J.D.B. Miller. 'Australasia and the world outside: foreign policies since world war II.' In *Tasman Relations: New Zealand and Australia, 1788–1988*, edited by Keith Sinclair, 183–201. Auckland: Auckland University Press, 1987: 192.

40 This is one of the main arguments in Lowe, *Menzies and the 'Great World Struggle.'*

Chapter Four

[1]   A. Shboul. 'Arabic-speaking Immigrants in Australia: Cultural Background, Image, Self-Image and Reality.' In *The Arabic Community Realities and Challenges: Seminar Proceedings NSW Arabic Welfare Inter-Agency*: 1985.

[2]   Australian Bureau of Statistics. *Australian Census 2001*. Canberra: ABS: 2001.

[3]   L. Foster and D. Stockley. *Multiculturalism: the Changing Australian Paradigm*. Clevedon, Avon, England: Multilingual Matters Ltd, 1984: 22.

[4]   J. Jupp. *Immigration*. Sydney: Sydney University Press, 1991: 46.

[5]   A.T. Yarwood. *Asian Migration to Australia: the background to exclusion, 1896–1923*. Melbourne: Melbourne University Press, 1964: 145.

[6]   A. Batrouney and T. Batrouney. *The Lebanese in Australia*. Melbourne: AE Press, 1985: 23–7.

[7]   L.E. Foster. *Diversity & Multicultural Education: A Sociological Perspective*. Sydney: Allen & Unwin, 1978: 6.

[8]   A. Jordens. *Redefining Australians: Immigration, Citizenship and National Identity*. Sydney: Hale and Iremonger Pty Ltd, 1995: 1.

[9]   J. Jupp. *Understanding Australian Multiculturalism*. Canberra: AGPS, 1996: 2.

[10] J. Goldlust. *Understanding Citizenship in Australia*. Canberra: AGPS, 1996: 18.

[11] Jupp, *Immigration*, 87.

[12] Goldlust, *Understanding Citizenship in Australia*, 18–19.

[13] Source: Australian Bureau of Statistics. *Australian Census 1996*. Canberra: ABS, 1996: Matrix Table CSO70.

[14] J. Jupp. *From White Australia to Woomera: The Story of Australian Immigration*. Port Melbourne, Victoria: Cambridge University Press: 2002.

[15] T. Batrouney. 'Australia's Immigration Policies: A Loss of Consensus.' *NIRA Review* (Winter 1998): 11–15: 13.

[16] Jupp, *From White Australia to Woomera*, 138–9.

[17] Jupp, *From White Australia to Woomera*, 150–1.

[18] Jupp, *From White Australia to Woomera*, 153.

[19] Jupp, *From White Australia to Woomera*, 159.

[20] Jupp, *From White Australia to Woomera*, 196.

Chapter Five

[1]   Zachariah Matthews. 'Origins of Islam in Australia.' Salam Magazine, July–August 1997; DFAT (Australian Department of Foreign Affairs and Trade). Australia Now: Islam in Australia. Canberra: Commonwealth of Australia, 2005; Ridwaan Jadwat. 'Islam — fastest growing faith in Australia.' Arab News, 27 October 2002; Abdullah Saeed. Muslim Australians — their beliefs, practices and institutions. Canberra: DIMIA (Department of Immigration and Multiculturalism and Indigenous Affairs), 2004.

[2]   Lyn Leader-Elliot and Iris Iwanicki. 'Heritage of the Birdsville and Strzelecki Tracks.' Department of Environment and Heritage, 2002: 52–5.

[3]   Abdullah Saeed. Islam in Australia. Sydney: Allen and Unwin, 2003: 5.

[4]   Christine Stevens. 'Afghan Camel Drivers: Founders of Islam in Australia.' In An Australian pilgrimage: Muslims in Australia from the seventeenth century to the present, edited by Mary Lucille Jones, 49–62. Melbourne:

    Victoria Press, 1993: 52

5   Stevens, 'Afghan Camel Drivers,' 49.

6   Saeed, Islam in Australia, 6.

7   Matthews, 'Origins of Islam in Australia.'

8   The White Australia policy was recognised to be racist — see James Jupp. Arrivals and Departures. Melbourne: Cheshire-Lansdowne, 1966: 23.

9   A.C. Palfreeman. The Administration of the White Australia Policy. Melbourne: Melbourne University Press, 1967: 1–3.

10   DIMIA. Abolition of the 'White Australia' Policy. Canberra: Commonwealth of Australia, 6 October 2004.

11   DIMIA, Abolition of the 'White Australia' Policy.

12   Christine Stevens. Tin Mosques and Ghantowns: A History of Afghan Camel drivers in Australia. Melbourne: Oxford University Press, 1989.

13   Stevens, Tin Mosques and Ghantowns, 150.

14   Stevens, 'Afghan Camel Drivers.' 62.

15   Great Southern Railway, 'The Ghan,' 2005. See http://www.theghan.com.au/ghan/index.htm

16   Islamic Community Council, 'Between the World Wars,' 2005. See http://www.icv.org.au

17   Saeed, Muslim Australians, 7.

18   DIMIA, Abolition of the 'White Australia' Policy.

19   Jupp, Arrivals and Departures, 15–16;

20   Saeed, Muslim Australians, 7.

21   Saeed, Islam in Australia, 1–12.

22   Helen Cattalini. 'Moving the Debate forward in Australia: Multiculturalism Post-Mabo.' From the 1995 Global Cultural Diversity Conference Proceedings, Sydney. Canberra: Department of Immigration and Multicultural and Indigenous Affairs, 1995.

23   Mary Crock.. *Immigration and refugee law in Australia.* Leichhardt, NSW: Federation Press, 1998: 33–4.

24   Saeed, Muslim Australians, 7; DIMIA, Abolition of the White Australia Policy.

25   DIMIA. Adult Migrant Education Program. Canberra: Commonwealth of Australia, 18 March 2005.

26   SBS (Special Broadcasting Service). Home Page, 2005. See http://www20.sbs.com.au

27   The Department of Immigration and Multicultural and Indigenous Affairs (DIMIA) is the latest official title for Commonwealth department(s) that deal with Immigration and Multicultural Affairs – Department of Immigration and Multicultural and Indigenous Affairs. Home Page, 2005. See http://www.dimia.gov.au

28   DIMIA, Abolition of the White Australia Policy.

29   Saeed, Islam in Australia, 12.

30   Saeed, Islam in Australia, iv–vii.

31   An example of the communal development was the establishment of a Muslim communal roof body — the Australian Federation of Islamic

Councils. For further information on this organization, see Australian Federation of Islamic Councils, About Us, 2005 at http://www.afic.com.au

32   State Islamic Councils exist across Australia, for examples, see Islamic Council of Victoria, 'About ICV, 2005 at http://www.icv.org.au/

33   An example of the development of community leading to the development of mosques in Australia can be seen with the Lakemba mosque which was established by Sunni Muslims from Lebanon, see Saeed, Islam in Australia, 8.

34   Australian Federation of Islamic Councils; Saeed, Muslim Australians, 55.

35   Islamic Council of Victoria, 'Activities.'

36   Islamic Council of Victoria.

37   Australian Federation of Islamic Councils, 'Home Page.'

38   Australian Federation of Islamic Councils, 'Current Activities.'

39   Saeed, Islam in Australia, 149–151.

40   Saeed, Muslim Australians.

41   Saeed, Islam in Australia, 149–156.

42   Pamela Bone. 'A new school of social division.' *The Age*. 13 December 1996: 15.

43   Bone. 'A new school of social division.'

44   Irene Donohoue Clyne. 'Those preaching tolerance failed to extend it religious schools.' *The Age*, 8 January 1997: 11.

45   Clyne, 'Those preaching tolerance failed.'

46   Saeed, Muslim Australians, 75–7.

47   Saeed, Islam in Australia, 134–6.

48   MCCA (Muslim Community Cooperative (Australia Ltd.). 2004. See 'The MCCA Story' and 'Company Profile' at http://www.mcca.com.au/

49   MCCA, 'Financial Report — Quarterly Update.'

50   *The Age*, 19 January 2000, 5.

51   Hallam is a suburb of Melbourne. *The Age*, 17 August 1999, 13.

52   *The Age*, 11 February 1998, 9.

53   *The Age*, 22 June 1996.

54   *The Age*, 11 March 1993.

55   *The Age*, 5 February 1991, 13.

56   *The Age*, 11 February 1998.

57   *The Age*, 13 August 1998, 13.

58   HREOC (Human Rights and Equal Opportunity Commission). 'National consultations on eliminating prejudice against Arab & Muslim Australians'. Newsletter No.6, October 2003.

Chapter Six

1   C. Hathaway. 'What's in a label?' *European Journal of Migration and Law*, 5: 1–21, 2003: 1.

2   C. Tazreiter. *Asylum Seekers and the State: The Politics of Protection in a Security Conscious World*. Hampshire, UK: Ashgate Publishing, 2004: 13.

3   C. Levy. 'The European Union after 9/11: The Demise of a Liberal Democratic Asylum Regime?' In *Government and Opposition*, Vol. 40 (1)

(2005): 26–59: 59.

4   See D. Marr and M. Wilkinson. *Dark Victory*. Sydney: Allen & Unwin, 2003, for a comprehensive discussion.

5   Prime Minister John Howard quoted in M. Leach. '"Disturbing Practices": Dehumanizing Asylum Seekers in the Refugee "Crisis" in Australia, 2001– 2002.' *Refuge,* Vol. 21, No. 3 (2003): 25–33: 26.

6   For a good outline of refugee policies, see M. Leach. and F. Mansouri. 'Critical perspectives on refugee policy in Australia.' An edited volume, Melbourne: Centre for Citizenship & Human Rights (CCHR) Deakin University, 2003.

7   J. Jupp. *From White Australia to Woomera: The Story of Australian Immigration.* Cambridge: Cambridge University Press, 2002: 183.

8   Jupp, *From White Australia to Woomera,* 182.

9   M. Gibney. *The Ethics and politics of Asylum: Liberal Democracy and the Response to Refugees.* Cambridge: Cambridge University Press, 2004: 176.

10   Klaus Neumann. *Refuge Australia: Australia's Humanitarian Record.* Sydney: UNSW Press, 2004 and Jupp, *From White Australia to Woomera,* 17.

11   Neuman, *Refuge Australia,* 32.

12   Dr Barry York. 'Australia and Refugees, 1901–2002: An Annotated Chronology Based on Official Sources.' Canberra: Parliamentary Library, Parliament of Australia, 2003: 15.

13   York, 'Australia and Refugees, 1901–2002,' 18.

14   York, 'Australia and Refugees, 1901–2002,' 20.

15   York, 'Australia and Refugees, 1901–2002,' 1–28.

16   Don McMaster. *Asylum Seekers: Australia's Response to Refugees.* Melbourne: Melbourne University Press, 2001: 6.

17   Robert Ray, Labor Immigration Minister, in York, 'Australia and Refugees, 1901–2002,' 40.

18   York, 'Australia and Refugees, 1901–2002,' 47.

19   P. Mares. *Borderline: Australia's Treatment of Refugees and Asylum Seekers.* Sydney: UNSW Press, 2001: 78.

20   M. Leach. Hansonism, Political Discourse and Australian Identity. In *The Rise and Fall of One Nation,* edited by M. Leach, G. Stokes and I. Ward, 42– 56. Queensland: Queensland University Press, 2000: 42.

21   A. Markus. *Race: John Howard and the Remaking of Australia.* Sydney: Allen & Unwin, 2001: 183–5.

22   Markus, *Race* , 183.

23   Leach, *Hansonism,* 43.

24   R. Manne, 'The Howard Years: A political interpretations', in R. Manned (ed) *The Hoard Years.* Melbourne: Black Inc, 2004: 14.

25   Leach *Hansonism,* 42.

26   R. Manne with David Corlett. 'Sending them home — refugees and the new politics of indifference.' *Quarterly Essay,* Issue 13 (2004): 31.

27   York, 'Australia and Refugees, 1901–2002,' 50–1.

28   York, 'Australia and Refugees, 1901–2002,' 51.

29   Refugee Council of Australia, Asylum Statistics accessed through website:

    http://www.refugeecouncil.org.au/html/facts_and_stats/stats.html
30 McMaster. *Asylum Seekers.*
31 See M. Leach and F. Mansouri. 'Lives in limbo: voices of refugees under temporary protection.' Sydney: University of New South Wales Press, 2004.
32 UNHCR (United Nations High Commission for Refugees). 1951 Convention Relating to the Status of Refugees. 28 July 1951: Article 31.
33 See F. Mansouri and M. Bagdas. *Politics of Social Exclusion: Refugees on Temporary Protection Visa in Victoria.* Geelong: Deakin University, 2002.
34 One Nation, 2002. *Immigration Policy,* 10 October 2003. http://vic.onenation.com.au/onenation3.1.htm [accessed July 2005]
35 'World Refugee Survey.' *United States Committee for Refugees.* (USCR) 2002: 110.
36 Tazreiter. *Asylum Seekers and the State,* 10.
37 M. Steketee. 'Door opens for 4000 Iraqis.' *The Weekend Australian,* 10 April 2004.
38 *The Age.* '9,500 Refugees can apply to stay.' *The Age,* 13 July 2004. Available from: http://theage.com.au/articles/2004/07/13/1089484342243.html [accessed 28 July 2004]
39 Personal communication with DIMIA staff October 2004.
40 Quoted in Arnold Zable. 'Prolonging the Agony.' *The Age,* 28 July 2004.
41 Senator Bob Brown, quoted in the *Herald Sun,* 'Refugee move met with cynicism.' 14 July 2004. Available from: http://heraldsun.news.com.au/printpage/0,5481,10133996,00.html [accessed 28 July 2004]
42 David Manne quoted in Zable, 'Prolonging the Agony.'
43 P. Mares. 'Quick fix better than nothing.' Melbourne: Institute for Social Research, Swinburne University of Technology, 16 July 2004.
44 A. Vanstone. 'Visas opportunities for TPV holders in Regional Australia.' Ministerial Press Release, 14 July 2004.
45 Zable, 'Prolonging the Agony.'
46 Mares, 'Quick fix better than nothing' and Zable, 'Prolonging the Agony.'
47 Zable, 'Prolonging the Agony.'
48 M. Phillips. 'Keep asylum seekers in Australia, pleads Iraq.' *The Advertiser* (Adelaide), 1 January 2004.
49 4269 TPVs have been issued to Iraqis since 1999, and as of 31 December 2003 there were 3346 Iraqis on TPVs in Australia, 923 less than the total number of visas issued since 1999.
50 Manne with Corlett, 'Sending them home,' 73.
51 DIMIA. *Iraqi Returnees.* Media Statement, 31 December 2003.
52 A. Vanstone. 'Decisions Handed Down on Nauru.' Ministerial Press Release, 2 December 2004.
53 UNCHR. *Iraq: security an issue for returnees too.* United Nations High Commissioner for Refugees. 2 April 2004.
54 M. Foucault. *The Archaeology of Knowledge.* London: Tavistock, 1977: 49.
55 C. Tazreiter. *Asylum seekers as Pariahs in the Australian State: Security Against the Few.* World Institute for Development Economics Research (WIDER),

Discussion Paper No.19 (2003): 01.

56 See Leach, M & Mansouri, 'Lives in limbo.'

57 As the former human rights commissioner Chris Sidoti noted, 'no other western country permits incommunicado detention of asylum-seekers.' See Chris Sidoti. *For those who come across the seas: The detention of unauthorised arrivals in Australia*. Canberra: HREOC, 1998: 224.

58 See, for example, Sharon Pickering. 'Common Sense and Original Deviancy: News Discourses and Asylum Seekers in Australia.' *Journal of Refugee Studies*, 14(2) (2001): 169–186.

59 For example, Australia has accepted only two UNHCR processed asylum seekers directly from Indonesia in recent years.

60 See Leach, 'Disturbing Practices,' 25–33.

61 Parliament of Australia: Hansard. 'Senate Select Committee on a Certain Maritime Incident.' 25 March 2002.

62 Matt Price, 'Strangling claims unsupported.' *The Australian*, 6 April 2002.

63 See, for example, Australian Broadcasting Commission. 'Woomera hunger strike continues as talks fail.' *ABC Online News,* 25 January 2002.

64 See A. Tay and Sev Ozdowski. 'Media Statement by President Professor Alice Tay AM and Dr Sev Ozdowski, Human Rights Commissioner.' *Human Rights and Equal Opportunity Commission*, 6 February 2002.

65 Andrew West. 'This isn't a camp, its an oven and we are burning.' *Sun Herald*, 17 February 2002. The United Nations Association of Australia argued that the government should apologise to asylum seekers wrongly accused of child neglect. See United Nations Association of Australia. *Unity*, 288 (22 February 2002).

66 Howard quoted in Leach, 'Disturbing Practices,' 26.

67 Leach, 'Disturbing Practices,' 27.

68 See Leach, 'Disturbing Practices.'

69 See Howard quoted in Hanifa Deen. *Caravanserai: Journey Among Australian Muslims*. Fremantle: Fremantle Arts Centre Press, 2003: 286.

70 Deen, *Caravanserai*, 285.

71 See Leach, 'Disturbing Practices,' 29.

72 G. Hage. 'Postscript: Arab-Australian belonging after September 11.' In *Arab-Australians Today: Citizenship and Belonging*, edited by G. Hage, 241–8. Melbourne: Melbourne University Press, 2002: 242.

73 Sharon Pickering. 'The Hard Press of Asylum.' *Forced Migration Review*, Issue 8 (August 2000): 33.

74 C. Sidoti. 'A nation of Thugs.' University of Sydney Seminar, 27 September 2001. Paper available through the website: http://www.hrca.org.au/nation%20of%20thugs.htm

75 K. Suter. 'Australia and asylum seekers.' *Contemporary Review*, Vol.279 Issue 630 (November 2001).

76 Refugee Review Tribunal, *Cases Finalised by Country in 2004/05*. See http://www.rrt.gov.au/ (accessed 23 June 2005]

77 A. Markus. 'Racism and refugees: an Australian tradition'. *Australian Rationalist*, Numbers 60/61 (2002): 16–22.

78   W. Maley quoted in Gibney, *The Ethics and Politics of Asylum*, 191.
79   Gibney, *The Ethics and Politics of Asylum*, 193.
80   Manne with Corlett, 'Sending them home.'
81   Gibney, *The Ethics and Politics of Asylum*, 54.
82   B. Sutcliffe. 'Crossing Borders in the New Imperialism.' In *The New Imperial Challenge — Socialist Register 2004*, edited by L. Panitch and S. Leys. London: Merlin Press, 2003: 277.
83   Gibney, *The Ethics and Politics of Asylum*, 51.

Chapter Seven

1   Clifford Geertz. *The Religion of Java*. New York: Free Press, 1960.
2   B. J. Boland *The Struggle of Islam in Modern Indonesia*. The Hague: Martinus Nijhoff, 1971.
3   For a thoughtful reflection on uncertainties about the real nature of al-Qaeda see Jason Burke. *Al-Qaeda: Casting a Shadow of Terror*. London: I.B. Tauris, 2003.
4   Iman Feisal Abdul Rauf. *What is right with Islam: a new vision for Muslims and the West*. San Francisco: Harper Collins, 2004.
5   Thomas L. Friedman. *Longitudes and Attitudes*. New York: Anchor Books, 2003.
6   John L. Esposito. *Unholy War: Terror in the Name of Islam*. New York: Oxford University Press, 2002.
7   Burke, *Al-Qaeda*; Malise Ruthven. *A Fury for God: The Islamist Attack on America*. London and New York: Granta Books, 2002.
8   Burke, *Al Qaeda*; Maria Ressa. *Seeds of Terror: An Eyewitness Account of al-Qaeda's Newest Center of Operations in Southeast Asia*, New York: Free Press, 2003.
9   Burke, *Al-Qaeda*; Ruthven, *A Fury for God*.
10 Pew Charitable Trust. The Pew Global Attitudes Project: Views of a Changing World 2003 (The full report is at: http://people-press.org/reports/pdf/185.pdf); Friedman, *Longitudes and Attitudes*; Gilles Kepel, translated by Pascale Ghazaleh. *The War for Muslim Minds: Islam and the West*. Cambridge, Mass.: The Belknap Press of Harvard University Press, 2004.
11 John L. Esposito. *The Islamic Threat: Myth or Reality?* New York: Oxford University Press, 1992; Gilles Kepel. translated by Anthony F. Roberts. *Jihad: The Trail of Political Islam*. Cambridge: The Belknap Press of Harvard University Press, 2002.
12 Robert W. Hefner. *Civil Islam: Muslims and Democratization in Indonesia*. Princeton: Princeton University Press, 2000; Kepel, *The War for Muslim Minds*; Olivier Roy. *Globalised Islam*. London: Hurst & Company, 2004; Emmanuel Sivan. *Radical Islam: Medieval Theology and Modern Politics* (enlarged edition) New Haven: Yale University Press, 1990.
13 Burke, *Al-Qaeda*; William Maley ed. *Fundamentalism Reborn? Afghanistan and the Taliban*. New York: New York University Press, 2001; Ahmed Rashid. *Taliban*. London: I.B. Tauris, 2001; Olivier Roy and Mariam Abou Zahab.

Islamist Networks: the Pakistan-Afghan Connection. New York: Columbia University Press, 2004.

14 Mark Juergensmeyer. *The New Cold War? Religious Nationalism Confronts the Secular State*. Berkeley: University of California Press, 1994.

15 Francis Fukuyama. *The End of History and the Last Man*. New York: Maxwell Macmillan International, 1992.

16 Rashid, *Taliban*; Roy and Abou Zahab, *Islamist Networks*.

17 Burke, *Al-Qaeda*; Rashid, *Taliban*.

18 Paul Berman. *Terror and Liberalism*. New York: W. W. Norton & Company, 2002; Ahmed Rashid. *Jihad: The Rise of Militant Islam in Central Asia*. New York: Penguin, 2003.

19 Roy, *Globalised Islam*; Giora Eliraz. *Islam in Indonesia: Modernism, Radicalism, and the Middle East Dimension*. Brighton: Sussex Academic Press, 2004.

20 Jessica Stern. *Terror in the Name of God: Why Religious Militants Kill*. New York: Harper Collins, 2003.

21 Eliraz, *Islam in Indonesia*; ICG (International Crisis Group). *Indonesia Backgrounder: Why Salafism and Terrorism Mostly Don't Mix*. Asia Report No.83, 13 September 2004.

22 Greg Barton. *Indonesia's Struggle: Jemaah Islamiah and radical Islamism*. Sydney and Singapore: UNSW Press and NUS Press, 2004; ICG. *Understanding Islamism*. Middle East/North Africa Report No.37, 2 March 2005; William Shepard. 'The Diversity of Islamic Thought in the 20th Century: Towards a Typology.' In *Islamic Thought in the Twentieth Century* edited by Suha Taji-Farouki and Basheer Nafi, London: I.B. Tauris, 2004.

23 Malise Ruthven. *Islam in the World* (2nd edition). New York: Oxford University Press, 2000.

24 Ibrahim Abu-Rabi'. *Intellectual Origins of Islamic Resurgence in the Modern Arab World*. Albany: State University of New York Press, 1995; Berman, *Terror and Liberalism*; Caryle Murphy. *Passion for Islam: Shaping the Modern Middle East — the Egyptian Experience*. New York: Scribner, 2002; William E. Shepard. 'Sayyid Qutb's Doctrine of *Jahiliyya*.' International Journal of Middle East Studies, 35(4) (November 2003): 521–45.

25 Ziauddin Sardar. *Desperately Seeking Paradise: Journeys of a Sceptical Muslim*. London: Granta Books, 2004.

26 Robert W. Hefner. 'Shariah Formalism or Democratic Communitarianism? The Islamic Resurgence and Political Theory.' In *Democracy and Communitarianism in Asia*, edited by Chua Beng-Huat, 122–47. London and New York: Routledge Curzon, 2004.

27 Bassam Tibi. *Islam and the Cultural Accommodation of Social Change*. Boulder, Colorado: West, 1991.

28 Laura Guazzone, ed. *The Islamist dilemma : the political role of Islamist movements in the contemporary Arab world*. Reading, Berkshire: Ithaca Press, 1995.

29 M. Hakan Yavuz. *Islamic Political Identity in Turkey*. London: Oxford University Press, 2003.

30 Greg Barton. 'Islam and Politics in Malaysia.' In *Islam in Asia: Changing Political Realities*, edited by Jason F. Issacson and Colin Rubenstein, 95–164.

New Jersey: Transaction Press, 2002; Hefner, 'Shariah Formalism or Democratic Communitarianism?'; Robert W. Hefner and Patricia Horvatich, eds. *Islam in an Era of Nation States: Politics and Religious Revival in Muslim Southeast Asia*. Honolulu: University of Hawai'i Press, 1997.

31 Greg Barton. 'Islam and Democratic Transition in Indonesia.' In *Religious Organizations and Democracy in Contemporary Asia*, edited by Deborah A. Brown and Tun-jen Cheng. New York: M. E. Sharpe, 2005.

32 Barton, 'Islam and Democratic Transition in Indonesia'; Greg Fealy. 'Islamic Politics: A Rising or Declining Force?' In *Indonesia: The Uncertain Transition*, edited by Damien Kingsbury and Arief Budiman, 119–136. Adelaide: Crawford House, 2001.

33 Barton: *Indonesia's Struggle*; and 'Making sense of Jemaah Islamiyah terrorism and radical Islamism in Indonesia.' In *Islam and the West Reflections from Australia*, edited by Shahram Akbarzadeh and Samina Yasmeen, 114–31. Sydney: UNSW Press, 2005; Robert W. Hefner. 'Civil Islam and Political Violence in Indonesia.' *Congress Monthly* 70:6 (November–December 2003): 3–5; ICG. *Al-Qaeda in Southeast Asia: The case of the 'Ngruki Network' in Indonesia*. (Corrected on 10 January 2003), Asia Briefing No.20, 8 August 2002; ICG. *Impact Of The Bali Bombings*. Asia Briefing No.23, 24 October 2002; ICG. *Indonesia Backgrounder: How The Jemaah Islamiyah Terrorist Network Operates*. Asia Report No.43, 11 December 2002'; and ICG. *Jemaah Islamiyah in South East Asia: Damaged but Still Dangerous*. Asia Report No.63, 26 August 2003.

34 ICG: *Indonesia Backgrounder: Jihad in Central Sulawesi*. Asia Report No.74, 3 February 2004; and *Recycling Militants in Indonesia: Darul Islam and the Australian Embassy Bombing*. Asia Report No.92, 22 February 2005.

35 Barton, *Indonesia's Struggle*; ICG: *Impact Of The Bali Bombings*; and *Indonesia Backgrounder: How The Jemaah Islamiyah Terrorist Network Operates*.

36 ICG: *Indonesia Backgrounder: How The Jemaah Islamiyah Terrorist Network Operates*; *Jemaah Islamiyah in South East Asia*; and *Recycling Militants in Indonesia*.

37 Martin van Bruinessen. 'Genealogies of Islamic Radicalism in Indonesia.' South East Asia Research, 10(2) (2002) 117–54: 53.

38 Robert W. Hefner. 'Civic Pluralism Denied? The New Media and Jihadi Violence in Indonesia.' In *New Media in the Muslim World: The Emerging Public Sphere*, edited by Dale F. Eickelman and Jon W. Anderson, 158–179. Bloomington: Indiana University, 2003.

Chapter Eight

1 John Howard, 23 October 2001, interview on Perth's Radio 6PR. http://www.pm.gov.au/news/interviews/2001/interview1413.htm

2 John Howard, 9 April 2003, address to Queensland press forum. http://www.pm.gov.au/news/speeches/speech87.html

3 Bill Clinton, *My Life*, London: Hutchinson, 2004, 924.

4 John Howard, 4 February 2003, Ministerial Statement to Parliament on Iraq. http://www.pm.gov.au/news/speeches/speech69.html Almost identical words were used in a speech to the National Press Club on 14 March 2003.

http://www.pm.gov.au/news/speeches/speech74.html
5 John Howard, 2 May 2000, press conference in Jerusalem.
   http://www.pm.gov.au/news/speeches/2000/jerusalem0205.htm
6 John Howard, 23 October 2001, interview on Perth's Radio 6PR.
   http://www.pm.gov.au/news/speeches/2000/jerusalem0205.htm
7 John Howard, 1 July 2003, address to the Sydney Institute.
   http://www.pm.gov.au/news/speeches/speech323.html
8 John Howard, 11 September 2003, interview on Sydney's Radio 2UE.
   http://www.pm.gov.au/news/interviews/Interview480.html
9 A comparative content analysis of US and subsequent Australian
   Government press releases and announcements following each Palestinian
   attack since 2001 would reveal a similarity of language bordering on
   plagiarism.
10 Alexander Downer, 23 March 2004, interview on Perth's Radio 6PR.
   http://www.foreignminister.gov.au/transcripts/2004/040323_6pr_perth.ht
   ml
11 John Howard, 23 October 2001, interview on Perth's Radio 6PR.
   http://www.pm.gov.au/news/interviews/2001/interview1413.htm; John
   Howard, 31 March 2002, press conference.
   http://www.pm.gov.au/news/interviews/2002/interview1576.htm; John
   Howard, 1 September, 2002, interview in Melbourne ABC Radio 774.
   http://www.pm.gov.au/news/interviews/2002/interview1810.htm; John
   Howard, 4 February 2003, Ministerial Statement to Parliament on Iraq.
   http://www.pm.gov.au/news/speeches/speech69.html
12 Greg Sheridan, 'Peace not included in Arafat's plans' and Dennis Ross, *The
   Missing Peace*. Curiously in an article published the previous day, Sheridan
   quotes Ross claiming the Israelis offered the Palestinians an even greater
   share of their territory — '97 per cent of the West Bank...' See Sheridan,
   'Powerful symbol but weak leader.'
13 Clinton, *My Life*, 915 and 936–7. Like Ross, Clinton is remarkably unspecific
   about what Arafat was effectively conceding later at Taba, 944.
14 Roane Carey, ed. *The New Intifada*. London: Verso, 2001, 36.
15 David Hirst. *The Gun and the Olive Branch: The Roots of Violence in the Middle
   East*. New York, Thunder Mouth Press/Nation Books, 2003, 24–5. The
   foreword to this (third) edition is a brilliant survey of the Palestinian–Israeli
   dispute since the 9/11 attacks. See also Noam Chomsky. *Middle East Illusions*.
   Lanham: Rowman & Littlefield, 2003.
16 Robert Fisk. 'Fear and Learning in America.' *The Independent*, 17 April 2002,
   25.
17 Noam Chomsky. 'Foreign Policy: Arafat' *Z Magazine*, Volume 17, Number
   12, December 2004, 37.
18 Tanya Reinhart. *Israel/Palestine*. Crows Nest: Allen & Unwin, 2003, 21–60.
19 Alexander Downer, 5 July 2004, interview ITN.
   http://www.foreignminister.gov.au/transcripts/2004/040705_itn.html
20 Alexander Downer, 13 April 2004, National Press Club.
   http://www.foreignminister.gov.au/speeches/2004/040413_global_terroris

m.html
21 John Howard, 7 April 2002, press conference.
    http://www.pm.gov.au/news/interviews/2002/interview1589.htm
22 John Howard, 12 November 2004, media release.
    http://www.pm.gov.au/news/media_releases/media_Release1145.html
23 Alexander Downer, 7 November 2004, ABC News online.
    http://www.abc.net.au/news

Chapter Nine

1   Peter Londey. *Other People's Wars: A History of Australian Peacekeeping.* Sydney: Allen & Unwin, 2004: 108–116.
2   Gareth Evans and Bruce Grant. *Australia's Foreign Relations in the World of the 1990s.* Melbourne: Melbourne University Press, 1992: 40–1.
3   Coral Bell. *Dependent Ally: A Study in Australian Foreign Policy.* Melbourne: Oxford University Press, 1988.
4   Margaret MacMillan. *Peacemakers: The Paris Conference of 1919 and Its Attempt to End War.* London: John Murray, 2001: 52.
5   Kosmas Tsokhas. Markets, Money and Empire: The Political Economy of the Australian Wool Industry. Melbourne: Melbourne University Press, 1990.
6   Philip Ayres. *Owen Dixon.* Melbourne: Miegunyah Press, 2003.
7   J.G. Starke. *The ANZUS Treaty Alliance.* Melbourne: Melbourne University Press, 1965.
8   See Garry Woodard. *Asian Alternatives: Australia's Vietnam Decision and Lessons on Going to War.* Melbourne: Melbourne University Press, 2004: 290–2.
9   Alan Renouf. *Malcolm Fraser and Australian Foreign Policy.* Sydney: Australian Professional Publications, 1986: 157.
10 See William Maley. 'The Gulf and the Australian Peace Movement.' *Quadrant*, Vol.35 No.10 (1991): 41–4.
11 Stewart Firth. *Australia in International Politics: An Introduction to Australian Foreign Policy.* Sydney: Allen & Unwin, 1999: 41.
12 William Maley. 'Australia and the East Timor Crisis: Some Critical Comments.' *Australian Journal of International Affairs*, Vol.54 No.2 (2000): 151–61.
13 Owen Harries. *Benign or Imperial? Reflections on American Hegemony.* Sydney: ABC Books: 2004.
14 Stefan Halper and Jonathan Clarke. *America Alone: The Neo-Conservatives and the Global Order.* Cambridge: Cambridge University Press, 2004: 134–5.
15 See Peter L. Bergen Holy War, Inc.: Inside the Secret World of Osama Bin Laden. New York: The Free Press, 2001; Steve Coll. *Ghost Wars: The Secret History of the CIA, Afghanistan, and Bin Laden, From the Soviet Invasion to September 10, 2001.* New York: The Penguin Press, 2004; Jonathan Randal. *Osama: The Making of a Terrorist.* New York: Alfred A. Knopf, 2004.
16 Richard A. Clarke. *Against All Enemies: Inside America's War on Terror.* New York: The Free Press, 2004.
17 William Maley. *The Foreign Policy of the Taliban.* New York: Council on

Foreign Relations, 2000: 13–14.

18 Rupert Colville. 'One Massacre That Didn't Grab the World's Attention.' *International Herald Tribune*, 7 August 1999.

19 William Maley. 'Security, People-Smuggling and Australia's New Afghan Refugees.' *Australian Journal of International Affairs*, Vol.55 No.3 (2001): 351–70.

20 Robert Garran. *True Believer: John Howard, George Bush & the American alliance.* Sydney: Allen & Unwin, 2004: 68–9.

21 Alan Sipress. 'Peacekeepers Won't Go Beyond Kabul, Cheney Says.' *The Washington Post*, 20 March 2002.

22 William Maley. 'Confronting Creeping Invasions: Afghanistan, the UN and the World Community.' In *The Afghanistan Crisis: Issues and Perspectives*, edited by K. Warikoo, 256–274. New Delhi: Bhavana Books, 2002: 256–74.

23 Rüdiger Wolfrum and Christiane E. Philipp. 'The Status of the Taliban: Their Obligations and Rights under International Law.' *Max Planck Yearbook of United Nations Law*. The Hague: Kluwer Law International, Vol.VI (2002): 559–97.

24 Gerry Simpson. Great Powers and Outlaw States: Unequal Sovereigns in the International Legal Order. Cambridge: Cambridge University Press, 2004: 334.

25 William Maley. *The Afghanistan Wars*. London: Palgrave Macmillan, 2002: 240–3.

26 William Maley. 'State-Building and Political Development in Afghanistan.' In *Between Knowledge and Commitment: Post-Conflict Peace-Building and Reconstruction in Regional Contexts*, edited by Masako Ishii and Jacqueline A. Siapno, 165–83. (Osaka: JCAS Symposium Series 21, The Japan Center for Area Studies, National Museum of Ethnology, 2004.

27 Barnett R. Rubin. *Road to Ruin: Afghanistan's Booming Opium Industry*. Washington DC: Center for American Progress; and New York: Center on International Cooperation, New York University, 2004; Matt Weiner. *An Afghan 'Narco-State'? Dynamics, Assessment and Security Implications of the Afghan Opium Industry*. Canberra: Canberra Papers on Strategy & Defence no.158, Strategic and Defence Studies Centre, The Australian National University, 2004.

28 See Madeleine Albright and Robin Cook. 'The world needs to step it up in Afghanistan,' *International Herald Tribune*, 5 October 2004; William Maley. 'Political Transition in Afghanistan: The State, Religion and Civil Society.' In *Political Transition in Afghanistan: The State, Islam and Civil Society*, 9–14. Washington DC: Asia Program Special Report no.122, Woodrow Wilson International Centre for Scholars, 2004; United States General Accounting Office. *Afghanistan Reconstruction: Deteriorating Security and Limited Resources Have Impeded Progress; Improvements in US Strategy Needed*. Washington DC: United States General Accounting Office, 2004.

29 Khalil, Samir al-. *Republic of Fear: The Inside Story of Saddam's Iraq*. Berkeley & Los Angeles: University of California Press, 1989.

30 Clarke, *Against All Enemies*, 41–2.

31   For example Daniel Pipes and Laurie Mylroie. 'Back Iraq.' *The New Republic*, Vol.196 No.17 (1987): 14–15.

32   Lawrence Freedman and Efraim Karsh. *The Gulf Conflict 1990–1991: Diplomacy and War in the New World Order*. London: Faber & Faber, 1993.

33   John J. Mearsheimer and Stephen M. Walt. 'An Unnecessary War.' *Foreign Policy* 134 (2003): 50–9.

34   See Hans Blix. Disarming Iraq: The Search for Weapons of Mass Destruction. London: Bloomsbury, 2004.

35   Philip H. Gordon and Jeremy Shapiro. *Allies at War: America, Europe and the Crisis over Iraq*. New York: McGraw-Hill, 2004.

36   Mann, James. *Rise of the Vulcans: The History of Bush's War Cabinet*. New York: Viking, 2004; Bob Woodward. *Plan of Attack*. New York: Simon & Schuster, 2004.

37   Olivier Roy. 'Europe Won't Be Fooled Again.' *The New York Times*, 13 May 2003.

38   Parliamentary Joint Committee on ASIO, ASIS, and DSD. *Intelligence on Iraq's weapons of mass destruction*. Canberra: The Parliament of the Commonwealth of Australia, 2003.

39   Parliamentary Joint Committee, *Intelligence on Iraq's weapons of mass destruction*, 97.

40   See William Maley. 'Tough words, limited action on terrorism.' *The Sydney Morning Herald*, 15 July 2004.

41   William H. Taft IV and Todd F. Buchwald. 'Preemption, Iraq and International Law.' *American Journal of International Law*, Vol.97 No.3 (2003): 557–63.

42   Danesh Sarooshi. The United Nations and the Development of Collective Security: The Delegation by the UN Security Council of its Chapter VII Powers, 178–185. Oxford: Oxford University Press, 1999; Simon Chesterman. *Just War or Just Peace? Humanitarian Intervention and International Law*. Oxford: Oxford University Press, 2001: 201–203; John F. Murphy. *The United States and the Rule of Law in International Affairs*. Cambridge: Cambridge University Press, 2004: 169–72.

43   Joseph Cirincione, Jessica Tuchman Mathews and George Perkovich. *WMD in Iraq: Evidence and Implications*. Washington DC: Carnegie Endowment for International Peace, 2004.

44   David Rieff. 'Blueprint for a Mess.' *The New York Times*, 2 November 2003.

45   Jeffrey Record. *Dark Victory: America's Second War against Iraq*. Annapolis: Naval Institute Press, 2004: 139.

46   International Crisis Group. *Iraq's Transition: On a Knife Edge*. Baghdad and Brussels: ICG Middle East Report No.27, International Crisis Group, 2004.

47   Human Rights Watch. *The Road to Abu Ghraib*. New York: Human Rights Watch, 2004; Mark Danner. *Torture and Truth: America, Abu Ghraib, and the War on Terror*. New York: New York Review Books, 2004.

48   Gertrude Himmelfarb. On Looking into the Abyss: Untimely Thoughts on Culture and Society. New York: Vintage Books, 1994: 107–21.

49   Mark Danner. 'Iraq: The Real Election.' *New York Review of Books*, 28 April

2005.

50 Les Roberts, Riyadh Lafta, Richard Garfield, Jamal Khudhairi, and Gilbert Burnham. 'Mortality before and after the 2003 invasion of Iraq: cluster sample survey.' *The Lancet,* 29 October 2004.

51 Christian Reus-Smit. *American Power and World Order.* Cambridge: Polity Press, 2004: 149.

52 Capling, Ann. All the Way with the USA: Australia, the US and Free Trade. Sydney, UNSW Press, 2005: 57.

53 Forbes, Mark. 'US has changed the world order: strategist.' *The Age,* 13 March 2003.

54 See Joseph S. Nye Jr. *Soft Power: The Means to Success in World Politics.* New York: Public Affairs, 2004.

55 Harries, *Benign or Imperial?* 90.

56 See Task Force on Strategic Communication. *Report of the Defense Science Board Task Force on Strategic Communication.* Washington DC: Office of the Under Secretary of Defense for Acquisition, Technology, and Logistics, 2004.

57 William Maley. 'There are risks in the company we keep.' *The Canberra Times,* 19 March 2004.

58 David Halberstam. *The Making of a Quagmire.* New York: Random House, 1965; Townsend Hoopes. *The Limits of Intervention.* New York: David Mackay, 1969; Bernard Brodie. *War and Politics.* New York: Macmillan, 1973: 157–222; Martin van Creveld. 'The Blemish of Conquest'. *Boston Review,* Vol.30 No.1 (February–March 2005).

Chapter Ten

1 For this examination, we shall focus on Morocco, Algeria, Tunisia and Libya as members of the 'Arab Maghrib Union' (AMU). Mauritania is also a member of the AMU, however, is not included here due to the negligible contact between Australia and the West African state. The trends highlighted in relation to the four core countries of this analysis can be extended to Mauritania. Also, Egypt is not included in our outline of North Africa as it is dealt with elsewhere in this volume. Geographically, Egypt is part of North Africa, however, politically it considers itself part of the 'core' of the Arab World and separate from the Maghrib states.

2 See: DFAT (Department of Foreign Affairs and Trade). 'Accessing Middle East Growth: Business Opportunities in the Arabian Peninsula and Iran.' Canberra: Commonwealth of Australia, 2000; Joint Standing Committee on Foreign Affairs, Defence and Trade. Australia's Relations with the Middle East. Canberra: Commonwealth of Australia, 2001 and DFAT. 'Advancing the National Interest: Australia's Foreign and Trade Policy White Paper,.' 2003.

3 For an outline of this, see DFAT. *In the National Interest.* Canberra: Commonwealth of Australia, 1997 and DFAT, 'Advancing the National Interest.'

4 Rawdon Dalrymple. *Looking for Theory in Australian Foreign Policy,* Symposium: Advancing the National Interest? 28 April 2003 *Australian Review of Public*

Affairs.

5   Both Howard Government foreign policy White Papers, in 1997 and 2003, are driven by this theme of only acting what is in the 'national interest.'

6   Samuel Huntington. 'The Clash of Civilizations?' *Foreign Affairs*, **72**:1, 1993: 22–49.

7   Huntington. 'The Clash of Civilizations?' 24

8   DFAT, 'Advancing the National Interest,' x–xiii.

9   For an overview of human needs theory, see: John Burton, ed. *Conflict: Human Needs Theory.* London: Macmillan, 1990.

10   DFAT, 'Advancing the National Interest,' vii.

11   DFAT, 'Advancing the National Interest,' xiii–xiv and 7.

12   DFAT, 'Advancing the National Interest,' 5.

13   The 'eastern' Arab states is in reference to those states east of (and including) Egypt (Yemen, Oman, Saudi Arabia, the UAE, Qatar, Bahrain, Kuwait, Jordan, Iraq, Syria, and Lebanon).

14   Gareth Evans and Bruce Grant. *Australia's Foreign Relations: in the World of the 1990s.* Melbourne: Melbourne University Press, 1995: 285.

15   DFAT, 'Advancing the National Interest,' 114.

16   Tom Allard. 'You're against us, Arab leaders tell Australia.' *Sydney Morning Herald*, 31 July 2004.

17   United Nations, Press Release GA/10248, 20 July 2004. http://www.un.org/News/Press/docs/2004/ga10248.doc.htm

18   DFAT, 'Advancing the National Interest,' xviii.

19   Figures sourced from DFAT. These trade figures mirror those to the eastern Arab states where Australia is far more dependant on exports to the Middle East than vice-versa. See: DFAT, 'Accessing Middle East Growth.'

20   Exports to Tunisia in 2003 were AUD $5 million, AUD $7 million to Morocco, and AUD $9 million to Libya.

21   The import of fertiliser products from Morocco are predominantly sourced from the Western Sahara. The contested status of the Western Sahara and Moroccan authority there makes this export product (a significant one for the Moroccan economy) tenuous.

22   Moroccan exports were AUD $29 million in 2003, AUD $5 million from Tunisia, whilst no exports to Australia were recorded from either Algeria or Libya. Libya was under a UN sanction regime in relation to its alleged participation in the 1988 Lockerbie bombing. The Libyan Government's compensation to victims of the bombing led to the lifting of UN sanctions in September, 2003. This, combined with substantial trade missions from Australian business and government officials in 2003, looks set to promote a growing relationship between Australia and Libya.

23   Karim Nashashibi. *Algeria: Stabilisation and Transition to the Market.* Washington D.C.: International Monetary Fund, 1998.

24   The ROD Integrated Development project is scheduled for completion in late 2004. See: BHP–Billiton. *The ROD Integrated Development Project — Algeria.* Briefing Paper, June 2000.

25   BHP–Billiton holds a 45 per cent stake in the Ohanet project whilst

Woodside holds a 15 per cent stake. See: BHP–Billion. *The Ohanet Development — Algeria*, October 2003.

26 DFAT. *Constructive Engagement on Two Fronts*. Media Release by Trade Minister Mark Vaile, 23 May 2003.

27 Saudi Arabia, Oman, the UAE, Qatar, and Bahrain specifically.

28 DFAT, 'Accessing Middle East Growth,' 25.

29 Trade between Australia and the Gulf economies has grown at an average of 11 per cent per-annum since 1990 whilst it has fallen dramatically in the same time between Australia and North Africa. For instance, exports to Morocco have fallen from nearly AUD $50 million to under AUD $10 million between 1998 and 2003. See DFAT, 'Accessing Middle East Growth.'

30 The United Nations Population Fund highlights the four Arab North African states as having some of the highest population growth rates globally (Algeria at 1.82 per cent, Libya at 2.1 per cent, Morocco at 1.87 per cent and Tunisia at 1.12 per cent). See: http://www.unfpa.org/profile. For information on North African trade liberalisation, see Nashashibi, *Algeria*.

31 For an analysis of the economic downturn in Algeria and the political consequences of this, see Pradeep Chhibber. 'State Policy, Rent Seeking, and the Electoral Success of a Religious Party in Algeria.' *Journal of Politics*, 58:1, 1996: 126–149. The impacts of such forces in Algeria are more pronounced that in the other North African states, however, there are similar trends, particularly in Morocco and Tunisia.

32 DFAT, 'Advancing the National Interest,' 114.

33 Evans and Grant, *Australia's Foreign Relations: in the World of the 1990s*, 282. For a detailed discussion of Australian military involvement in the Middle East, see Chapters 3 and 10 in this volume.

34 All trade figures sourced from DFAT, Commonwealth of Australia, Canberra — http://www.dfat.gov.au

35 DFAT, 'Advancing the National Interest,' 114.

36 The conflict in Algeria broke out in 1992 after the cancellation of the second round of national parliamentary elections in which the Islamist *Front Islamique du Salut* (FIS) were poised to win. Whilst there has been a notable abating of the violence in Algeria, there is still no formal end to the conflict as well as a lack of a mechanism for the re-integration of those groups alienated during the conflict back into Algerian political life. External parties have been reticent to pressure the Algerian regime to pursue this, particularly in the political atmosphere post–11 September where the Algerian Government has been able to operate under the rubric of the 'War on Terrorism' in its continued suppression of Islamist groups. This is a counter-productive stance as the government, with external support, is able to exclude these groups from the political life of the country.

37 Political pluralism, to some extent, does exist in Algeria. Alongside the *Front de Liberation Nationale* (FLN), the party of revolution against the French, multiple parties constitute the Algerian political scene, including the Trotskyist *Parti du Travailleurs* (PT), the socialist *Front des Forces Socialistes*

(FFS), the Islamist *an-Nahda*, as well as a variety of other groups. In Morocco, the Islamist Justice and Development Party and the Socialist Union of Popular Forces operate alongside a variety of smaller groups. In Tunisia, the ruling Democratic Constitutional Rally dominates the political scene, however, other groups, mostly moderate leftist, liberal, or Islamist, also operate. In Libya, there are no legal political parties due to the political structure of the Government of the Socialist People's Libyan Arab Jamahiriya.

[38]   DFAT, 'Advancing the National Interest,' 115.

[39]   These figures represent migration not only from Morocco, Algeria, Tunisia, and Libya but also from Sudan, Mauritania, Djibouti, and Western Sahara. One may speculate that even within this modest figure, a large proportion would be constituted by Sudanese migrants and refugees. See: Human Rights and Equal Opportunities Commission.
http://www.hreoc.gov.au/racial_discrimination/isma/consultations/

[40]   DFAT, 'Accessing Middle East Growth,' 74.

[41]   The announcement of the opening of an Australian embassy in Libya came in May 2004. The embassy is to be headed by an Australian Trade Commissioner and focus on the establishment of a trade-based relationship between Australia and Libya. The announcement was based on talks between Australian Trade Minister Mark Vaile and the Libyan Government held in 2002 with follow-up talks held in early 2004. See DFAT. *Australia to Open Diplomatic Mission in Libya.* Joint Media Release, Minister for Foreign Affairs Alexander Downer and Minister for Trade Mark Vaile, 21 May, 2004.
http:/www.foreignminister.gov.au/releases/2004/joint_open_libya_mission.html

[42]   For instance, see Mohammed Ayoob. *The Third World Security Predicament: State Making, Regional Conflict, and the International System.* Boulder: Lynne Rienner, 1995.

[43]   See Ayoob, *The Third World Security Predicament* for these issues in relation to North Africa. Specifically, see, amongst others, Nazih Ayubi. *Over-stating the Arab State: Politics and Society in the Middle East.* London: I.B. Taurus, 1995.

[44]   Algeria first applied to join the WTO in 1987 and is currently on the verge of accession whilst Libya applied in 2001 and is being fast-tracked, with accession likely some time toward 2007. For information, see WTO website — http://www.wto.org

[45]   DFAT, *Accessing Middle East Growth*, 167.

[46]   According to DFAT, automotive exports to the Gulf have risen from almost 0 in 1995 to over AUD $800 million in 1999, with the Australian-made Toyota Camry now the largest selling car in Saudi Arabia. DFAT, *Accessing Middle East Growth*, xiv.

[47]   DFAT, *Accessing Middle East Growth*, 70.

[48]   DFAT, *Accessing Middle East Growth*, 16.

[49]   There were 5593 North African students in US universities and 5545 in Canadian universities in 2001. US statistics from the National Centre for

Education Statistics. See
http://www.nces.ed.gov/programs/digest/d03/tables/dt417 Canadian
statistics from Statistics Canada, communication with Katie Davis,
Enhanced Student Information Systems, Statistics Canada, 22 March 2005.

50 For these organisations, see: CAAR http://www.dfat.gov.au/caar; AACCI
http://www.austarab.com.au; AACC http://www.arabcouncil.org.au and
AAC http://www.aac.org.au

Chapter Eleven

1 Edward Said. *Covering Islam: How the Media and the Experts Determine How We See the Rest of the World.* New York: Vintage Books. 1997: 13.

2 R.A. Falk. *Human Rights Horizons: The Pursuit of Justice in a Globalizing World.* New York: Routledge, 2002: 2.

3 C.M. Henry and R. Springbok. *Globalization and the Politics of Development in the Middle East.* Cambridge: Cambridge University Press, 2001: xiv.

4 See extensive Australian press coverage of this issue since December 2005 and throughout 2006.

5 Gordon, M. '*Why PM must act to broaden Cole probe*', *The Age*, 1 February 2006.

6 M.J. Bolle. *Middle East Free Trade Area: Progress Report.* Congressional Research Services (CRS), the Library of Congress, 8 February 2005: 1.

7 E. Gresser. *Blank Spot on the Map: How Trade Policy is Working Against the War on Terror.* Public Policy Institute, February 2003. Cited in M.J. Bolle, *Middle East Free Trade*, 2.

8 National Commission on Terrorist Attacks Upon the United States. *The 9-11 Commission Report*, released on August 29, 2004. Cited in M.J. Bolle, *Middle East Free Trade*, 2.

9 D. Rumley. 'The geopolitics of Australia's Regional Relations'. The Netherlands: Kluwer Academic Publishers, 2001: 85.

10 Rumley, 'The geopolitics of Australia's Regional Relations,' 85.

11 B. Turner. 'Cosmopolitan Virtue, Globalization and Patriotism.' In *Theory, Culture and Society.* 19(1–2), 45–63. London: SAGE Publications, 2002.

12 T. Abed and H.R. Davood. *Challenges of Growth and Globalization in the Middle East and North Africa.* International Monetary Fund (IMF), External Relations Department Publications, 2003: 1.

13 See studies undertaken by J. Li and S. E. Guisinger. 'Comparative Business Failures of Foreign-Controlled Firms in the United States.' *Journal of International Business Studies.* (22) 2, 1991: 209–24; O. Shenkar and Y. Zeria. 'Role Conflict and Role Ambiguity of Chief Executive Officers in International Joint Ventures.' *Journal of International Business Studies.* (23) 1, 1992: 55–75; K. Jones and W. Shill. 'The Dilemma of Foreign Affiliated Companies: Surviving Middle Age in Japan.' In *Collaborating to Compete*, edited by J. Bleeke and D. Ernst. New York: John Wiley and Sons, 1993; J.M. Pennings, H. Barkema and S. Douma. 'Organisation Learning and Diversification.' *Academy of Management Review.* (37) 3, 1994: 608–40; and J. F. Hennart and M. Zeng. 'Is Cross-Cultural Conflict Driving International Joint Venture Instability? A Comparative Study of Japanese-Japanese and

Japanese-American IJVs in the United States.' Paper presented at 1997
Academy of Management Meeting, Boston, MA, 1997.

14   Department of Foreign Affairs and Trade (DFAT). Inquiry 'Australia's
relations with the Middle East.' Joint Standing Committee on Foreign
Affairs Defence and Trade. Canberra: Parliament of Australia, 2001: 115–16
http://www.aph.gov.au/house/committee/jfadt/Mideast/MERptindx.htm

15   T. Harcourt. *Cars, Camels and Currencies — Australian Exporters and the Middle
East.* The *Australian.* 3 August 2004.

16   DFAT, 'Australia's relations with the Middle East,' 120.

17   DFAT, 'Australia's relations with the Middle East.'

18   DFAT. United Arab Emirates Fact Sheet. May 2005.
http://www.dfat.gov.au/geo/fs/uaem.pdf

19   According to the 2000 Index of Economic Freedom (Gerald P. O'Driscoll
Jr., Kim R. Holmes and Melanie Kirkpatrick. *2000 Index of Economic Freedom.*
Washington DC: The heritage Foundation, 2000) an extract of which is
found in Clement M. Henry and Robert Springborg. *Globalization and the
Politics of Development in the Middle* East. Cambridge: Cambridge University
Press, 2001: 197

20   DFAT. Jordan Fact Sheet. May 2005.
http://www.dfat.gov.au/geo/fs/jord.pdf

21   DFAT, 'Australia's relations with the Middle East,' xiv

22   DFAT, 'Australia's relations with the Middle East.'

23   Cf. Bolle. *Middle East Free Trade Area.*

24   For studies on Orientalism, see: E. Said, *Orientalism,* London: Routledge and
Kegan Paul, 1978; A. Hussain, R. Olson & J. (eds.) *Qureshi, Orientalism, Islam
and Islamists,* Barattleboro: Amana Books, 1984; S. Amin, *Eurocentricism,* New
York: Monthly Review Press, 1989.

25   H. Barakat. *The Arab World.* Berkeley: University of California Press, 1993:
12–13.

26   For a scholarly discussion of democracy, see K. Abou el-Fadl (et. al.), ed.
Islam and the Challenge of Democracy, Princeton: Princeton University Press,
2004; J. L. Esposito & J.V. Voll. *Islam and Democracy.* Oxford: Oxford
University Press, 1996; A. Tamimi, ed. *Power-Sharing Islam?* London: Liberty
for Muslim World, 1993. For a solid discussion of the views of Islamic
intellectuals on human rights, see: K. Dalacoura. *Islam, Liberalism and Human
Rights.* London: I.B. Tauris, 2003.

27   For details on some of the most recent achievements of civil society
organizations in various Arab countries, see: Gulf Research Center, *Arab
Human Development Report.* 2004.
http://www.grc.ae/?sec=Arab+Human+Development+Report

28   As Marwan Muasher, the Jordanian Foreign Minister, rightly pointed out:
'the idea is to come up with a homegrown process in order that others not
impose something from the outside.' Quoted from 'Arab Leaders Seek to
Counter US Plan for Mideast Overhaul.' *New York Times,* 4 March 2004,
cited by J. M. Sharp. 'The Broader Middle East and North Africa Initiative:
An Overview.' CRS Report for Congress, 15 February 2005: 3.

29 A. A. An-Na'im. 'Human Rights in the Muslim World: Socio-Political Conditions and Scriptural Imperatives.' *Harvard Human Rights Journal.* Vol.3 (Spring 1990): 15.

30 United Nations Development Programme (UNDP). '"The Time Has Come": A Call for Freedom and Good Governance in the Arab World.' 5 April 2005. http://www.undp.org/rbas/ahdr

31 D.P. Forsyth. *Human Rights in International Relations.* Cambridge: Cambridge University Press, 2000: 34–35.

32 DFAT. *Human Rights Manual 2004.* Canberra: DFAT, 2004: 9. http://www.dfat.gov.au/hr/hr_manual_2004/index.html

33 I. Khan. 'Don't turn a blind eye to the UN.' The *Australian.* 9 September 2004: 13.

34 E. Evatt. 'Australia's Performances in Human Rights.' *Alternative Law Journal.* Vol. 26 No.1, February 2001: 11.

35 A. Downer. 'Strengthening Australia's Human Rights Credentials.' Address at the Forum on Australia's Human Rights Obligations For Human Rights Day, National Press Club, 10 December 1996. http://www.dfat.gov.au/media/speeches/foreign/1996/AMNESTY_.html

36 DFAT, *Human Rights Manual 2004*, 4 and 12; Rumley, 'The geopolitics of Australia's Regional Relations,' 85.

37 Evatt, 'Australia's Performances in Human Rights,' 15.

38 J. Burnside. 'Hypocrisy and Human Rights.' *Law Society Bulletin.* November 2002: 12–15.

39 Evatt, 'Australia's Performances in Human Rights,' 15.

40 D. Hovell. 'The Sovereignty Stratagem: Australia's response to UN human rights treaty bodies.' *Alternative Law Journal.* Vol. 28 No.6, December 2003: 298.

41 Commonwealth of Australia. *Advancing the National Interest: Australia's Foreign and Trade Policy White Paper.* Canberra: Commonwealth of Australia, 2003. www.dfat.gov.au/ani

42 Downer, 'Strengthening Australia's Human Rights Credentials'.

43 Downer, 'Strengthening Australia's Human Rights Credentials'.

44 Downer, 'Strengthening Australia's Human Rights Credentials'.

45 Rumley, 'The geopolitics of Australia's Regional Relations,' 98.

46 DFAT, *Human Rights Manual 2004.*

47 Falk, *Human Rights Horizons*, 40.

48 A. Gyngell and M. Wesley. *Making Australian Foreign Policy.* Melbourne, 2003: 26. For an insightful study of national interest discourse, see: J. A. Camilleri. 'A Leap into the Past — in the name of the 'National Interest.' *Australian Journal of International Affairs,* Vol.57 No.3 (November 2003): 431–53.

49 Camilleri, 'A Leap into the Past.'

50 Forsyth, *Human Rights in International Relations*, 146.

51 Forsyth, *Human Rights in International Relations*, 13.

52 S. Loosley. 'Human Rights and Aid: An Australian Parliamentary Perspective.' 1998. www.hrca.org.au/symposium.htm

53 L. Chun. 'Human Rights and Democracy.' *The International Journal of Human*

Rights, Vol.5 No.3 (Autumn 2001): 19.

54 A. Downer. 'Securing Australia's Interests — Australian Foreign Policy Priorities.' *Australian Journal of International Affairs*. Vol. 59, No.1 (March 2005): 7–12: 8.

55 Lowy Institute for International Policy and UMR Research Pty Ltd. 'The Lowy Institute Poll 2005 Data Book.' February 2005: 6. http://www.lowyinstitute.org/

56 A. Downer, in '*Human Rights Manual*', DFAT, 2004.

57 Broinowski, 'Delinking trade from human rights,' 49.

58 AusAID. 'Australian Humanitarian Aid to Iraq.' Report updated 13 December 2004. http://www.ausaid.gov.au/hottopics/topic.cfm?Id=8614_8794_4510_8987 _445

59 See AusAID, 'Australian Humanitarian Aid to Iraq' and DFAT. 'Iraq — The Path Ahead.' Canberra: Australian Government, 2004: iv http://www.dfat.gov.au/publications/iraq_the_path_ahead/iraq_path_ahea d_web.pdf

60 DFAT, 'Iraq — The Path Ahead,' 16.

61 AusAID. Media release by the Minister for Foreign Affairs Alexander Downer. '2005–06 Aid Budget: Iraq Reconstruction Assistance.' 10 May 2005. www.ausaid.gov.au/media/release.cfm?BC=Media&Id=4856_6997_4327_7 366_4352; DFAT. 'Country Programs — Iraq'. 11 May 2005. www.ausaid.gov.au/country/country.cfm?CountryId=54777444

62 Amnesty International Australia. 'Iraq Memorandum on concerns relating to law and order.' 23 July 2003. http://www.amnesty.org.au/whats_happening/CounterTerrorism/article?ci d=12&pid=149

63 Human Rights Watch. World Report 2002. 'Iraq and Iraqi Kurdistan.' http://www.hrw.org/wr2k2/mena4.html

64 AusAID. 'Australian Development Co-operation in the Middle East: Strategy for 2004–2006.' Canberra: Australian Government, nd: 3. http://www.ausaid.gov.au/publications/pdf/me_strat_0406.pdf

65 AusAID. 'Australian Development Co-operation in the Middle East,' 1 and 2.

66 AusAID. 'Australian Development Co-operation in the Middle East,' 2.

67 Canadian International Development Agency. West Bank and Gaza Projects. http://www.acdi-cida.gc.ca/CIDAWEB/webcountry.nsf/vLUDocEn/ D370CB2ACF2EB43785256D6C004C82CB?OpenDocument#3 Lynne Cohen. 'Martin, Pettigrew disagree on Hamas.' *Jewish Tribune*. 2 June 2005. http://www.jewishtribune.ca/tribune/jt-050602-01.html

68 Cohen. 'Martin, Pettigrew disagree on Hamas.'

69 DFAT, *Human Rights Manual 2004*, 6.

70 M. Yacoubian. 'Promoting Middle East Democracy: European Initiatives.' United Sates Institute of Peace, Special Report. No.127, October 2004: 6.

71 Australian Lawyers for Human Rights. Media Release 'Australia's Human Rights Dialogues.' 16 April 2004.
http://www.alhr.asn.au/html/documents/HR_DialogueInquiry16APR04.ht ml
http://www.hrca.org.au/The_Rights_Way_to_Development_Manual.htm .

73 A. E. Frankovitas, E. Sidoti, and P. Earle. 'The Rights Way to Development: A Human Rights Approach to Development Assistance: Policy and Practice.' Human Rights Council of Australia, New South Wales, 1998.

74 The Human Rights Council of Australia. 'The Rights Way to Development Manual.' 1 June 1998.
http://www.hrca.org.au/The_Rights_Way_to_Development_Manual.htm

75 T. Kelly. 'Access to Justice: The Palestinian Legal System and the Fragmentation of Coercive Power.' Working Paper No.41, Development Research Centre, LSE, March 2004.

76 UN Secretary-General, Kofi Annan, reporting to the UN General Assembly in September 2003 on the implementation of the United Nations Millennium Declaration.

77 cf, A.J. Ali, 'Organizational development in the Arab world.' *Journal of Management Development.* Vol.15 No.5, 1996: 4–21.

BIBLIOGRAPHY

Abed, T. and H.R. Davood. *Challenges of Growth and Globalization in the Middle East and North Africa.* International Monetary Fund (IMF), External Relations Department Publications, 2003.

Abou el-Fadl, K. (et. al.), ed. *Islam and the Challenge of Democracy.* Princeton: Princeton University Press, 2004.

Abu-Rabi', Ibrahim. *Intellectual Origins of Islamic Resurgence in the Modern Arab World.* Albany: State University of New York Press, 1995.

The Age. 'Mr. Rudyard Kipling: An Interesting Interview', 13 November 1891: 5.

——. '9,500 Refugees can apply to stay.' *The Age*, 13 July 2004. Available from: http://theage.com.au/articles/2004/07/13/1089484342243.html [accessed 28 July 2004]

——. 'PM admits public don't support Iraq decision.' 15 March 2005.

Albright, Madeleine and Robin Cook. 'The world needs to step it up in Afghanistan,' *International Herald Tribune*, 5 October 2004.

Ali, A.J. 'Organizational development in the Arab world.' *Journal of Management Development*, Vol.15 No.5 (1996): 4–21.

Al-Jazeera. 'Iraq urges Australia to keep refugees.' 31 December 2003. http://english.aljazeera.net

Allard, Tom. 'You're against us, Arab leaders tell Australia.' *Sydney Morning Herald*, 31 July 2004.

Amnesty International Australia. 'Iraq Memorandum on concerns relating to law and order.' 23 July 2003. http://www.amnesty.org.au/whats_happening/CounterTerrorism/article?cid=12&pid=149

Amin, S. *Eurocentricism,* New York: Monthly Review Press, 1989.

An-Na'im, A. A. 'Human Rights in the Muslim World: Socio-Political Conditions and Scriptural Imperatives.' *Harvard Human Rights Journal,* Vol.3 (Spring 1990).

AusAID. 'Australia's Overseas Aid Program 2005–06.' Statement by the Honourable Alexander Downer MP Minister for Foreign Affairs. 10 May 2005. http://www.ausaid.gov.au/budget05/budget_2005_2006.html

——. '2005–06 Aid Budget: Iraq Reconstruction Assistance.' Media release by the Minister for Foreign Affairs Alexander Downer. 10 May 2005. http://www.ausaid.gov.au/media/release.cfm?BC=Media&Id=4856_6997_4327_7366_4352

——. 'Australian Development Co-operation in the Middle East: Strategy for 2004–2006.' http://www.ausaid.gov.au/publications/pdf/me_strat_0406.pdf

——. 'Country Programs — Iraq', 11 May 2005. http://www.ausaid.gov.au/country/country.cfm?CountryId=54777444

——. 'Country Programs — Middle East', 11 May 2005 http://www.ausaid.gov.au/country/country.cfm?CountryId=98411310

——. 'Guidelines for the Human Rights Small Grants Scheme.' September 2004. http://www.ausaid.gov.au/partner/global/hrsg_guidelines.pdf

——. Australian Government Aid Program, 'Australian Development Co-operation Strategy in the Middle East: 2004–2006'
http://www.ausaid.gov.au/publications/pdf/me_strat_0406.pdf
——. Australian Government Aid Program, 'Country Programs — Indonesia', 10 February 2005
http://www.ausaid.gov.au/country/country.cfm?CountryId=30
——. Australian Government Aid Program, 'Country Programs — Iraq', 11 May 2005 http://www.ausaid.gov.au/country/country.cfm?CountryId=54777444
——. Australian Government Aid Program, 'Country Programs — Papua New Guinea', Estimate Total Aid 2005.
http://www.ausaid.gov.au/country/papua.cfm
Austrade, 'Camels, Cars and Currencies — Australian Exporters and the Middle East.' Australian Trade Commission, 2004.
http://www.austrade.gov.au/corporate/
Australian Arabic Council. 'Racial Vilification against Arabic and Muslim Australians in light of the September 11th Terrorist Attacks in the United States.' Melbourne: 2001.
Australian Broadcasting Corporation. 'Woomera hunger strike continues as talks fail.' *ABC Online News*, 25 January 2002.
http://www.abc.net.au/news/newsitems/200201/s466756.htm
——. Radio National. 'Osama Bin Laden in the Suburbs.' *The Religion Report*, 13 October 2004.
Australian Bureau of Statistics. *Australian Census 1996*. Canberra: ABS, 1996.
——. *Australian Census 2001*. Canberra: ABS, 2001.
Australian Government's Inquiry into Australian Intelligence Agencies. *Report of the Inquiry into Australian Intelligence Agencies.*
http://www.pmc.gov.au/publications/intelligence_inquiry/
Australian Human Rights and Equal Opportunity Commission. 'Fact Sheet: Australians of Arab, Middle Eastern and North African Birth and Ancestry.' 21 March 2003.
http://www.hreoc.gov.au/racial_discrimination/isma/fact_arab.html
Australian Lawyers for Human Rights. Media Release 'Australia's Human Rights Dialogues.'16 April 2004.
http://www.alhr.asn.au/html/documents/HR_DialogueInquiry16APR04.html
Ayoob, Mohammed. *The Third World Security Predicament: State Making, Regional Conflict, and the International System*. Boulder: Lynne Rienner, 1995.
Ayres, Philip., *Owen Dixon*. Melbourne: Miegunyah Press, 2003.
Ayubi, Nazih. *Over-stating the Arab State: Politics and Society in the Middle East.* London: I.B. Taurus, 1995.
Barakat, H. *The Arab World*. Berkeley: University of California Press, 1993.
Barton, Greg. 'The Liberal, Progressive Roots of Abdurrahman Wahid's Thought.' In *Nahdlatul Ulama, Traditional Islam and Modernity in Indonesia*, edited by Greg Barton and Greg Fealy, 190–226. Clayton: Monash Asia Institute, 1996.

——. 'The Origins of Islamic Liberalism in Indonesia and its Contribution to Democratisation.' *Democracy in Asia*, New York: St Martins Press 1997: 427–51.

——. 'Indonesia's Nurcholish Madjid and Abdurrahman Wahid as Intellectual Ulama: The Meeting of Islamic Traditionalism and Modernism in neo-Modernist thought.' *Islam and Christian–Muslim Relations*, Vol.8 No.3 (October 1997): 323–50.

——. 'The Prospects for Islam.' In *Indonesia Today: Challenges of History*, Grayson Lloyd and Shannon Smith, 244–255. Singapore: Institute of Southeast Asian Studies, 2001.

——. 'Islam and Politics in Malaysia.' In *Islam in Asia: Changing Political Realities*, edited by Jason F. Issacson and Colin Rubenstein, 95–164. New Jersey: Transaction Press, 2002.

——. *Abdurrahman Wahid, Indonesian President, Muslim Democrat: a view from the inside*. Sydney and Honolulu: UNSW Press and University of Hawai'i Press, 2002.

——. 'The Wahid Presidency in Context: Regime Change, Inflated Expectations, Islam and the Promise of Democracy.' In *Indonesia Matters: Diversity, Unity, and Stability in Fragile Times*, edited by Thang D. Nguyen and Frank-Jurgen Richter, 28–38. Singapore: Times Editions, 2003.

——. *Indonesia's Struggle: Jemaah Islamiah and radical Islamism*. Sydney and Singapore: UNSW Press and NUS Press, 2004.

——. 'Islam and Democratic Transition in Indonesia.' In *Religious Organizations and Democracy in Contemporary Asia*, edited by Deborah A. Brown and Tun-jen Cheng, . New York: M. E. Sharpe, 2005.

——. 'Making sense of Jemaah Islamiyah terrorism and radical Islamism in Indonesia.' In *Islam and the West Reflections from Australia*, edited by Shahram Akbarzadeh and Samina Yasmeen, 114–31. Sydney: UNSW Press, 2005.

Batrouney, A. 'Arabic Immigration to Australia.' Conference paper presented at *Arabic Smoke Free Sunday*. Melbourne: 18 August 2003.

Batrouney A. and T. Batrouney. *The Lebanese in Australia*. Melbourne: AE Press, 1985.

Batrouney, T. 'The Lebanese in Australia.' In *The Lebanese in the World: A Century of Migration*, edited by A. Hourani and N. Shehadie, 413–42. London: Centre for Lebanese Studies and I. B. Tauris, 1992.

——. 'Australia's Immigration Policies: A loss of Consensus.' *NIRA Review* (Winter 1998): 11–15.

——. 'Lebanese Community Life in Melbourne.' In *The Australian People*, edited by J. Jupp, 567–9. Oakleigh, Victoria: Cambridge University Press, 2001.

——. 'Arab-Australians: From White Australia to Multiculturalism: Citizenship and Identity.' In *Arab Australians To-day: Citizenship and Belonging* edited by G. Hage, 37–62. Carlton South, Victoria: Melbourne University Press, 2002.

Batrouney, T. and R. Lampugnani. 'Citizenship in Australia: The Roles of Government and the Voluntary Sector.' Proceedings ANZTSR Conference, Victoria University of Wellington, New Zealand, 1996.

Bean, C.E.W. *What to Know in Egypt: a Guide for Australian Soldiers*, 1915, extracted in *On the War-path: An Anthology of Australian Military Travel*, edited by Robin

Gerster and Peter Pierce, 85–8. Melbourne: Melbourne University Press, 2004.

Beaumont, Joan. 'Australia's War.' In *Australia's War 1914–18*, edited by Joan Beaumont, 8–14. St Leonards: Allen & Unwin, 1995.

——. 'Europe and the Middle East.' In *Australia's War 1939–45*, edited by Joan Beaumont, 9–12. St Leonards: Allen and Unwin, 1996.

Bedford, Randolph. *Explorations in Civilization*. Sydney: Angus & Robertson, 1914[?].

Bell, Coral. *Dependent Ally: A Study in Australian Foreign Policy*. Melbourne: Oxford University Press, 1988.

Benjamin, Roger, ed. *Orientalism: Delacroix to Klee*. Sydney: Art Gallery of New South Wales, 1997.

Bergen, Peter L. *Holy War, Inc.: Inside the Secret World of Osama Bin Laden*. New York: The Free Press, 2001.

Berman, Paul. *Terror and Liberalism*. New York: W. W. Norton & Company, 2002.

BHP–Billion. *The ROD Integrated Development Project — Algeria*. Briefing Paper, June 2000. http://www.bhpbilliton.com/bbContentRepository/BriefingPapers/RODBriefingPaper.pdf

——. *The Ohanet Development — Algeria*, October 2003. http://www.bhpbilliton.com/bbContentRepository/News/RelatedContent/OhanetDevelopment.pdf

Binder, Leonard. *Islamic Liberalism: A Critique of Development Ideologies*. Chicago: University of Chicago Press, 1988.

Blix, Hans. *Disarming Iraq: The Search for Weapons of Mass Destruction*. London: Bloomsbury, 2004.

Boland, B. J. *The Struggle of Islam in Modern Indonesia*. The Hague: Martinus Nijhoff, 1971.

Bolle, M.J. *Middle East Free Trade Area: Progress Report*. Congressional Research Services (CRS), the Library of Congress, 8 February 2005.

Bone, Pamela. 'A new school of social division.' *The Age*. 13 December 1996: 15.

Bowes, Joseph. *The Aussie Crusaders: With Allenby in Palestine*. London: Oxford University Press, 1920.

Bridge, Carl. 'Poland to Pearl Harbor.' In *Munich to Vietnam: Australia's Relations with Britain and the United States since the 1930*, edited by Carl Bridge, 38–51. Melbourne: Melbourne University Press, 1991.

Brodie, Bernard. *War and Politics*. New York: Macmillan, 1973.

Broinowski, R. 'Delinking trade from human rights: The Australian approach.' *Australian Rationalist*, No. 24, 1998: 47–52.

Brown, Senator Bob. 'Refugee move met with cynicism.' *Herald* Sun. 14 July 2004.

Burke, Jason. *Al-Qaeda: Casting a Shadow of Terror*. London: I.B. Tauris, 2003.

Burnside, J. 'Hypocrisy and Human Rights.' *Law Society Bulletin*. November 2002: 12–15.

Burton, John. ed. *Conflict: Human Needs Theory*. London: Macmillan, 1990.

Camilleri, J. A. 'A Leap into the Past — In the name of the 'National Interest.' *Australian Journal of International Affairs,* Vol.57 No.3 (November 2003): 431–453.

Campbell, D. *Writing Security: United States Foreign Policy and the Politics of Identity.* Minneapolis: University of Minnesota Press, 1992.

Canadian International Development Agency. West Bank and Gaza Projects. http://www.acdi-cida.gc.ca/CIDAWEB/webcountry.nsf/vLUDocEn/D370CB2ACF2EB43785256D6C004C82CB?OpenDocument#3

Capling, Ann. *All the Way with the USA: Australia, the US and Free Trade.* Sydney, UNSW Press, 2005.

Carey, Roane, ed. *The New Intifada.* London: Verso, 2001.

Carlyon, Les. *Gallipoli.* Sydney: Macmillan, 2001.

Castles, S. and M. Miller. *The Age of Migration: International Population Movements in the Modern World.* New York: Guilford Press, 1993.

Castles, S., W. Foster, R. Iredale and G. Withers. *Immigration and Australia: Myths and Realities.* St Leonards, NSW: Allen and Unwin, 1998.

Cattalini, Helen. 'Moving the Debate forward in Australia: Multiculturalism Post-Mabo.' From the 1995 Global Cultural Diversity Conference Proceedings, Sydney. Canberra: Department of Immigration and Multicultural and Indigenous Affairs, 1995. http://www.immi.gov.au/multicultural/_inc/publications/confer/06/speech27a.htm

Chesterman, Simon. *Just War or Just Peace? Humanitarian Intervention and International Law.* Oxford: Oxford University Press, 2001.

Chhibber, Pradeep. 'State Policy, Rent Seeking, and the Electoral Success of a Religious Party in Algeria.' *Journal of Politics,* 58:1 (1996): 126–49.

Chomsky, N. *Middle East Illusions.* Lanham: Rowman & Littlefield, 2003.

——. 'Foreign Policy: Arafat' *Z Magazine,* Vol.17 No.12 (December 2004).

Chun, L. 'Human Rights and Democracy.' *The International Journal of Human Rights,* Vol.5 No.3 (Autumn 2001): 19.

Cigler, Michael J. *The Afghans in Australia.* Blackburn: Australasian Educa Press, 1986.

Cirincione, Joseph, Jessica Tuchman Mathews and George Perkovich. *WMD in Iraq: Evidence and Implications.* Washington DC: Carnegie Endowment for International Peace, 2004.

Clarke, Richard A. *Against All Enemies: Inside America's War on Terror.* New York: The Free Press, 2004.

Cleland, Bilal. *The Muslims in Australia: A Brief History.* Melbourne: Islamic Council of Victoria, 2002.

Clinton, Bill. *My Life.* London: Hutchinson, 2004.

Clune, Frank. *Tobruk to Turkey: With the Army of the Nile.* Sydney: Angus and Robertson, 1943.

——. *Song of India,* Sydney: Invincible Press, 1946.

——. *To the Isles of Spice.* Sydney: Angus and Robertson, 1948.

Cohen, Lynne. 'Martin, Pettigrew disagree on Hamas.' *Jewish Tribune.* 2 June 2005. http://www.jewishtribune.ca/tribune/jt-050602-01.html

'Cold War — Outline Notes' prepared for a conference on Cold War Planning, Department of External Affairs, 20 December 1954, Series A7936/2, Item B/4/2 Part1, National Archives of Australia.

Coll, Steve. *Ghost Wars: The Secret History of the CIA, Afghanistan, and Bin Laden, From the Soviet Invasion to September 10, 2001.* New York: The Penguin Press, 2004.

Collins, J., G. Noble, S. Poynting and P. Tabar. *Kebabs, Kids, Cops and Crime.* Annandale NSW: Pluto Press, 2000.

Colville, Rupert. 'One Massacre That Didn't Grab the World's Attention.' *International Herald Tribune,* 7 August 1999.

Commission on the Intelligence Capabilities of the United States Regarding Weapons of Mass Destruction 'Overview — Report to the President.' 31 March 2005. http://www.wmd.gov/report/overview_fm.pdf

Crawford, Robert. 'A Slow Coming of Age: Advertising and the Little Boy from Manly in the Twentieth Century.' *Journal of Australian Studies,* March 2001.

Crock, Mary. *Immigration and refugee law in Australia.* Leichhardt, NSW: Federation Press, 1998.

Crocker, W.R. *The Racial Factor in International Relations.* Canberra: Australian National University, 1956.

Dalacoura, K. *Islam, Liberalism and Human Rights.* London: I.B. Tauris, 2003.

Dalrymple, Rawdon. 'Looking for Theory in Australian Foreign Policy.' *Australian Review of Public Affairs.* Symposium: Advancing the National Interest? 28 April 2003. www.econ.usyd.edu.au/drawingboard/digest/0304/dalrymple.html

Danner, Mark. *Torture and Truth: America, Abu Ghraib, and the War on Terror.* New York: New York Review Books, 2004.

Danner, Mark. 'Iraq: The Real Election.' *New York Review of Books,* 28 April 2005.

David, Edgeworth. 'A Wilderness: Australia's Arid Centre.' *Sydney Morning Herald,* 13 August 1924: 12.

Day, David. *The Politics of War.* Pymble: Harper Collins, 2003.

Deen, Hanifa. *Caravanserai: Journey Among Australian Muslims.* Fremantle: Fremantle Arts Centre Press, 2003.

Department of the Prime Minister and Cabinet. *National Agenda for a Multicultural Australia … Sharing our Future.* Canberra: AGPS, 1989.

DFAT (Australian Department of Foreign Affairs and Trade). *In the National Interest.* Canberra: Commonwealth of Australia, 1997. http://www.dfat.gov.au/ini/whitepaper.pdf

——. *Accessing Middle East Growth: Business Opportunities in the Arabian Peninsula and Iran.* Canberra: Commonwealth of Australia, 2000. http://www.dfat.gov.au/publications/megrowth/index.html

——. Joint Standing Committee on Foreign Affairs, Defence and Trade. *Australia's Relations with the Middle East.* Canberra: Commonwealth of Australia, 2001. http://www.aph.gov.au/house/committee/jfadt/Mideast/MERptindx.htm

——. 'Advancing the National Interest: Australia's Foreign and Trade Policy White Paper,.' 2003.

——. *Advancing the National Interest*. Canberra: Commonwealth of Australia, 2003. http://ww.dfat.gov.au/ani/

——. *Constructive Engagement on Two Fronts*. Media Release by Trade Minister Mark Vaile, 23 May 2003. http://www.trademinister.gov.au/releases/2003/mvt096_03.html

——. *Human Rights Manual 2004*. Canberra: DFAT, 2004. http://www.dfat.gov.au/hr/hr_manual_2004/index.html

——. 'Iraq — The Path Ahead.' Canberra: Australian Government, 2004. http://www.dfat.gov.au/publications/iraq_the_path_ahead/iraq_path_ahead_web.pdf

——. *Australia to Open Diplomatic Mission in Libya*. Joint Media Release, Minister for Foreign Affairs Alexander Downer and Minister for Trade Mark Vaile, 21 May 2004. http://www.foreignminister.gov.au/releases/2004/joint_open_libya_mission.html

——. *Doing Business with Qatar*, *Doing Business with Saudi Arabia*, and *Doing Business with United Arab Emirates*, March 2005.

——. Australia Now: *Islam in Australia*. Canberra: Commonwealth of Australia, 2005. http://www.dfat.gov.au/facts/islam_in_australia.html

——. Joint Media Release, 'Australia Indonesia Partnership for Reconstruction and Development — Inaugural Joint Commission Meeting.' 17 March 2005. http://www.foreignminister.gov.au/releases/2005/jointpr170305_aus-ind.html

——. United Arab Emirates 'Fact Sheet.' May 2005, at http://www.dfat.gov.au/geo/uae/

DIMIA (Department of Immigration and Ethnic Affairs). *Australian Citizenship Ceremonies*. Canberra: AGPS, 1994.

——. *Iraqi Returnees*. Media Statement, 31 December 2003. http://www.immi.gov.au/media_releases/media03/d03ms2.htm

——. *Abolition of the 'White Australia' Policy*. Canberra: Commonwealth of Australia, 6 October 2004. http://www.immi.gov.au/facts/08abolition.htm

——. Fact Sheet 82. Immigration Detention, 14 October 2004. http://www.dimia.gov.au/facts/82detention.htm

Dinning, Hector. *By-Ways on Service: Notes from an Australian Journal*, 1918, in *On the War-Path* edited by Gerster and Pierce, Melbourne: Melbourne University Press, 2004: 87–96.

Diosy, Arthur. *The New Far East*. London: Cassell and Company Ltd, 1904.

Donohoue Clyne, Irene. 'Those preaching tolerance failed to extend it religious schools.' *The Age*, 8 January 1997: 11.

Dorrington, Albert. *The Radium Terrors: A Mystery Story*. New York: W.R. Caldwell & Co., 1910.

Dow, D. 'A note on psychological distance and export market selection.' *Journal of International Marketing*, Vol.8 No.1 (2000): 51–64.

Downer, A. Address, 10 December 1996. www.dfat.gov.au/hr/#speeches

——. 'Human Rights: A Record of Achievement.' *Foreign Affairs and Trade Record*, September 1998: 15–18.

——. 'Securing Australia's Interests — Australian Foreign Policy Priorities.' *Australian Journal of International Affairs*, Vol.59 No.1 (March 2005): 7–12.

Eliraz, Giora. *Islam in Indonesia: Modernism, Radicalism, and the Middle East Dimension.* Brighton: Sussex Academic Press, 2004.

Elliott, Brian. *The Landscape of Australian Poetry.* Melbourne: F.W. Cheshire, 1967.

Ellis, M.H. *Express to Hindustan: An Account of a Motor-Car Journey from London to Delhi.* London: John Lane the Bodley Head Limited, 1929.

Esposito, John L. *The Islamic Threat: Myth or Reality?* New York: Oxford University Press, 1992.

——. *Unholy War: Terror in the Name of Islam.* New York: Oxford University Press, 2002.

Esposito, John L. and John Voll. *Islam and Democracy.* New York: Oxford University Press, 1996.

Evans, Gareth and Bruce Grant. *Australia's Foreign Relations: in the World of the 1990s.* Melbourne: Melbourne University Press, 1995.

Evatt, E. 'Australia's Performances in Human Rights.' *Alternative Law Journal*, Vol.26 No.1 (February 2001): 11–15.

Falk, R. *Human Rights Horizons: The Pursuit of Justice in a Globalizing World.* London: Routledge, 2000.

Fealy, Greg. 'Islamic Politics: A Rising or Declining Force?' In *Indonesia: The Uncertain Transition*, edited by Damien Kingsbury and Arief Budiman, 119–136. Adelaide: Crawford House, 2001.

Firth, Stewart. *Australia in International Politics: An Introduction to Australian Foreign Policy.* Sydney: Allen & Unwin, 1999.

Fisk, Robert. 'Fear and Learning in America.' *The Independent*, 17 April 2002.

Forbes, Mark. 'US has changed the world order: strategist.' *The Age*, 13 March 2003.

Forsyth, D.P. *Human Rights in International Relations.* Cambridge: Cambridge University Press, 2000.

Foster, L. and D. Stockley. *Multiculturalism: the Changing Australian Paradigm.* Clevedon, Avon, England: Multilingual Matters Ltd, 1984.

Foster, L.E. *Diversity & Multicultural Education: A Sociological Perspective.* Sydney: Allen & Unwin, 1978.

Foucault, M. *The Archaeology of Knowledge.* London: Tavistock, 1977/

Frankovitas, A., E. Sidoti and P. Earle. 'The Rights Way to Development: A Human Rights Approach to Development Assistance: Policy and Practice.' Human Rights Council of Australia, New South Wales, 1998. www.grc-exchange.org/info.data/record.cfm?Id=626

Freedman, Lawrence and Efraim Karsh. *The Gulf Conflict 1990–1991: Diplomacy and War in the New World Order.* London: Faber & Faber, 1993.

Friedman, Thomas L. *Longitudes and Attitudes.* New York: Anchor Books, 2003.

Fukuyama, Francis. *The End of History and the Last Man.* New York : Maxwell Macmillan International, 1992.

Garran, Robert. *True Believer: John Howard, George Bush & the American alliance.* Sydney: Allen & Unwin, 2004.

Geertz, Clifford. *The Religion of Java.* New York: Free Press, 1960.

Gerster, Robin. *Big-Noting: The Heroic Theme in Australian War Writing.* Melbourne: Melbourne University Press, 1987.

Gibney, M.J. *The Ethics and politics of Asylum: Liberal Democracy and the Response to Refugees.* Cambridge: Cambridge University Press, 2004.

Glassop, Lawson. *We Were the Rats.* Sydney: Angus and Robertson, 1944.

Goldlust, J. *Understanding Citizenship in Australia.* Canberra: AGPS, 1996.

Goldlust, J. and T. Batrouney. 'Immigrants, Australian Citizenship and National Identity.' *Migration Action,* October 1996.

Gordon, Philip H. and Jeremy Shapiro. *Allies at War: America, Europe and the Crisis over Iraq.* New York: McGraw-Hill, 2004.

Gray, Christine. *International Law and the Use of Force.* Oxford: Oxford University Press, 2000.

Greenwood, G. and Charles Grimshaw, eds. *Documents on Australian International Affairs 1901–1918.* West Melbourne: Nelson, 1977.

Guardian Unlimited. Special Reports. 'Iraq timeline: July 16 1979 to January 31 2004.' 29 July 2003. www.guardian.co.uk/Iraq/page/0,12438,793802,00.html

——. Special Reports. 'Chronology of Terror.' *Guardian Unlimited,* 2003. http://www.guardian.co.uk/wtccrash/story/0,1300,550230,00.html

——. 'Timeline: terror and its aftermath (part 1).' *Guardian Unlimited,* 2003. http://www.guardian.co.uk/Print/0,3858,4259753,00.html

Guazzone, Laura ed. *The Islamist dilemma : the political role of Islamist movements in the contemporary Arab world.* Reading, Berkshire: Ithaca Press, 1995.

Gullett, H.S and Chas Barrett. eds. *Australia in Palestine.* Sydney: Angus & Robertson, 1919.

Gullett, Henry. *The Australian Imperial Force in Sinai and Palestine 1914–1918.* (Sydney: Angus & Robertson, 1923). In *On the War-Path,* edited by R. Gerster and P. Pierce, 100–2. Melbourne: Melbourne University Press, 2004.

Gyngell, A. and M. Wesley. *Making Australian Foreign Policy.* Melbourne, 2003.

Hage, G. *White Nation.* Annandale NSW: Pluto Press, 1998.

——. 'The Differential Intensities of Social Reality: migration, participation and guilt.' In *Arab-Australians Today: Citizenship and Belonging,* edited by G. Hage, 192–205. Melbourne: Melbourne University Press, 2002.

——. *Arab Australians To-day: Citizenship and Belonging.* Carlton South, Victoria: Melbourne University Press, 2002.

Halberstam, David. *The Making of a Quagmire.* New York: Random House, 1965.

Hall, S. and S. Maharaj. 'Modernity and difference.' *Annotations,* 6. London: Iniva Publication (2001): 36–66.

Halper, Stefan and Jonathan Clarke. *America Alone: The Neo-Conservatives and the Global Order.* Cambridge: Cambridge University Press, 2004.

Harcourt, T. *Cars, Camels and Currencies — Australian Exporters and the Middle East.* The *Australian.* 3 August 2004.

Harcourt, Tim. 'The Middle East — A Mecca for our Exports.' Australian Trade Commission, 2005. www.austrade.gov.au/corporate/

Harries, Owen. *Benign or Imperial? Reflections on American Hegemony.* Sydney: ABC Books, 2004.

Hathaway, C. 'What's in a label?' *European Journal of Migration and Law,* 5 (2003): 1–21.

Hefner, Robert W. *Civil Islam: Muslims and Democratization in Indonesia.* Princeton: Princeton University Press, 2000.

——. 'Civic Pluralism Denied? The New Media and Jihadi Violence in Indonesia.' In *New Media in the Muslim World: The Emerging Public Sphere*, edited by Dale F. Eickelman and Jon W. Anderson, 158–79. Bloomington: Indiana University, 2003.

——. 'Civil Islam and Political Violence in Indonesia.' *Congress Monthly* 70:6 (November–December 2003): 3–5.

——. 'Shariah Formalism or Democratic Communitarianism? The Islamic Resurgence and Political Theory.' In *Democracy and Communitarianism in Asia*, edited by Chua Beng-Huat, 122–47. London and New York: Routledge Curzon, 2004.

Hefner, Robert W. and Patricia Horvatich, eds. *Islam in an Era of Nation States: Politics and Religious Revival in Muslim Southeast Asia.* Honolulu: University of Hawai'i Press, 1997.

Hennart, J. F. and M. Zeng. 'Is Cross-Cultural Conflict Driving International Joint Venture Instability? A Comparative Study of Japanese-Japanese and Japanese-American IJVs in the United States.' Paper presented at 1997 Academy of Management Meeting, Boston, MA, 1997.

Henry, C.M. and R. Springbok. *Globalization and the Politics of Development in the Middle East.* Cambridge: Cambridge University Press, 2001.

Hickey, Michael. *Gallipoli.* London: John Murray, 1995.

Himmelfarb, Gertrude. *On Looking into the Abyss: Untimely Thoughts on Culture and Society.* New York: Vintage Books, 1994.

Hirst, David. *The Gun and the Olive Branch: The Roots of Violence in the Middle East.* New York, Thunder Mouth Press/Nation Books, 2003.

Hoopes, Townsend. *The Limits of Intervention.* New York: David Mackay, 1969.

Hovell, D. 'The Sovereignty Stratagem: Australia's response to UN human rights treaty bodies.' *Alternative Law Journal*, Vol.28 No.6 (December 2003): 297–301.

Howard, The Hon John MP. 'Australia in the World.' Address by the Prime Minister to the Lowy Institute for International Policy. 31 March 2005, 7.

HREOC (Human Rights and Equal Opportunity Commission). 'Fact Sheet: Australians of Arab, Middle Eastern and North African Birth and Ancestry.' 21 March 2003.

Hudson, W. J. *Blind Loyalty: Australia and the Suez Crisis.* Melbourne: Melbourne University Press, 1989.

Human Rights Council of Australia. 'The Rights Way to Development Manual.' 1 June 1998. http://www.hrca.org.au/The_Rights_Way_to_Development_Manual.htm

Human Rights Watch. World Report 2002 'Iraq and Iraqi Kurdistan.' http://www.hrw.org/wr2k2/mena4.html

——. Policy Paper 'Justice for Iraq.' December 2002. http://www.hrw.org/backgrounder/mena/iraq1217bg.htm

——. *The Road to Abu Ghraib.* New York: Human Rights Watch, 2004. http://www.hrw.org/reports/2004/usa0604/

Humphrey, M. *Islam, Multiculturalism and Transnationalism: From the Lebanese Diaspora.* London, UK: Centre for Lebanese Studies and I.B. Tauris & Co Ltd, 1998.

——. 'Injuries and Identities: authorising Arab diasporic difference in crisis.' In *Arab-Australians Today: Citizenship and Belonging,* edited by G. Hage, 206–224. Melbourne: Melbourne University Press, 2002.

Huntington, Samuel P. 'The Clash of Civilizations?' *Foreign Affairs,* 72:1, 1993: 22–49.

Hussain, A., R. Olson & J. (eds.) *Orientalism, Islam and Islamists,* Barattleboro: Amana Books, 1984.

ICG (International Crisis Group). *Al-Qaeda in Southeast Asia: The case of the 'Ngruki Network' in Indonesia.* (Corrected on 10 January 2003), Asia Briefing No.20, 8 August 2002.

——. *Impact Of The Bali Bombings.* Asia Briefing No.23, 24 October 2002.

——. *Indonesia Backgrounder: How The Jemaah Islamiyah Terrorist Network Operates.* Asia Report No.43, 11 December 2002.

——. *Jemaah Islamiyah in South East Asia: Damaged but Still Dangerous.* Asia Report No.63, 26 August 2003.

——. *Iraq's Transition: On a Knife Edge.* Baghdad and Brussels: ICG Middle East Report No.27, International Crisis Group, 2004.

——. *Indonesia Backgrounder: Jihad in Central Sulawesi.* Asia Report No.74, 3 February 2004.

——. *Indonesia Backgrounder: Why Salafism and Terrorism Mostly Don't Mix.* Asia Report No.83, 13 September 2004.

——. *Recycling Militants in Indonesia: Darul Islam and the Australian Embassy Bombing.* Asia Report No.92, 22 February 2005.

——. *Understanding Islamism.* Middle East/North Africa Report No.37, 2 March 2005.

Inglis, K.S. *The Rehearsal: Australians at War in the Sudan 1885.* McMahons's Point: Rigby, 1985.

International Monetary Fund. Yearbook, 2001

Iriye, Akira. 'The International Order.' In *The Columbia History of the Twentieth Century,* edited by Richard W. Bullit, 229–47. New York: Columbia University Press, 1998.

Ishay, M.R.. 'What are Human Rights? Six Historical Controversies.' *Journal of Human Rights,* Vol.3 No.3 (September 2004): 359–71.

Jadwat, Ridwaan. 'Islam — fastest growing faith in Australia.' *Arab News,* 27 October 2002. http://www.arabnews.com/

Joint Standing Committee of the Parliament of Australia. *Australians All: Enhancing Australian Citizenship.* Canberra: AGPS, September 1994.

Jones, K. and W. Shill. 'The Dilemma of Foreign Affiliated Companies: Surviving Middle Age in Japan.' In *Collaborating to Compete,* edited by J. Bleeke and D. Ernst, . New York: John Wiley and Sons, 1993.

Jones, S. 'Regional Institutions for Protecting Human Rights in Asia.' *Australian Journal of International Affairs,* Vol.50 No.3 (1996): 269–77.

Jordens, A. *Promoting Australian Citizenship 1949–71*. Canberra: Administration, Compliance and Governability Program, Research School of Social Sciences, Australian National University, 1994.

——. *Redefining Australians: Immigration, Citizenship and National Identity*. Sydney: Hale and Iremonger Pty Ltd, 1995.

Juergensmeyer, Mark. *The New Cold War? Religious Nationalism Confronts the Secular State*. Berkeley: University of California Press, 1994.

Jupp, James. *Arrivals and Departures*. Melbourne: Cheshire-Lansdowne, 1966.

——. *Immigration*. Sydney: Sydney University Press, 1991.

——. *Understanding Australian Multiculturalism*. Canberra: AGPS, 1996.

——. 'Afghans.' In *The Australian People: An Encyclopedia of the Nation, Its People and Their Origins*, edited by James Jupp, 164. Cambridge: Cambridge University Press, 2001.

——. 'Lebanese.' In *The Australian People: An Encyclopedia of the Nation, Its People and Their Origins*, edited by James Jupp, 554–69. Cambridge: Cambridge University Press, 2001.

——. 'Turks.' In *The Australian People: An Encyclopedia of the Nation, Its People and Their Origins*, edited by James Jupp, 709–716. Cambridge: Cambridge University Press, 2001.

——. *From White Australia to Woomera: The Story of Australian Immigration*. Port Melbourne, Victoria: Cambridge University Press, 2002.

Karim, H.K. *Islamic Peril: Media and Global Violence*. Montreal: Black Rose Books, 2000.

Kelly, T. 'Access to Justice: The Palestinian Legal System and the Fragmentation of Coercive Power.' Working Paper No.41, Development Research Centre, LSE, March 2004. www.crisisstates.com/download/wp/wp41.pdf

Kepel, Gilles, translated by Anthony F. Roberts. *Jihad: The Trail of Political Islam*. Cambridge: The Belknap Press of Harvard University Press, 2002.

——. translated by Pascale Ghazaleh. *The war for Muslim minds: Islam and the West*. Cambridge, Mass.: The Belknap Press of Harvard University Press, 2004.

Khaleej Times. 'UAE, Australia to negotiate a free trade agreement.' 15 March 2005. http://www.khaleejtimes.com/

Khalil, Samir al-. *Republic of Fear: The Inside Story of Saddam's Iraq*. Berkeley & Los Angeles: University of California Press, 1989.

Khan, I.. *The Australian*, 9 September 2004.

Knight, J. and G. Patz, eds. *Australia and the Middle East: Papers and Documents*. Canberra: the Canberra Branch of the Australian Institute of International Affairs, 1976.

Kumar, V. and V. Subramaniam 'A contingency framework for the mode of entry decision.' *Journal of World Business*, Vol.32 No.1 (1997): 29–53.

Kurzman, Charles. *Liberal Islam*. Oxford: Oxford University Press, 1998.

Lambert, Eric. *The Twenty Thousand Thieves*, Melbourne: Newport, 1951.

Langlois, A. J. *The Politics of Justice and Human Rights*. Cambridge: Cambridge University Press: 2001.

Lea, Homer. *The Day of the Saxon*. New York: Harper & Brothers Publishers, 1912.

——. *The Valor of Ignorance*. New York: Harper & Brothers Publishers, 1909.

Leach, M. 'Hansonism, Political Discourse and Australian Identity'. In *The Rise and Fall of One Nation*, edited by M. Leach, G. Stokes and I. Ward, 42–56. Queensland: Queensland University Press, 2000.

——. '"Disturbing Practices": Dehumanizing Asylum Seekers in the Refugee "Crisis" in Australia, 2001–2002.' *Refuge,* Vol.21 No.3 (2003): 25–33.

Leach, M. and F. Mansouri. 'Critical perspectives on refugee policy in Australia.' An edited volume, Melbourne: Centre for Citizenship & Human Rights (CCHR) Deakin University, 2003.

——. 'Lives in limbo: voices of refugees under temporary protection.' Sydney: University of New South Wales Press, 2004.

Leach, M., G. Stokes and I. Ward. *The Rise and Fall of One Nation.* Queensland: Queensland University Press, 2000.

Leader-Elliot, Lyn and Iris Iwanicki. 'Heritage of the Birdsville and Strzelecki Tracks.' Canberra: Department of Environment and Heritage, 2002: 52–5. http://www.environment.sa.gov.au/heritage/pdfs/surveys/birdsville/sectio ns_1–2.pdf

Levy, C. 'The European Union after 9/11: The Demise of a Liberal Democratic Asylum Regime?' In *Government and Opposition,* Vol.40(1) 2005: 26–59.

Li, J. and S. E. Guisinger. 'Comparative Business Failures of Foreign-Controlled Firms in the United States.' *Journal of International Business Studies,* (22) 2 (1991): 209–24.

Londey, Peter. *Other People's Wars: A History of Australian Peacekeeping.* Sydney: Allen & Unwin, 2004.

Loosley, S. 'Human Rights and Aid: An Australian Parliamentary Perspective.' 1998. www.hrca.org.au/symposium.htm

Lowe, David. *Menzies and the 'Great World Struggle': Australia's Cold War, 1948–1954.* Kensington: UNSW Press, 1999.

Lowy Institute for International Policy and UMR Research Pty Ltd. 'The Lowy Institute Poll 2005 Data Book.' February 2005: 6. http://www.lowyinstitute.org/

MacMillan, Margaret. *Peacemakers: The Paris Conference of 1919 and Its Attempt to End War.* London: John Murray, 2001.

Maigan, I. and B.A. Lukas. 'Entry mode decisions: the role of managers' mental modes.' *Journal of Global Marketing,* Vol.4 (1997): 7–22.

Maley, William. 'The Gulf and the Australian Peace Movement.' *Quadrant,* Vol.35 No.10 (1991): 41–4.

——. 'Australia and the East Timor Crisis: Some Critical Comments.' *Australian Journal of International Affairs,* Vol.54 No.2 (2000): 151–61.

——. *The Foreign Policy of the Taliban.* New York: Council on Foreign Relations, 2000.

——. ed. *Fundamentalism Reborn? Afghanistan and the Taliban.* New York: New York University Press., 2001.

——. 'Security, People-Smuggling and Australia's New Afghan Refugees.' *Australian Journal of International Affairs,* Vol.55 No.3 (2001): 351–70.

——. 'Confronting Creeping Invasions: Afghanistan, the UN and the World Community.' In *The Afghanistan Crisis: Issues and Perspectives*, edited by K. Warikoo, 256–274. New Delhi: Bhavana Books, 2002.

——. *The Afghanistan Wars*. London: Palgrave Macmillan, 2002.

——. 'Political Transition in Afghanistan: The State, Religion and Civil Society.' In *Political Transition in Afghanistan: The State, Islam and Civil Society*, 9–14. Washington DC: Asia Program Special Report no.122, Woodrow Wilson International Centre for Scholars, 2004.

——. 'State-Building and Political Development in Afghanistan.' In *Between Knowledge and Commitment: Post-Conflict Peace-Building and Reconstruction in Regional Contexts,* edited by Masako Ishii and Jacqueline A. Siapno, 165–83. (Osaka: JCAS Symposium Series 21, The Japan Center for Area Studies, National Museum of Ethnology, 2004.

——. 'There are risks in the company we keep.' *The Canberra Times*, 19 March 2004.

——. 'Tough words, limited action on terrorism.' *The Sydney Morning Herald*, 15 July 2004.

Malone, Rev. J.J. *The Purple East: Notes of Travel.* Melbourne: W.P. Linehan, 1911.

Mann, James. *Rise of the Vulcans: The History of Bush's War Cabinet.* New York: Viking, 2004.

Manne, Robert with David Corlett. 'Sending them home — refugees and the new politics of indifference.' *Quarterly Essay.* Issue 13: 2004.

Mansouri, F. 'Citizenship, identity and belonging in contemporary Australia.' In *Islam and the West: Reflections from Australia,* edited by S. Akbarzadeh and S. Yasmeen, 114–132. Sydney: UNSW Press, 2005.

Mansouri, F. and M. Bagdas. *Politics of Social Exclusion: Refugees on Temporary Protection Visa in Victoria.* Melbourne: Centre for Citizenship and Human Rights (CCHR), Deakin University, 2002.

Mares, P. 'Quick fix better than nothing.' Institute for Social Research, Swinburne University of Technology, 16 July 2004. http://www.apo.org.au/webboard/print-version.chtml?filename_num=00766

——. *Borderline: Australia's Treatment of Refugees and Asylum Seekers.* Sydney: UNSW Press, 2001.

Markus, A. *Race: John Howard and the Remaking of Australia.* Sydney: Allen & Unwin, 2001.

——. *Racism and refugees: an Australian tradition.* Australian Rationalist, Numbers 60/61 (2002): 16–22.

Marr, D. and M. Wilkinson. *Dark Victory.* Sydney: Allen & Unwin, 2003.

Matthews, Ken. *The Gulf Conflict and International Relations.* London: Routledge, 1993.

Matthews, Zachariah. 'Origins of Islam in Australia.' *Salam Magazine*, July–August 1997. http://www.famsy.com/salam/Origins.htm

McGuire, Paul. *Westward the Course: The New World of Oceania.* Melbourne: Leighton House, 1946.

McIntyre, L. 'Introduction'. In *Australia and the Middle East: Papers and Documents*, edited by J. Knight and G. Patz, 1–3. Canberra: the Canberra Branch of the Australian Institute of International Affairs, 1976.

McKay, J. *Phoenician Farewell: Three Generations of Lebanese Christians in Australia.* Melbourne: Ashwood House, 1989.

McMaster, Don. *Asylum Seekers: Australia's Response to Refugees*. Melbourne: Melbourne University Press, 2001.

McKay, J. and T. Batrouney. 'Lebanese Immigration until the 1990s.' In *The Australian People*, edited by J. Jupp, 554–8. North Ryde, NSW: Angus and Robertson, 1988.

McMaster, Don. *Asylum Seekers: Australia's Response to Refugees*. Melbourne: Melbourne University Press, 2001.

Mearsheimer, John J. and Stephen M. Walt. 'An Unnecessary War.' *Foreign Policy* 134 (2003): 50–9.

Menzies' trip diary, 1950, Menzies Papers, MS4936, Series 13, National Library of Australia.

Miller, J.D.B. 'Australasia and the world outside: foreign policies since world war II.' In *Tasman Relations: New Zealand and Australia, 1788–1988*, edited by Keith Sinclair, 183–201. Auckland: Auckland University Press, 1987.

Mohammadi, A. *Islam Encountering Globalization*. London: Routledge Curzon, 2002.

Moodie, C.T. to Secretary, Department of External Affairs, 18 May 1955, 'Buddhism in Burma', Series A 1838/283, Item 563/10/2/ Part1, National Archives of Australia.

Morrison, George Ernest. *An Australian in China*. Oxford: Oxford University Press, 1985.

Morrison, H. 'Beyond Universalism.' *Muslim World Journal of Human Rights*. Vol.1 No.1, 2004: 1–21.

Murphy, Caryle. *Passion for Islam: Shaping the Modern Middle East — the Egyptian Experience*. New York: Scribner, 2002.

Murphy, John F. *The United States and the Rule of Law in International Affairs*. Cambridge: Cambridge University Press, 2004.

Nairn, Bede and Geoffrey Serle, eds. *Australian Dictionary of Biography*. Vol.7: 1891–1939, A-Ch, Melbourne: Melbourne University Press, 1979.

Nashashibi, Karim. *Algeria: Stabilisation and Transition to the Market*. Washington D.C.: International Monetary Fund, 1998.

Neumann, Klaus. *Refuge Australia: Australia's Humanitarian Record*. Sydney: UNSW Press, 2004.

Nye, Joseph S. Jr. *Soft Power: The Means to Success in World Politics*. New York: Public Affairs, 2004.

One Nation, 2002. *Immigration Policy,* 10 October 2003. http://vic.onenation.com.au/onenation3.1.htm [accessed July 2005]

Osland, G.E., C.R. Taylor and S. Zou. 'Selecting international modes of entry and expansion.' *Marketing Intelligence & Planning*. 19/3, 2001: 153–61.

Palfreeman, A.C. *The Administration of the White Australia Policy*. Melbourne: Melbourne University Press, 1967.

Park, S. H. and G.R. Ungson. 'The Effect of National Culture, Organisational Complementarity and Economic Motivation on Joint Venture Dissolution.' *Academy of Management Journal*, (40) 2 (1997): 279–308.

Parliament of Australia: Hansard. 'Senate Select Committee on a Certain Maritime Incident.' 25 March 2002. http://www.aph.gov.au/hansard/senate/commttee/s5409.pdf

Parliamentary Joint Committee on ASIO, ASIS, and DSD. *Intelligence on Iraq's weapons of mass destruction*. Canberra: The Parliament of the Commonwealth of Australia, 2003.

Pearl, Cyril. *Morrison of Peking*, Ringwood: Penguin, 1970.

Pearson, Charles H. *National Life and Character: A Forecast*. London: Macmillan & Co., 1893.

Pennings, J. M., H. Barkema and S. Douma. 'Organisation Learning and Diversification.' *Academy of Management Review*. (37) 3, 1994: 608–40.

Peres, Shimon. *The New Middle East*, New York: Holt, 1993.

Pew Charitable Trust. *The Pew Global Attitudes Project: Views of a Changing World 2003*. The full report is at:
http://people-press.org/reports/pdf/185.pdf

Phillips, M. 'Keep asylum seekers in Australia, pleads Iraq.' *The Advertiser* (Adelaide), 1 January 2004.

Pickering, S. 'The Hard Press of Asylum.' *Forced Migration Review*, Issue 8 (August 2000): 32–3.

——. 'Common Sense and Original Deviancy: News Discourses and Asylum Seekers in Australia.' *Journal of Refugee Studies*, 14(2) (2001): 169–86.

Pipes, Daniel and Laurie Mylroie. 'Back Iraq.' *The New Republic*, Vol.196 No.17 (1987): 14–15.

Plimsoll J. to posts in Asia, 'Buddhism in Asia', 25 January 1955, Series A 1838/283, Item TS383/1/1/1 Part1, National Archives of Australia.

Ponder, H.W. *Java Pageant: a description of one of the world's richest, most beautiful, yet little known islands of the world*. London: Seeley Service & Co., 1934.

——. *Javanese Panorama: a further account of the world's richest island with some intimate pictures of life among the people of its lesser known regions*. London: Seeley Service & Co., nd.

Price, Matt. 'Strangling claims unsupported.' *The Australian*, 6 April 2002.

Raffaelli, J.F. 'A Picture by Emperor William.' *Harper's Weekly*, 22 January 1898: 76.

Rahman, Fazlur. *Islam and Modernity: Transformation of an Intellectual Tradition*. Chicago: University of Chicago Press, 1982.

Ramage, Douglas E. *Politics in Indonesia: Democracy, Islam and the Ideology of Tolerance*. London: Routledge, 1995.

Randal, Jonathan. *Osama: The Making of a Terrorist*. New York: Alfred A. Knopf, 2004.

Rashid, Ahmed. *Taliban*. London: I.B. Tauris, 2001.

——. *Jihad: The Rise of Militant Islam in Central Asia*. New York: Penguin, 2003.

Rauf, Iman Feisal Abdul. *What is right with Islam: a new vision for Muslims and the West*. San Francisco: Harper Collins, 2004.

Record, Jeffrey. *Dark Victory: America's Second War against Iraq*. Annapolis: Naval Institute Press, 2004.

Refugee Council of Australia, Asylum Statistics. May 2005.
http://www.refugeecouncil.org.au/html/facts_and_stats/stats.html

Refugee Review Tribunal, *Cases Finalised by Country in 2004/05*. See http://www.rrt.gov.au/ [accessed 23 June 2005]

Reinhart, Tanya. *Israel/Palestine*. Crows Nest: Allen & Unwin, 2003.

Renouf, Alan. *Malcolm Fraser and Australian Foreign Policy.* Sydney: Australian Professional Publications, 1986.

Ressa, Maria. *Seeds of Terror: An Eyewitness Account of al-Qaeda's Newest Center of Operations in Southeast Asia,* New York: Free Press, 2003.

Reus-Smit, Christian. *American Power and World Order.* Cambridge: Polity Press, 2004.

Rieff, David. 'Blueprint for a Mess.' *The New York Times,* 2 November 2003.

Rittner, S. and W.R. Pitt. *War On Iraq: What Team Bush Doesn't Want You to Know.* USA/Australia: Allen & Unwin, 2002.

Roberts, Les, Riyadh Lafta, Richard Garfield, Jamal Khudhairi and Gilbert Burnham. 'Mortality before and after the 2003 invasion of Iraq: cluster sample survey.' *The Lancet,* 29 October 2004.

Rohmer, Sax. *The Mystery of Dr Fu Manchu.* London: J.M. Dent & Sons Ltd, 1985.

Rolls, Eric. *Sojourners: The epic story of China's centuries-old relationship with Australia.* Brisbane: University of Queensland Press, 1992.

Root, F.R. 'Entry strategies for international markets.' Lexingon, MA: Lexingon Books, 1994.

Ross, Dennis. *The Missing Peace.* London: St Martins Press, 2004.

Rourke, Brigadier. 21 June 1950. Notes of Council of Defence Meeting, CRS AA1971/216, Australian Archives, Canberra (AA).

Rowell memo for McBride, 28 February 1952. 'Citizen Military Forces — Survey', CRS A5954 item 2291/4 (AA).

Roy Morgan Research. 'Refugees Not Welcome' Australians Say.' 25 September 2001. http://www.roymorgan.com/news/polls/2001/3446/

Roy, Olivier. 'Europe Won't Be Fooled Again.' *The New York Times,* 13 May 2003.

— . *Globalised Islam.* London: Hurst & Company, 2004.

Roy, Olivier and Mariam Abou Zahab. *Islamist Networks: the Pakistan–Afghan Connection.* New York: Columbia University Press, 2004.

Roydhouse, T.R. *The Coloured Conquest.* Sydney: New South Wales Bookstall Company, 1903.

Rubin, Barnett R. *Road to Ruin: Afghanistan's Booming Opium Industry.* Washington DC: Center for American Progress; and New York: Center on International Cooperation, New York University, 2004.

Rumley, D. 'The geopolitics of Australia's Regional Relations'. The Netherlands: Kluwer Academic Publishers, 2001

Russow L.C. and S.C. Okoroafo. 'On the way towards developing a global screening model'. *International Marketing Review,* Vol.13 No.1 (1996): 46–64.

Ruthven, Malise. *Islam in the World* (2nd edition). New York: Oxford University Press, 2000.

— . *A Fury for God: The Islamist Attack on America.* London and New York: Granta Books, 2002.

Saeed, A. *Islam in Australia.* Sydney: Allen & Unwin, 2003.

— . *Muslim Australians — their beliefs, practices and institutions.* Canberra: DIMIA, 2004.

Said, Edward. *Orientalism: Western Conceptions of the Orient.* London: Penguin, 1995.

——. *Covering Islam: How the Media and the Experts Determine How We See the Rest of the World*. London: Vintage Books, 1997.

——. *From Oslo to Iraq and the Roadmap*, London Bloomsbury 2004.

Sardar, Ziauddin. *Desperately Seeking Paradise: Journeys of a Sceptical Muslim*. London: Granta Books, 2004.

Sarooshi, Danesh. *The United Nations and the Development of Collective Security: The Delegation by the UN Security Council of its Chapter VII Powers*. Oxford: Oxford University Press, 1999.

Scheffer, Thomas. '"Fertile Crescent", "Orient", "Middle East": The Changing Mental Maps of Southwest Asia.' *European Review of History*, Vol.10 No.2 (2003): 253–72.

Seth, S.P. 'What sort of self-image do Australians seek?' *Khaleej Times*. 9 April 2002.

Sharp, J.M. *The Broader Middle East and North Africa Initiative: An Overview*. CRS Report for Congress, 15 February 2005.

Shaw, M. 'Activists hope UN refugee chief will push for asylum seeker solutions.' *The Age*, 22 March 2004.

Shboul, A. 'Arabic-speaking Immigrants In Australia: Cultural Background, Image, Self-Image and Reality.' In *The Arabic Community Realities and Challenges: Seminar Proceedings NSW Arabic Welfare Inter-Agency*, 1985.

Shenkar, O. and Y. Zeria. 'Role Conflict and Role Ambiguity of Chief Executive Officers in International Joint Ventures.' *Journal of International Business Studies*, (23) 1 (1992): 55–75.

Shepard, William E. 'Sayyid Qutb's Doctrine of *Jahiliyya*.' *International Journal of Middle East Studies*, 35(4) (November 2003): 521–45.

——. 'The Diversity of Islami Thought in the 20th Century: Towards a Typology.' In *Islamic Thought in the Twentieth Century* edited by Suha Taji-Farouki and Basheer Nafi, London: I.B. Tauris, 2004.

Sheridan, Greg. 'Powerful symbol but weak leader.' *The Australian*, 12 November 2004.

——. 'Peace not included in Arafat's plans.' *The Australian*, 13 November 2004.

Sidoti, Chris. *For those who come across the seas: The detention of unauthorised arrivals in Australia*. Canberra: HREOC, 1998.

——. 'A nation of Thugs.' University of Sydney Seminar, 27 September 2001. Paper available through the website: http://www.hrca.org.au/nation%20of%20thugs.htm

Simpson, Gerry. *Great Powers and Outlaw States: Unequal Sovereigns in the International Legal Order*. Cambridge: Cambridge University Press, 2004.

Sipress, Alan. 'Peacekeepers Won't Go Beyond Kabul, Cheney Says.' *The Washington Post*, 20 March 2002.

Sivan, Emmanuel. *Radical Islam: Medieval Theology and Modern Politics* (enlarged edition) New Haven: Yale University Press, 1990.

Starke, J.G. *The ANZUS Treaty Alliance*. Melbourne: Melbourne University Press, 1965.

Steketee, M. 'Door opens for 4000 Iraqis.' *The Weekend Australian*, 10 April 2004.

Stephensen, P. R. Papers, 1905–1965, 62 (127), item 1, ML MSS 1284, Mitchell Library, Sydney

Stern, Jessica. *Terror in the Name of God: Why Religious Militants Kill*. New York: Harper Collins, 2003.

Stevens, C. *Tin mosques & Ghantowns: a history of Afghan camel drivers in Australia*. Melbourne: Oxford University Press, 1989.

——. 'Afghan Camel Drivers: Founders of Islam in Australia.' In *An Australian pilgrimage: Muslims in Australia from the seventeenth century to the present*, edited by Mary Lucille Jones, 49–62. Melbourne: Victoria Press, 1993.

Suter, K. 'Australia and asylum seekers.' *Contemporary Review*. Vol.279 Issue 630 (November 2001).

Taft, William H. IV and Todd F. Buchwald. 'Preemption, Iraq and International Law.' *American Journal of International Law*, Vol.97 No.3 (2003): 557–63.

Tamimi, A. ed. *Power-Sharing Islam?* London: Liberty for Muslim World, 1993.

Task Force on Strategic Communication. *Report of the Defense Science Board Task Force on Strategic Communication*. Washington DC: Office of the Under Secretary of Defense for Acquisition, Technology, and Logistics, 2004.

Tay, A. and Sev Ozdowski. 'Media Statement by President Professor Alice Tay AM and Dr Sev Ozdowski, Human Rights Commissioner.' *Human Rights and Equal Opportunity Commission*, 6 February 2002. http://www.hreoc.gov.au/media_releases/2002/05_02.html

Taylor, Florence M. *A Pot-Pourri of Eastern Australia with Comparisons and Reflections*. Sydney: Building Publishing Co. Ltd., 1935.

Tazreiter, C. *Asylum seekers as Pariahs in the Australian State: Security Against the Few*. World Institute for Development Economics Research (WIDER), Discussion Paper No.19 (2003).

——. *Asylum Seekers and the State: The Politics of Protection in a Security Conscious World*. Hampshire, UK: Ashgate Publishing, 2004.

Templeton, M. *Ties of Blood and Empire: New Zealand's Involvement in the Middle East Defence and the Suez Crisis 1947–57*. Auckland NZ: Auckland University Press, 1994.

Thompson, R., *Australian Imperialism in the Pacific: The Expansionist Era 1820–1920*. Melbourne: Melbourne University Press, 1980.

Tibi, Bassam. *Islam and the Cultural Accommodation of Social Change*. Boulder, Colorado: West, 1991.

Tsokhas, Kosmas. *Markets, Money and Empire: The Political Economy of the Australian Wool Industry*. Melbourne: Melbourne University Press, 1990.

Turner, B. 'Cosmopolitan Virtue, Globalization and Patriotism.' In *Theory, Culture and Society* 19(1–2), 45–63. London: SAGE Publications, 2002.

United Nations Development Programme (UNDP). '"The Time Has Come": A Call for Freedom and Good Governance in the Arab World.' 5 April 2005. http://www.undp.org/rbas/ahdr

UNHCR (United Nations High Commission for Refugees). 1951 Convention Relating to the Status of Refugees. 28 July 1951. http://www.unhchr.ch/html/menu3/b/o_c_ref.htm

——. *Iraq: security an issue for returnees too*. United Nations High Commissioner for Refugees. 2 April 2004. http://www.unhcr.ch/cgi-bin/texis/vtx/news/opendoc.htm?tbl=NEWS&page=home&id=406d38465

United Nations Association of Australia. *Unity*, 288 (22 February 2002)
    http://www.unaa.org.au/praxis.php/category/view/12
United States General Accounting Office. *Afghanistan Reconstruction: Deteriorating
    Security and Limited Resources Have Impeded Progress; Improvements in US Strategy
    Needed.* Washington DC: United States General Accounting Office, 2004.
van Bruinessen, Martin. 'Genealogies of Islamic Radicalism in Indonesia.' South
    East Asia Research, 10(2) (2002) 117–54.
van Creveld, Martin. 'The Blemish of Conquest'. *Boston Review*, Vol.30 No.1
    (February–March 2005).
Vanstone, A. 'Visas opportunities for TPV holders in Regional Australia.'
    Ministerial Press Release, 14 July 2004.
    http://www.minister.immi.gov.au/media_releases/media04/v04101.htm
——. 'Decisions Handed Down on Nauru.' Ministerial Press Release, 2
    December 2004.
    http://www.minister.immi.gov.au/media_releases/media04/v04142.htm
Vasta, E. and S. Castles, eds. *The Teeth are Smiling: The Persistence of Racism in
    Multicultural Australia.* Sydney: Allen & Unwin, 1996.
Walker, David. 'The Writer's War.' In *Australia's War 1939–45*, edited by Joan
    Beaumont, 136–61. St Leonards: Allen and Unwin, 1996.
——. 'Cultural Change and the Response to Asia: 1945 to the Present.' In
    Australia and Asia, edited by Mark McGillivray and Gary Smith, 11–27.
    Melbourne: Oxford University Press, 1997.
——. *Anxious Nation: Australia and the rise of Asia 1850–1939.* Queensland:
    University of Queensland Press, 1999.
——. 'Survivalist Anxieties: Australian Responses to Asia, 1890s to the Present.'
    Australian Historical Studies, Vol.31 (120) (October 2002).
Weiner, Matt. *An Afghan 'Narco-State'? Dynamics, Assessment and Security Implications
    of the Afghan Opium Industry.* Canberra: Canberra Papers on Strategy &
    Defence no.158, Strategic and Defence Studies Centre, The Australian
    National University, 2004.
West, Andrew. 'This isn't a camp, it's an oven and we are burning.' *Sun Herald*,
    17 February 2002.
White, Richard. 'Sun, Sand and Syphilis: Australian Soldiers and the Orient,
    Egypt 1914.' *Australian Cultural History*, No.9 (1990).
Wilkie, Andrew. 'A lack of intelligence.' *Sydney Morning Herald*. 31 May 2003.
    http://www.smh.com.au/articles/2003/05/30/1054177726543.html
Wilton, J. *Hawking to Haberdashery: Immigrants in the Bush*, Armidale, NSW:
    Armidale C.A.E., 1987.
Wolfrum, Rüdiger and Christiane E. Philipp. 'The Status of the Taliban: Their
    Obligations and Rights under International Law.' *Max Planck Yearbook of
    United Nations Law.* The Hague: Kluwer Law International, Vol.VI (2002):
    559–97.
Woodard, Garry. *Asian Alternatives: Australia's Vietnam Decision and Lessons on
    Going to War.* Melbourne: Melbourne University Press, 2004.
Woodward, Bob. *Plan of Attack.* New York: Simon & Schuster, 2004.
'World Refugee Survey.' *United States Committee for Refugees.* (USCR) 2002

Yacoubian, M. 'Promoting Middle East Democracy: European Initiatives.'
    United Sates Institute of Peace, Special Report. No.127, October 2004.
Yarwood, A.T. *Asian Migration to Australia: the background to exclusion, 1896–1923.*
    Melbourne: Melbourne University Press, 1964
Yavuz, M. Hakan. *Islamic Political Identity in Turkey.* London: Oxford University
    Press, 2003.
York, Barry. 'Australia and Refugees, 1901–2002: An Annotated Chronology
    Based on Official Sources.' Canberra: Parliamentary Library, Parliament of
    Australia, 2003.
Zable, Arnold. 'Prolonging the Agony.' *The Age*, 28 July 2004.

Internet References

Australian Federation of Islamic Councils. Home Page, 2005.
    http://www.afic.com.au
DIMIA (Department of Immigration and Multiculturalism and Indigenous
    Affairs. *Adult Migrant Education Program.* Canberra: Commonwealth of
    Australia, 18 March 2005. http://www.immi.gov.au/amep/
Great Southern Railway, 'The Ghan,' 2005.
    http://www.theghan.com.au/ghan/index.htm
Human Rights Council of Australia.
    www.hrca.org.au/activities.htm#Development
Islamic Council of Victoria Inc. Home Page, 2005. http://www.icv.org.au/
Lowy Institute for International Policy and UMR Research Pty Ltd, February
    2005. http://www.lowyinstitute.org/
MCCA (Muslim Community Cooperative (Australia Ltd.). Home Page, 2004.
    http://www.mcca.com.au/
Refugee Council of Australia. June 2005.
    http://www.refugeecouncil.org.au/html/facts_and_stats/stats.html
SBS (Special Broadcasting Service). Home Page, 2005.
    http://www20.sbs.com.au

NAME INDEX

SUBJECT INDEX

Victoria 53, 66–8, 75, 77, 78, 79, 80
Victorian Arabic and Social Services (VASS) 66, 67, 68, 71
Vietnam 4, 186
Vietnam War 88, 110, 136, 138, 138, 151–2
Visas *see* Humanitarian visa; Migrant visa; Permanent migration visa; Return pending visa; Temporary protection visa (TPV)

Wahhabi Movement 53
'War on terror' viii, 8, 9, 12, 19, 23, 83, 105, 112, 124, 141, 143, 155, 175

weapons of mass destruction (WMD) 12, 13, 125, 144, 145, 147, 151
West Bank 123, 124, 127, 129–31, 183, 184, 185
Western Australia 24, 73, 75, 78
White Australia Policy 2, 8, 31, 33, 52–7, 58, 59, 70, 73–6, 87
Whitlam Government 59, 76, 87
Woodside Petroleum 158
World Food Programme (WFP) 4, 185
World Refugee Survey 91
World Trade Organization (WTO) 156, 164

'Yellow Peril' 19–21, 25, 37, 97
Yemen 6, 107